AI-DRIVEN EDUCATION 4.0

(*Innovating Education & Research*)

AI-DRIVEN EDUCATION 4.0

(*Innovating Education & Research*)

Dr. Alok Kumar Srivastav
Dr. Tridib Singha
Dr. Priyanka Das
Dr. Poonam Jaiswal

NAMYA PRESS.com

Published by

Namya Press

India: 213, Vardan House, 7/28 Ansari Road Darya Ganj - Delhi India 110002
USA: 10685-B Hazelhurst Dr. # 31013 Houston, Texas USA - 77043
Email: namyapress@gmail.com
Website: https://namyapress.com

Edition	:	First Published in 2024 (Namya Press)
Title	:	AI-Driven Education 4.0 (Innovating Education & Research)
Authors	:	Dr. Alok Kumar Srivastav, Dr. Tridib Singha, Dr. Priyanka Das, Dr. Poonam Jaiswal
ISBN	:	978-93-5545-388-4
Copyright	:	© Dr. Alok Kumar Srivastav, Dr. Tridib Singha, Dr. Priyanka Das, Dr. Poonam Jaiswal. 2024 All Rights Reserved

Acknowledgement

Writing a book is a journey that often involves the support, encouragement, and contributions of many individuals and organizations. As we present this work on AI-Driven Education 4.0: Innovating Education & Research, we would like to express our heartfelt gratitude to those who have made this endeavor possible.

First and foremost, we extend our sincere appreciation to our families for their unwavering support, patience, and understanding throughout the writing process. Your encouragement has been a constant source of motivation. We are deeply thankful to our colleagues and mentors whose guidance and expertise have enriched this book. Your insights have shaped our understanding of AI-Driven Education 4.0: Innovating Education & Research. We would like to acknowledge the contributions of the research institutions and libraries that provided access to valuable resources, making our research more comprehensive and thorough. Our gratitude goes to the reviewers and experts in the field who provided valuable feedback and constructive criticism, helping us refine the content and ensure its accuracy.

We extend our thanks to the publishing team, editors, and designers who have worked diligently to transform our manuscript into a published book. Last but not least, we are grateful to our readers, students, and fellow researchers who find value in this book. Your interest and engagement in the subject of AI-Driven Education 4.0: Innovating Education & Research drive our commitment to promoting sustainable practices and environmental stewardship.

This book would not have been possible without the collective effort and support of these individuals and institutions. We humbly acknowledge your contributions and express our deepest appreciation.

Dr. Alok Kumar Srivastav
Dr. Tridib Singha
Dr. Priyanka Das
Dr. Poonam Jaiswal

Preface

The rapid advancement of Artificial Intelligence (AI) is reshaping various sectors globally, and education is no exception. This transformative technology promises to revolutionize how we teach, learn, and manage educational systems, offering unprecedented opportunities for innovation and improvement. However, alongside these opportunities come significant challenges and ethical considerations that must be addressed to ensure that AI's integration into education is equitable, inclusive, and beneficial for all.

This book, "AI-Driven Education 4.0: Innovating Education & Research," aims to provide a comprehensive exploration of the multifaceted impact of AI on education. It is designed to serve as a guide for educators, administrators, policymakers, researchers, and students who seek to understand and navigate the evolving landscape of AI-driven education.

- **Chapter 1- Introduction to AI-Driven Education:** We begin with an exploration of the evolution of education technology, laying the foundation for understanding AI and its diverse applications in education. This chapter discusses AI-powered learning platforms, personalized learning, AI in assessment and evaluation, and the crucial ethical considerations that accompany AI integration.
- **Chapter 2- Innovating Teaching Practices:** This chapter delves into how AI is revolutionizing teaching practices. It covers AI-driven curriculum development, enhancing teacher capabilities, student engagement through AI, virtual classrooms, and the role of AI in special education. Additionally, it emphasizes the importance of professional development and training for educators to effectively integrate AI into their teaching.
- **Chapter 3- Research and Future Directions:** The focus shifts to AI-driven educational research, predictive analytics, and the role of AI in lifelong learning and higher education. This chapter also explores global education trends and how AI is transforming research methods in education, providing valuable insights and directions for future research.

- **Chapter 4- Ethical and Social Considerations:** Ethics and social impact are at the heart of this chapter, which examines the ethical implications of AI in education, its social impact, policy and regulation, and the role of AI in workforce development. It also highlights the importance of community and stakeholder engagement in shaping ethical AI-driven educational practices.
- **Chapter 5- Practical Applications and Case Studies:** Through practical applications and case studies, this chapter illustrates the implementation of AI in K-12 education, educational content creation, classroom management, language learning, and gamification. It also explores how AI transforms special education, providing tailored learning experiences for diverse needs.
- **Chapter 6- Future Prospects and Innovations:** Looking ahead, this chapter discusses the future prospects of AI in education, including its impact on STEAM education, collaborative learning, learning analytics, creative arts education, and education for sustainable development. It also addresses how AI can promote educational equity and inclusion.
- **Chapter 7- Overcoming Challenges in AI-Driven Education:** This chapter tackles the challenges associated with AI in education, the role of educators, building AI-ready institutions, the future of AI in education policy, and preparing students for an AI-driven world. It underscores the importance of collaboration and partnerships in overcoming these challenges.
- **Chapter 8- AI and Global Education:** The global implications of AI in education are explored, focusing on international collaboration, global education equity, lifelong learning, and case studies from different countries. Strategies for implementing AI in diverse educational contexts and the future of AI in global education are also discussed.
- **Chapter 9- AI and Ethical Leadership in Education:** Ethical leadership is crucial in the age of AI. This chapter defines ethical leadership, develops ethical guidelines, and discusses training for ethical AI use. Case studies of ethical AI implementation and building trust in AI-driven education are provided, along with strategies for ensuring long-term ethical compliance.
- **Chapter 10- The Long-Term Impact of AI on Education:** In the final chapter, we explore the long-term impact of AI on education, including AI-driven innovation, its effects on learning and teaching, and future visions for AI in 2050. The chapter also examines the evolution of educational systems and the global implications of AI in education, providing a comprehensive outlook on the future.

This book aims to be a comprehensive resource, offering in-depth insights, practical strategies, and ethical considerations for integrating AI into education. As we stand on the cusp of a new era in education, it is crucial to embrace the potential of AI while addressing the challenges and responsibilities it brings. We hope this book serves as a valuable guide for all stakeholders in navigating the complex and exciting landscape of AI-driven education.

Dr. Alok Kumar Srivastav
Dr. Tridib Singha
Dr. Priyanka Das
Dr. Poonam Jaiswal

Book Description

"AI-Driven Education 4.0: Innovating Education & Research" offers a comprehensive exploration of the transformative impact of Artificial Intelligence (AI) on education. This essential guide navigates the evolving landscape of AI integration in educational systems, providing in-depth insights into its applications, benefits, and challenges. Covering a wide range of topics from AI-powered learning platforms and personalized learning to the ethical implications and global impacts of AI, this book addresses critical issues facing educators, administrators, policymakers, and researchers.

Each chapter delves into key aspects of AI in education, including innovative teaching practices, AI-driven educational research, and the future prospects of AI technologies. Real-world case studies illustrate practical applications, while discussions on ethical considerations ensure a balanced perspective on the responsible use of AI. The book also highlights the importance of collaboration and partnerships, offering strategies for effective implementation and long-term ethical compliance.

"AI-Driven Education" is a valuable resource for anyone seeking to understand and leverage AI's potential to enhance learning experiences, promote equity, and drive educational innovation. As we prepare for an AI-driven future, this book provides the knowledge and tools needed to navigate the complexities and opportunities that lie ahead.

Contents

1

Introduction to AI-Driven Education

THE EVOLUTION OF EDUCATION TECHNOLOGY

The evolution of education technology has been a journey marked by innovation and transformation. From the early days of chalkboards and printed textbooks to the current era of digital classrooms and interactive learning environments, the tools and methods used in education have continually evolved to meet the changing needs of society. This chapter delves into this fascinating journey, setting the stage for understanding the revolutionary impact of artificial intelligence (AI) on education today.

In the early 20th century, classrooms were primarily characterized by rote learning and teacher-centered instruction. The primary tools were chalkboards, textbooks, and handwritten notes. Education was largely a one-size-fits-all approach, with little consideration for individual learning styles and paces. However, the mid-20th century began to see the introduction of more dynamic teaching aids, such as overhead projectors, film strips, and audio-visual materials. These tools provided new ways to engage students and enhance the learning experience.

The advent of personal computers in the 1980s marked a significant turning point in educational technology. Computers introduced a level of interactivity and accessibility previously unimaginable. Programs like LOGO and early educational games allowed students to learn programming basics and develop problem-solving skills in an engaging and interactive manner. This era also saw the beginning of computer-assisted instruction (CAI), which provided students with personalized learning experiences tailored to their individual needs and progress.

As the internet became more widely available in the 1990s, it revolutionized the educational landscape once again. The introduction of online resources, digital libraries, and educational websites provided students and teachers with unprecedented access to information. Platforms like Blackboard and Moodle emerged, enabling schools and universities to offer online courses and manage learning materials digitally. The concept of e-learning started to take shape, allowing for flexible and distance learning opportunities.

The early 21st century saw the proliferation of mobile devices and the rise of digital content. Tablets, smartphones, and laptops became common in classrooms, and the use of interactive whiteboards replaced traditional chalkboards. This period also marked the beginning of blended learning, where traditional face-to-face instruction was combined with online and digital resources. Learning management systems (LMS) like Canvas and Google Classroom further streamlined the integration of technology in education, enabling more effective communication, collaboration, and assessment.

In recent years, the emergence of AI has brought about a new wave of transformation in education. AI technologies, such as machine learning, natural language processing, and computer vision, have the potential to revolutionize how we teach and learn. AI can analyze vast amounts of data to provide insights into student performance, personalize learning experiences, and automate administrative tasks. For instance, AI-powered tutoring systems can provide personalized feedback and guidance to students, helping them master complex subjects at their own pace.

One of the most significant advantages of AI in education is its ability to offer personalized learning experiences. Unlike traditional methods that often cater to the average student, AI can tailor educational content to meet the specific needs of each learner. By analyzing data on a student's learning style, strengths, and weaknesses, AI can create customized learning paths that optimize their educational experience. This level of personalization helps to ensure that no student is left behind and that each learner can achieve their full potential.

Another critical area where AI is making a significant impact is in assessment and evaluation. Traditional assessment methods, such as standardized tests, often fail to capture the full range of a student's abilities and knowledge. AI-driven assessment tools can provide more comprehensive and nuanced evaluations by analyzing various data points, including student interactions, written responses, and even emotional cues. These tools can offer real-time feedback, enabling educators to adjust their teaching strategies and provide targeted support to students who need it most.

Moreover, AI can help streamline administrative tasks, allowing educators to focus more on teaching and less on paperwork. Automated grading systems, for instance, can handle multiple-choice questions and even complex essay evaluations, saving teachers valuable time. AI can also assist in scheduling, attendance tracking, and resource management, making the overall educational process more efficient and effective.

As we move forward, it is essential to consider the ethical implications of integrating AI into education. While AI offers numerous benefits, it also raises questions about data privacy, algorithmic bias, and the role of human educators. Ensuring that AI is used responsibly and ethically will be crucial to maximizing its positive impact on education.

The journey of education technology has been one of continuous evolution and adaptation. From chalkboards to AI-driven platforms, each innovation has brought new opportunities and challenges. As we stand on the brink of a new era in education, driven by the power of AI, it is vital to reflect on this journey and prepare for the transformative changes that lie ahead.

UNDERSTANDING AI AND ITS APPLICATIONS IN EDUCATION

Artificial Intelligence (AI) is no longer a concept confined to science fiction; it is a transformative force reshaping various sectors, including education. To grasp the full potential of AI in education, it is essential to understand what AI is and how it can be applied to enhance teaching and learning processes.

At its core, AI refers to the simulation of human intelligence in machines designed to think and learn like humans. This involves capabilities such as reasoning, learning, problem-solving, perception, and language understanding. AI systems can perform tasks that typically require human intelligence, such as visual perception, speech recognition, decision-making, and language translation.

In education, AI can be broadly categorized into several applications, each serving a unique purpose:

- **Adaptive Learning Systems:** Adaptive learning systems use AI algorithms to personalize the learning experience for each student. These systems analyze data on a student's performance, learning style, and preferences to adjust the content, pace, and difficulty of lessons. By providing a tailored learning experience, adaptive learning systems help students achieve better outcomes and maintain engagement.
- **Intelligent Tutoring Systems (ITS):** Intelligent Tutoring Systems leverage AI to provide personalized instruction and feedback to students. These systems can simulate the one-on-one interaction between a tutor and a student, guiding learners through complex subjects, answering their questions, and providing instant feedback. ITS can identify areas where students struggle and offer targeted support, making learning more efficient and effective.
- **Automated Grading and Feedback:** One of the significant applications of AI in education is automated grading and feedback. AI-powered tools can grade multiple-choice tests, essays, and even complex assignments, providing instant feedback to students. This not only saves time for educators but also ensures that students receive timely feedback to improve their learning.
- **Natural Language Processing (NLP):** Natural Language Processing is a subset of AI that focuses on the interaction between computers and human language. In education, NLP can be used to develop applications such as automated essay scoring, language translation tools, and virtual teaching assistants. These applications can help break down language barriers, assist in grading complex written work, and provide additional support to students in real-time.
- **AI-Powered Analytics and Insights:** AI can analyze vast amounts of educational data to provide valuable insights into student performance, learning trends, and institutional efficiency. By examining patterns and correlations in the data, AI can help educators identify at-risk students, optimize curriculum design, and improve teaching strategies. Predictive analytics can also forecast student outcomes, enabling proactive interventions to enhance learning success.
- **Virtual and Augmented Reality (VR/AR):** While not exclusively an AI application, VR and AR technologies often incorporate AI to create immersive and interactive learning experiences. AI can enhance these environments by adapting the content to the

learner's progress, providing real-time feedback, and simulating real-world scenarios for hands-on learning. These technologies can make complex subjects more accessible and engaging for students.

- **Robotics in Education:** AI-powered robots are increasingly being used in classrooms to assist with teaching and learning. These robots can perform various tasks, from leading lessons and conducting experiments to offering personalized tutoring and engaging students in interactive activities. By integrating robotics into education, schools can provide unique and innovative learning experiences that enhance student engagement and understanding.
- **Chatbots and Virtual Assistants:** AI chatbots and virtual assistants can support both students and educators by answering questions, providing information, and assisting with administrative tasks. These tools can be available 24/7, offering instant support and reducing the workload on teachers. Chatbots can help with tasks such as scheduling, homework reminders, and providing study resources, making education more accessible and efficient.

The integration of AI in education is not without its challenges. Concerns about data privacy, algorithmic bias, and the digital divide must be addressed to ensure that AI benefits all students equitably. Furthermore, the role of human educators remains crucial; AI should be seen as a tool to augment and enhance their capabilities, not replace them.

Personalized Learning with AI

One of the most promising applications of AI in education is personalized learning. Traditional education systems often struggle to cater to the diverse needs of individual students, leading to a one-size-fits-all approach that may not be effective for everyone. AI has the potential to transform this by providing personalized learning experiences tailored to each student's unique needs, preferences, and abilities.

Benefits of Personalized Learning with AI

- **Tailored Learning Paths:** AI can create customized learning paths for students by analyzing their performance data, learning styles, and interests. This ensures that each student receives content and instruction that is most relevant and effective for their learning journey. Personalized learning paths can help students progress at their own pace, allowing them to master concepts before moving on to more advanced topics.
- **Engagement and Motivation:** Personalized learning experiences can significantly boost student engagement and motivation. When

students receive content that is aligned with their interests and learning preferences, they are more likely to stay engaged and motivated to learn. AI can adapt lessons to include interactive elements, gamified activities, and real-world applications, making learning more enjoyable and relevant.

- **Timely and Targeted Feedback:** AI can provide real-time feedback to students, helping them understand their strengths and areas for improvement. This immediate feedback allows students to adjust their learning strategies and seek help when needed, promoting a more effective and self-directed learning process. Teachers can also use this feedback to identify students who may need additional support or enrichment.
- **Reducing Learning Gaps:** By tailoring instruction to individual needs, AI can help reduce learning gaps and ensure that all students have the opportunity to succeed. Personalized learning can address the diverse needs of students, including those with learning disabilities, language barriers, or different cultural backgrounds. This inclusivity can help create a more equitable and effective education system.

Implementing Personalized Learning with AI

To implement personalized learning with AI effectively, several key components need to be in place:

- **Robust Data Infrastructure:** Collecting and analyzing data is essential for personalized learning. Schools and educational institutions need robust data infrastructure to gather information on student performance, behavior, and preferences. This data must be managed securely and ethically to protect student privacy.
- **Adaptive Learning Platforms:** AI-powered adaptive learning platforms are central to personalized learning. These platforms use algorithms to adjust content and instruction based on student data. Schools should invest in high-quality adaptive learning platforms that offer comprehensive features and support various subjects and grade levels.
- **Professional Development for Educators:** Teachers play a crucial role in personalized learning. Educators need training and professional development to effectively use AI tools and integrate personalized learning strategies into their teaching. Ongoing support and collaboration with AI experts can help teachers stay updated with the latest technologies and best practices.

- **Student and Parent Engagement:** For personalized learning to be successful, students and parents must be engaged and informed about the process. Schools should communicate the benefits of personalized learning and provide resources to help students and parents understand how AI tools work. Encouraging student feedback and involving parents in the learning process can enhance the effectiveness of personalized learning.

AI in Assessment and Evaluation

Assessment and evaluation are critical components of the education process. Traditional assessment methods, such as standardized tests and written exams, often provide limited insights into a student's true abilities and knowledge. AI can revolutionize assessment and evaluation by offering more comprehensive, accurate, and personalized feedback.

AI-Driven Assessment Tools

- **Automated Grading Systems:** AI-powered grading systems can quickly and accurately grade various types of assignments, from multiple-choice tests to complex essays. These systems use natural language processing and machine learning algorithms to evaluate student responses, providing instant feedback. Automated grading saves teachers time and allows them to focus on more meaningful interactions with students.
- **Adaptive Assessments:** Adaptive assessments adjust the difficulty of questions based on the student's responses. This approach provides a more accurate measure of a student's knowledge and abilities. AI can analyze response patterns to identify strengths and weaknesses, offering a personalized assessment experience that can inform instruction.
- **Formative Assessments:** Formative assessments are ongoing evaluations that provide real-time feedback to students and teachers. AI can facilitate formative assessments by analyzing student interactions with learning materials, tracking progress, and identifying areas where students may need additional support. This continuous feedback loop helps teachers adjust their teaching strategies and provides students with timely guidance.
- **Holistic Evaluation:** AI can support holistic evaluation by considering multiple data points, including student participation, collaboration, and creativity. AI tools can analyze various aspects of student performance, such as group projects, presentations, and class discussions, offering a more comprehensive view of their

abilities. This approach can help educators recognize and nurture a broader range of skills and talents.

Ethical Considerations in AI-Driven Assessments

While AI offers significant advantages in assessment and evaluation, ethical considerations must be addressed to ensure fairness and transparency:

- **Data Privacy:** Protecting student data is paramount. Schools and institutions must implement robust data security measures and adhere to privacy regulations to ensure that student information is handled responsibly.
- **Bias and Fairness:** AI algorithms can be susceptible to bias, which can affect the fairness of assessments. It is crucial to develop and implement AI systems that are transparent and free from bias. Ongoing monitoring and evaluation of AI tools can help identify and mitigate any biases that may arise.
- **Human Oversight:** Despite the capabilities of AI, human oversight remains essential. Educators should review AI-generated assessments and feedback to ensure accuracy and appropriateness. Combining AI with human judgment can lead to more effective and fair evaluations.

AI-POWERED LEARNING PLATFORMS

In recent years, the development of AI-powered learning platforms has revolutionized the educational landscape, offering innovative tools and resources that enhance the teaching and learning experience. These platforms leverage artificial intelligence to create more interactive, personalized, and efficient educational environments. In this section, we will explore the key features and benefits of AI-powered learning platforms and examine several prominent examples.

Key Features of AI-Powered Learning Platforms

- **Personalization and Adaptivity:** AI-powered learning platforms are designed to personalize the educational experience for each student. By analyzing data on student performance, preferences, and learning styles, these platforms can tailor content and instructional methods to meet individual needs. This adaptivity ensures that students receive the right level of challenge and support, helping them stay engaged and make progress at their own pace.
- **Interactive and Engaging Content:** AI technologies enable the creation of highly interactive and engaging learning materials.

Through the use of multimedia, simulations, and gamification, AI-powered platforms can make complex subjects more accessible and enjoyable. Interactive content not only enhances understanding but also motivates students to actively participate in their learning.

- **Real-Time Feedback and Assessment:** One of the significant advantages of AI-powered learning platforms is their ability to provide real-time feedback and assessment. These platforms can instantly analyze student responses and offer personalized feedback, helping learners understand their mistakes and improve. Real-time assessment allows educators to monitor student progress continuously and make data-driven decisions to support their learning.
- **Data-Driven Insights:** AI-powered platforms collect and analyze vast amounts of data on student interactions, performance, and behavior. This data provides valuable insights into learning patterns, strengths, and areas for improvement. Educators can use these insights to identify at-risk students, tailor instructional strategies, and optimize the overall learning experience.
- **Accessibility and Flexibility:** AI-powered learning platforms are accessible from various devices, including computers, tablets, and smartphones, allowing students to learn anytime and anywhere. This flexibility accommodates diverse learning environments and schedules, making education more inclusive and accessible to a broader range of learners.

Prominent AI-Powered Learning Platforms

- **Coursera:** Coursera is a widely recognized online learning platform that partners with top universities and organizations to offer courses, specializations, and degrees. The platform uses AI to recommend courses based on user interests and learning history, providing a personalized learning path. AI also powers the platform's assessment and grading systems, offering real-time feedback and personalized course recommendations.
- **Khan Academy:** Khan Academy is a non-profit educational platform that offers free, high-quality resources for students, teachers, and parents. The platform uses AI to personalize learning experiences, providing tailored recommendations and adaptive exercises based on individual student performance. Khan Academy's AI-driven analytics help educators track student progress and identify areas where additional support is needed.
- **Edmodo:** Edmodo is a social learning platform that connects teachers, students, and parents. The platform uses AI to enhance

communication and collaboration, offering personalized content recommendations and interactive learning tools. Edmodo's AI-driven analytics provide insights into student engagement and performance, helping educators create more effective and targeted instructional strategies.

- **Duolingo:** Duolingo is a popular language-learning platform that uses AI to create personalized and engaging language lessons. The platform adapts to the user's learning pace and preferences, providing tailored exercises and feedback. Duolingo's AI-driven assessment tools track progress and adjust the difficulty of lessons to ensure continuous improvement.
- **Socrative:** Socrative is an AI-powered platform designed to facilitate formative assessments and real-time feedback in the classroom. The platform allows educators to create quizzes, polls, and exit tickets that students can complete using their devices. Socrative's AI-driven analytics provide immediate insights into student understanding, helping teachers adjust their instruction accordingly.

The Impact of AI-Powered Learning Platforms

The integration of AI-powered learning platforms into education has profound implications for both students and educators. By providing personalized, interactive, and data-driven learning experiences, these platforms can significantly enhance educational outcomes and transform traditional teaching practices.

For Students

- **Enhanced Engagement:** AI-powered platforms offer engaging and interactive content that keeps students motivated and interested in learning.
- **Personalized Learning:** Tailored learning paths ensure that each student receives the right level of challenge and support, leading to better understanding and retention of knowledge.
- **Immediate Feedback:** Real-time feedback helps students quickly identify and address their mistakes, promoting continuous improvement and confidence in their abilities.
- **Flexible Learning:** The accessibility of AI-powered platforms allows students to learn at their own pace and on their own schedule, accommodating diverse learning needs and preferences.

For Educators

- **Data-Driven Decision Making:** AI-powered analytics provide valuable insights into student performance and behavior, enabling educators to make informed decisions about instruction and intervention.

- **Efficient Assessment:** Automated grading and assessment tools save educators time and effort, allowing them to focus more on teaching and student support.
- **Targeted Support:** Real-time data and insights help educators identify at-risk students and provide targeted support to address learning gaps and challenges.
- **Professional Development:** AI-powered platforms offer resources and tools for educator training and professional development, helping teachers stay updated with the latest technologies and best practices.

Challenges and Considerations

While AI-powered learning platforms offer numerous benefits, their implementation also presents challenges and considerations:

- **Data Privacy and Security:** Protecting student data is a critical concern when using AI-powered platforms. Schools and institutions must ensure that data is collected, stored, and used in compliance with privacy regulations and ethical standards. Implementing robust security measures and obtaining informed consent from students and parents are essential steps in safeguarding data privacy.
- **Digital Divide:** Access to AI-powered learning platforms depends on the availability of technology and internet connectivity. Addressing the digital divide is crucial to ensure that all students, regardless of their socioeconomic background, can benefit from these innovations. Schools and policymakers must work to provide equitable access to technology and resources.
- **Bias and Fairness:** AI algorithms can be susceptible to bias, which can impact the fairness of personalized learning experiences and assessments. It is essential to develop and implement AI systems that are transparent, unbiased, and regularly monitored for potential issues. Ensuring diversity in AI training data and involving diverse stakeholders in the development process can help mitigate bias.
- **Teacher Training and Support:** Integrating AI-powered learning platforms into education requires adequate training and support for educators. Teachers need to understand how to use these tools effectively and integrate them into their instructional practices. Ongoing professional development and collaboration

with AI experts can help educators harness the full potential of AI in education.

PERSONALIZED LEARNING WITH AI

Personalized learning has emerged as one of the most transformative applications of AI in education. Traditional educational systems often struggle to cater to the diverse needs of individual students, leading to a one-size-fits-all approach. AI offers the potential to revolutionize this by providing personalized learning experiences tailored to each student's unique needs, preferences, and abilities. This section delves into the various aspects of personalized learning with AI and its impact on education.

The Concept of Personalized Learning

Personalized learning refers to an educational approach that aims to customize learning experiences to individual student's needs, strengths, and interests. It moves away from the traditional model where all students follow the same curriculum at the same pace. Instead, personalized learning allows for flexibility in how, what, when, and where students learn.

AI's Role in Personalized Learning

AI plays a crucial role in enabling personalized learning by analyzing vast amounts of data on student performance, behavior, and preferences. Through advanced algorithms and machine learning techniques, AI systems can:

- **Analyze Learning Patterns:** AI can track and analyze how students interact with learning materials, identify patterns in their behavior, and detect areas where they excel or struggle. This analysis provides insights into each student's learning style and preferences.
- **Customize Learning Paths:** Based on the data analysis, AI can create customized learning paths for each student. These paths adapt to the student's pace, providing more challenging materials when they are ready or offering additional support when needed. This ensures that students remain engaged and motivated throughout their learning journey.
- **Provide Real-Time Feedback:** AI systems can provide immediate feedback on assignments and assessments. This real-time feedback helps students understand their mistakes and learn from them promptly. It also allows teachers to monitor student progress continuously and adjust their teaching strategies accordingly.

- **Predict Student Outcomes:** Predictive analytics can forecast student outcomes based on current performance and behavior. This allows educators to intervene early and provide targeted support to students who may be at risk of falling behind.

Benefits of Personalized Learning with AI

- **Improved Engagement and Motivation:** Personalized learning experiences align with students' interests and learning styles, keeping them engaged and motivated. When students feel that the content is relevant and tailored to their needs, they are more likely to participate actively and enjoy the learning process.
- **Better Academic Outcomes:** By providing customized support and challenging students at their appropriate levels, personalized learning can lead to better academic outcomes. Students can progress at their own pace, ensuring they fully understand each concept before moving on to the next.
- **Enhanced Self-Directed Learning:** Personalized learning encourages students to take ownership of their education. With AI providing guidance and feedback, students can develop self-directed learning skills, becoming more independent and responsible for their progress.
- **Equity in Education:** AI-powered personalized learning can help address educational inequities by providing tailored support to students from diverse backgrounds and with different learning needs. This inclusivity ensures that all students have the opportunity to succeed.

Implementing Personalized Learning with AI

To effectively implement personalized learning with AI, several key components are necessary:

- **Robust Data Collection and Analysis:** Collecting and analyzing comprehensive data on student performance and behavior is essential. This includes academic records, interaction with learning materials, assessment results, and even social-emotional indicators. Ensuring data privacy and security is paramount in this process.
- **Adaptive Learning Platforms:** AI-powered adaptive learning platforms are central to personalized learning. These platforms use algorithms to adjust content and instruction based on individual student data. They should be user-friendly, flexible, and capable of integrating various types of educational content.

- **Professional Development for Educators:** Teachers need training and professional development to effectively use AI tools and integrate personalized learning strategies into their teaching. This includes understanding how to interpret data, customize instruction, and use AI platforms to enhance student learning.
- **Student and Parent Engagement:** Engaging students and parents in the personalized learning process is crucial. Educators should communicate the benefits of personalized learning and provide resources to help students and parents understand how AI tools work. Encouraging student feedback and involving parents in the learning journey can enhance the effectiveness of personalized learning.

Challenges and Considerations

While personalized learning with AI offers numerous benefits, it also presents challenges and considerations that need to be addressed:

- **Data Privacy and Security:** Protecting student data is critical. Schools and institutions must implement robust security measures and comply with privacy regulations to ensure that data is handled responsibly.
- **Algorithmic Bias:** AI algorithms can be biased based on the data they are trained on. It is essential to develop transparent and unbiased AI systems. Regular monitoring and evaluation of AI tools can help identify and mitigate any biases that may arise.
- **Digital Divide:** Access to AI-powered personalized learning depends on the availability of technology and internet connectivity. Addressing the digital divide is crucial to ensure that all students, regardless of their socioeconomic background, can benefit from these innovations. Schools and policymakers must work to provide equitable access to technology and resources.
- **Teacher Training and Support:** Integrating AI-powered personalized learning into education requires adequate training and support for educators. Teachers need to understand how to use these tools effectively and integrate them into their instructional practices. Ongoing professional development and collaboration with AI experts can help educators harness the full potential of AI in education.

AI in Assessment and Evaluation

Assessment and evaluation are critical components of the education process. Traditional assessment methods, such as standardized tests and written exams, often provide limited insights into a student's true abilities and knowledge. AI can revolutionize assessment and evaluation by offering more comprehensive, accurate, and personalized feedback.

AI-Driven Assessment Tools

- **Automated Grading Systems:** AI-powered grading systems can quickly and accurately grade various types of assignments, from multiple-choice tests to complex essays. These systems use natural language processing and machine learning algorithms to evaluate student responses, providing instant feedback. Automated grading saves teachers time and allows them to focus on more meaningful interactions with students.
- **Adaptive Assessments:** Adaptive assessments adjust the difficulty of questions based on the student's responses. This approach provides a more accurate measure of a student's knowledge and abilities. AI can analyze response patterns to identify strengths and weaknesses, offering a personalized assessment experience that can inform instruction.
- **Formative Assessments:** Formative assessments are ongoing evaluations that provide real-time feedback to students and teachers. AI can facilitate formative assessments by analyzing student interactions with learning materials, tracking progress, and identifying areas where students may need additional support. This continuous feedback loop helps teachers adjust their teaching strategies and provides students with timely guidance.
- **Holistic Evaluation:** AI can support holistic evaluation by considering multiple data points, including student participation, collaboration, and creativity. AI tools can analyze various aspects of student performance, such as group projects, presentations, and class discussions, offering a more comprehensive view of their abilities. This approach can help educators recognize and nurture a broader range of skills and talents.

Ethical Considerations in AI-Driven Assessments

While AI offers significant advantages in assessment and evaluation, ethical considerations must be addressed to ensure fairness and transparency:

- **Data Privacy:** Protecting student data is paramount. Schools and institutions must implement robust data security measures and adhere to privacy regulations to ensure that student information is handled responsibly.

- **Bias and Fairness:** AI algorithms can be susceptible to bias, which can affect the fairness of assessments. It is crucial to develop and implement AI systems that are transparent and free from bias. Ongoing monitoring and evaluation of AI tools can help identify and mitigate any biases that may arise.
- **Human Oversight:** Despite the capabilities of AI, human oversight remains essential. Educators should review AI-generated assessments and feedback to ensure accuracy and appropriateness. Combining AI with human judgment can lead to more effective and fair evaluations.

AI IN ASSESSMENT AND EVALUATION

Assessment and evaluation are cornerstones of the educational process. Traditionally, these have been carried out through standardized tests, quizzes, assignments, and exams. However, such methods often provide limited insights into a student's comprehensive abilities and knowledge. The advent of AI offers a transformative potential in this domain, making assessments more comprehensive, personalized, and accurate.

AI-Driven Assessment Tools

- **Automated Grading Systems:** Automated grading systems utilize AI to evaluate student submissions quickly and accurately. These systems are especially effective for grading multiple-choice tests and even complex essays. Natural language processing (NLP) and machine learning algorithms analyze the content and structure of student responses, providing detailed feedback. This process saves educators considerable time and ensures consistent grading standards.
- **Adaptive Assessments:** Adaptive assessments adjust the difficulty of questions in real-time based on the student's responses. AI analyzes each answer to determine the student's understanding and subsequently selects questions that are appropriately challenging. This method provides a more precise measure of a student's knowledge and skills, catering to individual learning levels and identifying specific areas of strength and weakness.
- **Formative Assessments:** AI facilitates formative assessments by offering continuous, real-time evaluations of student performance. These assessments are integral to the learning process, providing immediate feedback that helps students identify their mistakes and understand concepts better. AI-driven formative assessments

can track progress over time, enabling educators to adjust their instructional strategies to meet the evolving needs of their students.

- **Holistic Evaluation:** AI supports holistic evaluation by considering various data points, including student participation, collaboration, and creativity. Traditional assessments often fail to capture these aspects, but AI tools can analyze diverse elements of student performance, such as group projects, presentations, and class discussions. This comprehensive view allows educators to recognize and nurture a broader range of skills and talents, providing a more well-rounded assessment of student abilities.

The Benefits of AI in Assessment

- **Efficiency and Consistency:** AI-driven assessment tools can process and evaluate large volumes of student work quickly and consistently. This efficiency reduces the administrative burden on educators, allowing them to focus more on teaching and interacting with students. Consistent grading also ensures fairness, as AI eliminates the subjective biases that can influence human grading.
- **Personalized Feedback:** AI can provide detailed, personalized feedback to students based on their performance. This feedback is specific and actionable, helping students understand their strengths and areas for improvement. Personalized feedback is crucial for promoting self-directed learning and helping students take ownership of their educational journey.
- **Enhanced Learning Outcomes:** By offering real-time feedback and adaptive assessments, AI helps students learn more effectively. Immediate feedback allows students to correct their mistakes and reinforce their understanding promptly. Adaptive assessments ensure that students are continually challenged at an appropriate level, promoting deeper learning and retention.
- **Data-Driven Insights:** AI-driven assessments generate a wealth of data on student performance. Educators can use this data to gain insights into learning patterns, identify at-risk students, and tailor their teaching strategies. Data-driven decision-making helps optimize the learning experience and improve overall educational outcomes.

Challenges and Ethical Considerations

While AI in assessment offers numerous benefits, it also presents challenges and ethical considerations that must be addressed to ensure its responsible and fair use:

- **Data Privacy and Security:** Protecting student data is of paramount importance. Schools and educational institutions must implement robust data security measures to safeguard sensitive information. Compliance with data privacy regulations, such as GDPR and FERPA, is essential to maintain trust and protect student rights.
- **Algorithmic Bias:** AI algorithms can be susceptible to biases based on the data they are trained on. If the training data contains biases, the AI system may perpetuate these biases in its assessments. It is crucial to develop AI systems that are transparent, unbiased, and regularly monitored for fairness. Involving diverse stakeholders in the development process can help mitigate biases and ensure more equitable outcomes.
- **Human Oversight:** Despite the advanced capabilities of AI, human oversight remains essential. Educators should review AI-generated assessments and feedback to ensure accuracy and appropriateness. Combining AI with human judgment can lead to more effective and fair evaluations. Teachers can interpret AI insights within the broader context of their students' learning experiences and provide the necessary emotional and pedagogical support.
- **Access and Equity:** The digital divide remains a significant barrier to the equitable implementation of AI-driven assessment tools. Students from underserved communities may lack access to the necessary technology and internet connectivity. Schools and policymakers must address these disparities to ensure that all students can benefit from AI advancements in education.

AI in Summative and Formative Assessments

AI's role in both summative and formative assessments enhances the educational process by providing a comprehensive evaluation framework:

- **Summative Assessments:** Summative assessments, such as final exams and standardized tests, evaluate student learning at the end of an instructional period. AI can enhance summative assessments by providing automated grading, detailed analytics, and comprehensive feedback. This helps educators identify trends and areas for curriculum improvement while ensuring timely and consistent evaluation.
- **Formative Assessments:** Formative assessments are ongoing and provide real-time insights into student learning. AI tools can track student progress, analyze learning behaviors, and offer immediate feedback. These assessments inform instructional adjustments

and support individualized learning paths, making formative assessments a powerful tool for improving student outcomes.

Future Directions in AI-Driven Assessment

The future of AI in assessment and evaluation holds exciting possibilities. Innovations such as emotion recognition, predictive analytics, and immersive technologies like virtual reality (VR) and augmented reality (AR) are poised to further transform educational assessments:

- **Emotion Recognition:** AI systems capable of recognizing and analyzing emotions can provide deeper insights into student engagement and well-being. By monitoring facial expressions, body language, and vocal tones, AI can assess students' emotional states and provide real-time interventions to support their learning and emotional health.
- **Predictive Analytics:** Predictive analytics can forecast student performance and identify potential challenges before they arise. By analyzing historical data and learning patterns, AI can predict outcomes and recommend proactive measures to ensure student success. This anticipatory approach can help educators provide targeted support and resources.
- **Immersive Technologies:** VR and AR technologies, powered by AI, offer immersive assessment experiences that simulate real-world scenarios. These technologies can assess practical skills, problem-solving abilities, and critical thinking in dynamic and interactive environments. Immersive assessments provide a more comprehensive evaluation of student capabilities and prepare them for real-life challenges.

AI in assessment and evaluation is a game-changer for education. By providing personalized, efficient, and comprehensive assessments, AI enhances the learning experience for students and supports educators in their mission to deliver high-quality education. However, it is essential to address the ethical considerations and challenges associated with AI implementation to ensure that its benefits are realized equitably and responsibly.

ETHICAL CONSIDERATIONS IN AI-DRIVEN EDUCATION

As Artificial Intelligence (AI) becomes increasingly integrated into education, it is essential to address the ethical considerations that arise. Ensuring that AI technologies are used responsibly and equitably is crucial for maintaining trust and maximizing their benefits. This section explores key ethical considerations in AI-driven education, including data privacy, algorithmic bias, transparency, accountability, and the human-centered approach.

Data Privacy and Security

- **Protecting Student Data:** The collection and analysis of student data are fundamental to AI-driven education. However, ensuring the privacy and security of this data is paramount. Educational institutions must implement robust data protection measures, including encryption, secure storage, and access controls, to safeguard sensitive information.
- **Compliance with Regulations:** Institutions must comply with relevant data privacy regulations, such as the General Data Protection Regulation (GDPR) and the Family Educational Rights and Privacy Act (FERPA). These regulations set standards for data collection, usage, and sharing, ensuring that student information is handled responsibly.
- **Informed Consent:** Obtaining informed consent from students and parents is essential when collecting and using data. Institutions should clearly explain what data will be collected, how it will be used, and the measures in place to protect privacy. Transparent communication builds trust and ensures that stakeholders are aware of their rights.

Algorithmic Bias and Fairness

- **Understanding Bias in AI:** AI systems can perpetuate biases present in the data they are trained on. These biases can lead to unfair outcomes, such as discrimination against certain groups of students. Understanding and addressing algorithmic bias is crucial for ensuring fairness and equity in AI-driven education.
- **Mitigating Bias:** To mitigate bias, institutions should use diverse and representative data sets when developing AI systems. Regular audits and evaluations of AI algorithms can help identify and address biases. Additionally, involving diverse stakeholders in the design and development process ensures that multiple perspectives are considered.
- **Promoting Inclusivity:** AI-driven educational tools should be designed to accommodate the diverse needs of all students, including those with disabilities and special educational needs. Promoting inclusivity ensures that AI technologies provide equitable support and opportunities for every learner.

Transparency and Accountability

- **Transparent AI Systems:** Transparency in AI systems involves openly sharing how algorithms work, what data they use, and how decisions are made. Institutions should provide clear and accessible information about AI technologies, ensuring that stakeholders understand and trust these systems.
- **Establishing Accountability:** Accountability mechanisms are essential for ensuring that AI systems are used responsibly. Institutions should establish clear roles and responsibilities for the development, deployment, and monitoring of AI technologies. Regular audits and assessments can help maintain accountability and address any issues that arise.
- **Feedback and Reporting Channels:** Creating channels for feedback and reporting concerns is crucial for maintaining transparency and accountability. Stakeholders should have the opportunity to voice their opinions and report any ethical concerns related to AI use. Institutions should actively respond to feedback and take corrective actions when necessary.

The Human-Centered Approach

- **Augmenting Human Capabilities:** AI should augment, not replace, human capabilities in education. While AI can handle routine tasks and provide personalized support, educators play a vital role in fostering relationships, providing emotional support, and guiding students' personal and social development. The human element remains central to the educational experience.
- **Balancing Technology and Human Interaction:** Striking a balance between technology and human interaction is essential for creating a supportive and effective learning environment. AI-driven tools should complement and enhance the work of educators, allowing them to focus on activities that require human judgment, creativity, and empathy.
- **Ethical AI Design:** Designing AI systems with ethical considerations in mind is crucial for ensuring their responsible use. Institutions should adopt ethical AI design principles, such as fairness, accountability, and transparency, throughout the development and deployment process. Engaging stakeholders in ethical decision-making fosters a culture of responsibility and integrity.

Long-Term Ethical Considerations

- **Sustainable AI Practices:** Ensuring the sustainability of AI-driven education involves addressing the long-term ethical implications of AI use. Institutions should consider the environmental impact of AI technologies, promote sustainable practices, and prioritize the well-being of future generations.
- **Continuous Ethical Reflection:** Ethical considerations in AI-driven education are not static; they evolve with technological advancements and societal changes. Institutions should engage in continuous ethical reflection, regularly reviewing and updating their ethical guidelines and practices to address emerging challenges and opportunities.
- **Building Ethical Awareness:** Fostering ethical awareness among all stakeholders is essential for creating a responsible AI-driven educational ecosystem. Institutions should provide training and resources on ethical AI use, encouraging students, educators, and administrators to engage with ethical issues critically and thoughtfully.

Conclusion

Addressing ethical considerations in AI-driven education is essential for ensuring that AI technologies are used responsibly, equitably, and transparently. By focusing on data privacy, algorithmic bias, transparency, accountability, and the human-centered approach, educational institutions can build trust and maximize the benefits of AI. Long-term ethical reflection and continuous engagement with ethical issues are crucial for navigating the dynamic nature of AI and fostering a sustainable and inclusive educational landscape. Through thoughtful and proactive ethical practices, we can harness the transformative potential of AI to enhance education while safeguarding the interests and well-being of all stakeholders.

QUESTIONNAIRE

Question 1: How has education technology evolved over the past decades?

Answer: Education technology has significantly evolved from traditional classroom tools to advanced digital platforms. Initially, it involved basic computer-assisted instruction and multimedia resources. With the advent of the internet, e-learning platforms emerged, offering online courses and interactive content. In recent years, advancements in AI have revolutionized education, enabling adaptive learning systems, virtual tutors, and sophisticated data analytics. These innovations provide personalized learning experiences and real-time feedback, enhancing student engagement and outcomes.

Question 2: What are some key milestones in the development of educational technology?

Answer: Key milestones include the introduction of personal computers in the 1980s, the rise of the internet and online learning platforms in the 1990s, the development of Learning Management Systems (LMS) in the 2000s, and the integration of AI and machine learning in education in the 2010s. Each milestone has progressively enhanced the accessibility, interactivity, and personalization of education.

Question 3: What is AI, and how is it applied in education?

Answer: AI, or Artificial Intelligence, refers to the simulation of human intelligence in machines designed to think and learn. In education, AI is applied through intelligent tutoring systems, adaptive learning platforms, and automated grading systems. These applications can analyze student data to provide personalized feedback, suggest tailored learning paths, and automate administrative tasks, thereby enhancing the efficiency and effectiveness of educational processes.

Question 4: What are the primary benefits of AI in education?

Answer: The primary benefits of AI in education include personalized learning experiences, improved student engagement, efficient assessment and feedback, and enhanced administrative efficiency. AI can adapt to individual learning styles, provide real-time support, and automate routine tasks, allowing educators to focus more on teaching and less on administrative duties. Additionally, AI-driven insights can help identify learning gaps and inform instructional strategies.

Question 5: What are AI-powered learning platforms, and how do they function?

Answer: AI-powered learning platforms are educational tools that leverage AI algorithms to enhance learning experiences. These platforms use data analytics to track student progress, identify learning patterns, and personalize content delivery. Functions include adaptive learning paths, real-time feedback, and interactive content. Examples include platforms like Coursera, Khan Academy, and Duolingo, which use AI to customize lessons based on individual performance and preferences.

Question 6: How do AI-powered learning platforms benefit students and educators?

Answer: AI-powered learning platforms benefit students by providing personalized learning experiences, immediate feedback, and engaging content. They adapt to each student's pace and style, ensuring that learning is optimized for individual needs. For educators, these platforms offer valuable insights into student performance, automate grading and administrative tasks, and enable more targeted instruction, freeing up time for more meaningful student interactions.

Question 7: What is personalized learning, and how does AI facilitate it?

Answer: Personalized learning tailors educational experiences to individual students' needs, preferences, and abilities. AI facilitates personalized learning by analyzing data on student performance and behavior to customize content delivery, suggest appropriate learning activities, and provide timely feedback. This approach ensures that each student can learn at their own pace and receive support that is specifically suited to their unique learning style.

Question 8: What are the key advantages of personalized learning with AI?

Answer: The key advantages of personalized learning with AI include improved student engagement, better learning outcomes, and enhanced motivation. AI can identify and address individual learning gaps, provide targeted resources, and adapt to different learning styles. This personalized approach fosters a more supportive and effective learning environment, allowing students to achieve their full potential.

Question 9: How is AI transforming assessment and evaluation in education?

Answer: AI is transforming assessment and evaluation by automating grading, providing instant feedback, and enabling more comprehensive and continuous assessment methods. AI-powered tools can evaluate not only multiple-choice questions but also written responses, projects, and even oral presentations. This allows for a more accurate and holistic assessment of student performance, reducing biases and enhancing objectivity.

Question 10: What are the challenges associated with using AI for assessment and evaluation?

Answer: Challenges associated with using AI for assessment and evaluation include concerns about data privacy, the potential for algorithmic bias, and the need for significant infrastructure and investment. Additionally, ensuring that AI systems are transparent and explainable is crucial to maintain trust and reliability in automated assessment processes. Addressing these challenges requires robust ethical guidelines, continuous monitoring, and collaboration between educators, technologists, and policymakers.

2

Innovating Teaching Practices

AI-DRIVEN CURRICULUM DEVELOPMENT

The integration of artificial intelligence into curriculum development marks a significant shift in how educational content is designed, implemented, and refined. AI-driven curriculum development leverages data analytics, machine learning, and natural language processing to create dynamic and adaptive curricula that cater to diverse student needs. This approach promises to enhance educational outcomes by ensuring that curricula are relevant, engaging, and personalized.

The Role of AI in Curriculum Design

- **Data-Driven Insights:** AI can analyze vast amounts of data from various sources, including student performance records, standardized test scores, and feedback from educators. By identifying patterns and trends, AI provides valuable insights that inform curriculum design. This data-driven approach ensures that the curriculum addresses the specific needs and challenges of students, making it more effective and impactful.

- **Personalization and Adaptivity:** One of the most significant advantages of AI in curriculum development is its ability to personalize learning experiences. AI can create adaptive curricula that adjust in real-time based on student performance and learning styles. This means that each student receives a tailored learning path that meets their unique needs, ensuring that they are appropriately challenged and supported.
- **Content Creation and Curation:** AI can assist in the creation and curation of educational content. Natural language processing algorithms can generate new learning materials, such as lesson plans, quizzes, and interactive exercises. Additionally, AI can curate existing content, selecting the most relevant and effective resources for inclusion in the curriculum. This ensures that the curriculum is always up-to-date and aligned with the latest educational standards and research.
- **Continuous Improvement:** AI enables continuous improvement of the curriculum by providing ongoing feedback and analysis. As students engage with the curriculum, AI systems collect data on their performance and interactions. This data is used to refine and optimize the curriculum, ensuring that it remains effective and responsive to student needs. Continuous improvement also allows educators to address emerging trends and challenges in real-time.

Benefits of AI-Driven Curriculum Development

- **Enhanced Student Engagement:** AI-driven curricula are designed to be interactive and engaging, incorporating multimedia elements, gamification, and real-world applications. This approach helps to capture students' interest and motivate them to actively participate in their learning. Engaged students are more likely to retain information and perform better academically.
- **Improved Learning Outcomes:** By personalizing the learning experience and providing targeted support, AI-driven curricula can significantly improve learning outcomes. Students receive the right level of challenge and support, helping them to master concepts more effectively. Additionally, continuous feedback ensures that learning gaps are identified and addressed promptly.

- **Efficiency and Scalability:** AI-driven curriculum development streamlines the process of creating and updating educational content. This efficiency allows educators to focus more on teaching and less on administrative tasks. Furthermore, AI systems can scale easily, making it possible to implement personalized curricula across large student populations without requiring additional resources.
- **Inclusivity and Equity:** AI-driven curricula can help to create a more inclusive and equitable education system. By personalizing learning experiences, AI ensures that all students, regardless of their background or abilities, receive the support they need to succeed. This inclusivity helps to close achievement gaps and promote educational equity.

Challenges and Considerations

- **Data Privacy and Security:** The use of AI in curriculum development involves collecting and analyzing large amounts of student data. Ensuring the privacy and security of this data is critical. Schools and institutions must implement robust data protection measures and comply with relevant privacy regulations to safeguard student information.
- **Bias and Fairness:** AI algorithms can be susceptible to bias, which can impact the fairness of the curriculum. It is essential to develop AI systems that are transparent and free from bias. This includes using diverse and representative training data and regularly auditing AI systems for potential biases.
- **Teacher Training and Support:** Successful implementation of AI-driven curricula requires that educators are adequately trained and supported. Teachers need to understand how to use AI tools and interpret the data they provide. Ongoing professional development and collaboration with AI experts can help educators integrate AI into their teaching practices effectively.
- **Ethical Considerations:** The use of AI in education raises important ethical considerations. These include ensuring that AI is used to enhance rather than replace human judgment, maintaining transparency in AI decision-making processes, and considering the broader societal implications of AI-driven education.

Case Studies and Examples

- **Carnegie Learning:** Carnegie Learning is an educational technology company that uses AI to develop personalized math curricula. Their AI-driven platform, MATHia, adapts to each student's learning pace and provides real-time feedback and support. This approach has been shown to improve student engagement and performance in mathematics.

- **Knewton:** Knewton is another example of an AI-powered platform that personalizes learning experiences. Knewton's adaptive learning technology analyzes student data to create customized learning paths. The platform continuously updates its recommendations based on student interactions, ensuring that the curriculum remains relevant and effective.
- **Smart Sparrow:** Smart Sparrow is an adaptive e-learning platform that uses AI to create interactive and personalized learning experiences. The platform allows educators to design adaptive lessons that respond to student performance. Smart Sparrow's AI-driven analytics provide insights into student learning, helping educators refine their teaching strategies.

The Future of AI-Driven Curriculum Development

The future of AI-driven curriculum development holds exciting possibilities. As AI technologies continue to advance, we can expect even more sophisticated and effective educational tools. Some potential future developments include:

- **Increased Interactivity:** Future AI-driven curricula may incorporate more advanced interactive elements, such as virtual reality (VR) and augmented reality (AR). These technologies can create immersive learning experiences that enhance understanding and engagement.
- **Integration with Other Technologies:** AI-driven curricula may integrate with other emerging technologies, such as the Internet of Things (IoT) and blockchain. IoT devices can provide real-time data on student interactions, while blockchain can ensure secure and transparent data management.
- **Greater Focus on Soft Skills:** In addition to academic content, future AI-driven curricula may place greater emphasis on developing soft skills, such as critical thinking, creativity, and collaboration. AI can help design activities and assessments that nurture these essential skills.
- **Global Collaboration:** AI-driven curriculum development can facilitate global collaboration among educators, researchers, and policymakers. By sharing data and best practices, we can create more effective and inclusive educational systems worldwide.

ENHANCING TEACHER CAPABILITIES WITH AI

Artificial Intelligence (AI) holds the promise of not only transforming student learning experiences but also significantly enhancing teacher capabilities. By leveraging AI, educators can access tools and resources that streamline administrative tasks, provide real-time insights, and enable more personalized and effective teaching strategies. This section explores the various ways AI can support and empower teachers in their professional roles.

AI Tools for Administrative Efficiency

- **Automated Grading:** One of the most time-consuming tasks for teachers is grading student assignments. AI-powered grading systems can automate this process, providing quick and accurate evaluations of student work. These systems are particularly effective for grading multiple-choice tests, short answers, and even complex essays. By using natural language processing (NLP) algorithms, AI can assess the content, structure, and coherence of student responses, offering detailed feedback. This automation allows teachers to focus more on instructional activities and student interaction.
- **Attendance Tracking and Record Keeping:** AI can streamline administrative tasks such as attendance tracking and record-keeping. Facial recognition technology and smart sensors can automatically monitor student attendance, reducing the need for manual record-keeping. AI-driven systems can also manage student records, track academic progress, and generate reports, making it easier for teachers to access and analyze important data.
- **Scheduling and Planning:** AI-powered scheduling tools can help teachers plan their classes and manage their time more effectively. These tools can optimize timetables, allocate resources, and coordinate activities, ensuring that teachers have the necessary support to deliver their lessons efficiently. By automating these administrative tasks, AI enables teachers to focus more on their core responsibilities of teaching and mentoring students.

Personalized Professional Development

- **Targeted Training Programs:** AI can identify areas where teachers may need additional training and professional development. By analyzing data on teaching practices and student outcomes, AI systems can recommend targeted training programs and resources.

This personalized approach ensures that teachers receive the support they need to improve their skills and effectiveness.

- **Mentorship and Coaching:** AI-powered platforms can facilitate mentorship and coaching for teachers. Virtual coaching systems use AI to provide real-time feedback and guidance, helping teachers refine their instructional techniques. These systems can analyze classroom interactions, suggest improvements, and offer strategies for engaging students more effectively. AI-driven mentorship programs can connect teachers with experienced educators and experts, fostering collaboration and knowledge sharing.
- **Resource Recommendation:** AI can recommend teaching resources, such as lesson plans, multimedia materials, and interactive activities, based on the specific needs and preferences of teachers. By curating high-quality resources, AI helps teachers enhance their instructional practices and provide more engaging and effective learning experiences for their students.

Enhanced Instructional Strategies

- **Adaptive Teaching Tools:** AI-powered adaptive teaching tools can provide real-time insights into student performance and learning needs. These tools can track student progress, identify areas of difficulty, and suggest personalized interventions. By using adaptive teaching tools, teachers can tailor their instruction to meet the diverse needs of their students, ensuring that each learner receives the appropriate level of support and challenge.
- **Interactive Learning Environments:** AI can create interactive and immersive learning environments that enhance student engagement and understanding. For example, AI-driven virtual reality (VR) and augmented reality (AR) applications can simulate real-world scenarios and provide hands-on learning experiences. These technologies can help teachers create more dynamic and engaging lessons, making complex concepts more accessible and interesting for students.
- **Data-Driven Decision Making:** AI provides teachers with valuable data-driven insights that inform instructional decision-making. By analyzing student performance data, AI systems can identify trends, highlight areas for improvement, and suggest effective teaching strategies. This data-driven approach enables teachers to make informed decisions that enhance the quality of education and improve student outcomes.

Challenges and Considerations

- **Data Privacy and Security:** The use of AI in education involves collecting and analyzing large amounts of student and teacher data. Ensuring the privacy and security of this data is crucial. Schools and institutions must implement robust data protection measures and comply with relevant privacy regulations to safeguard sensitive information.
- **Bias and Fairness:** AI algorithms can be susceptible to bias, which can impact the fairness of the insights and recommendations provided. It is essential to develop AI systems that are transparent and free from bias. Regular audits and evaluations of AI tools can help identify and address any biases, ensuring that AI supports equitable and fair educational practices.
- **Teacher Training and Support:** Successful integration of AI into teaching practices requires adequate training and support for educators. Teachers need to understand how to use AI tools effectively and interpret the data they provide. Ongoing professional development and collaboration with AI experts can help teachers harness the full potential of AI in education.
- **Ethical Considerations:** The use of AI in education raises important ethical considerations. These include ensuring that AI enhances rather than replaces human judgment, maintaining transparency in AI decision-making processes, and considering the broader societal implications of AI-driven education.

Case Studies and Examples

- **IBM Watson for Education:** IBM Watson for Education offers a suite of AI-powered tools designed to support teachers in various aspects of their professional roles. These tools provide personalized recommendations for lesson plans, student interventions, and professional development resources. By analyzing student data, Watson helps teachers identify learning gaps and tailor their instruction to meet individual student needs.
- **Google Classroom with AI:** Google Classroom integrates AI to streamline administrative tasks and enhance instructional practices. AI-powered features, such as automated grading and personalized feedback, help teachers manage their workloads more efficiently. Google Classroom's AI-driven analytics provide insights into student performance, enabling teachers to make data-informed decisions.

- **Century Tech:** Century Tech is an AI-powered platform that combines learning science, AI, and neuroscience to create personalized learning experiences. The platform provides real-time data and insights that help teachers understand student performance and tailor their instruction accordingly. Century Tech also offers professional development resources to support teachers in using AI effectively.

The Future of AI in Enhancing Teacher Capabilities

The future of AI in education holds exciting possibilities for enhancing teacher capabilities. As AI technologies continue to advance, we can expect even more sophisticated and effective tools that support teachers in their professional roles:

- **Increased Collaboration Future:** AI systems may facilitate greater collaboration among teachers, students, and parents. AI-driven platforms can support communication, resource sharing, and joint problem-solving, creating a more collaborative and supportive educational environment.
- **Advanced Personalization:** AI will continue to improve its ability to personalize learning experiences and professional development for teachers. Advanced AI systems can offer even more tailored recommendations and interventions, helping teachers address the unique needs of their students and enhance their instructional practices.
- **Integration with Emerging Technologies:** AI will increasingly integrate with other emerging technologies, such as IoT and blockchain, to provide comprehensive and secure educational solutions. These integrations will enhance data collection, analysis, and management, further supporting teachers in their roles.
- **Ethical AI Development:** As AI becomes more prevalent in education, there will be a growing emphasis on developing ethical AI systems. Ensuring transparency, fairness, and accountability in AI-driven education will be paramount to building trust and maximizing the benefits of AI for teachers and students alike.

AI AND STUDENT ENGAGEMENT

Student engagement is a critical factor in the learning process, influencing academic achievement, motivation, and overall educational outcomes. AI technologies offer innovative ways to enhance student engagement by creating interactive, personalized, and immersive learning experiences. This section explores how AI can boost student engagement and the benefits it brings to the educational landscape.

Interactive Learning Environments

- **Gamification:** Gamification involves incorporating game-like elements into educational activities to make learning more engaging and enjoyable. AI can enhance gamification by personalizing challenges, providing instant feedback, and adapting game difficulty based on student performance. This approach can motivate students to participate actively, complete tasks, and achieve learning goals. Examples of AI-driven gamified learning platforms include Duolingo for language learning and Kahoot! for interactive quizzes.
- **Virtual and Augmented Reality (VR/AR):** AI-powered VR and AR technologies create immersive learning environments that simulate real-world scenarios. These technologies can make complex subjects more accessible and engaging by allowing students to explore, interact, and experiment in a virtual space. For example, medical students can practice surgeries in a virtual operating room, and history students can explore ancient civilizations through AR. These immersive experiences can deepen understanding and retention of knowledge.
- **AI-Driven Simulations:** Simulations powered by AI provide realistic and interactive learning experiences. These simulations can replicate complex systems and processes, allowing students to experiment and learn in a risk-free environment. For instance, AI-driven flight simulators help aviation students practice piloting skills, while business simulations enable students to manage virtual companies. Such hands-on learning experiences can enhance engagement and develop critical thinking and problem-solving skills.

Personalized Learning Experiences

- **Adaptive Learning Platforms:** Adaptive learning platforms use AI to tailor educational content to individual student needs. By analyzing student performance data, these platforms adjust the difficulty, pace, and type of content presented. This personalization ensures that each student receives the appropriate level of challenge and support, keeping them engaged and motivated. Examples of adaptive learning platforms include DreamBox for mathematics and Smart Sparrow for interactive lessons.

- **Intelligent Tutoring Systems:** Intelligent Tutoring Systems (ITS) use AI to provide one-on-one tutoring tailored to each student's learning style and pace. ITS can offer personalized feedback, hints, and explanations, helping students understand complex concepts and stay engaged in their learning. These systems can identify areas where students struggle and provide targeted interventions, making learning more efficient and enjoyable. Notable ITS examples include Carnegie Learning's MATHia and the Virtual Learning Lab's ASSISTments.
- **Personalized Content Recommendations:** AI can recommend personalized learning resources based on student interests, performance, and learning history. These recommendations can include articles, videos, interactive exercises, and more. By presenting content that aligns with student preferences and needs, AI helps maintain engagement and fosters a love for learning. Platforms like Edmodo and Coursera utilize AI to provide personalized content recommendations.

Real-Time Feedback and Support

- **Instant Feedback Mechanisms:** AI-powered systems can provide immediate feedback on student assignments, quizzes, and activities. This real-time feedback helps students understand their mistakes and correct them promptly, reinforcing learning and maintaining engagement. Instant feedback also allows teachers to monitor student progress continuously and provide timely support when needed.
- **AI-Powered Chatbots and Virtual Assistants:** AI chatbots and virtual assistants offer real-time support to students, answering questions, providing explanations, and offering study tips. These tools are available 24/7, ensuring that students can receive help whenever they need it. By offering immediate assistance, AI-powered chatbots and virtual assistants help students stay on track and engaged in their studies.
- **Adaptive Assessments:** AI-driven adaptive assessments adjust the difficulty of questions based on student responses. This personalized approach ensures that students are continuously challenged at the right level, preventing boredom and frustration. Adaptive assessments provide a more accurate measure of student understanding and help maintain engagement throughout the learning process.

Collaborative Learning with AI

- **AI-Enhanced Group Projects:** AI can facilitate collaborative learning by enhancing group projects and activities. AI tools can help form diverse and balanced groups, manage project timelines, and provide real-time feedback on group dynamics and progress. By supporting effective collaboration, AI encourages student engagement and fosters teamwork skills.
- **Online Learning Communities:** AI can create and manage online learning communities where students can collaborate, share resources, and support each other. These communities provide a platform for peer-to-peer learning and engagement, making the educational experience more interactive and social. AI can moderate discussions, recommend relevant topics, and highlight key contributions, ensuring that the community remains active and focused.
- **Virtual Classrooms:** AI-powered virtual classrooms offer interactive and engaging online learning experiences. These platforms support live video lessons, interactive whiteboards, and real-time collaboration tools. AI can enhance virtual classrooms by personalizing content, providing instant feedback, and facilitating group activities. Examples of AI-powered virtual classroom platforms include Zoom with AI enhancements and Microsoft Teams with AI-driven features.

Benefits of AI-Enhanced Student Engagement

- **Increased Motivation:** AI technologies that provide personalized and interactive learning experiences can significantly boost student motivation. When students feel that the content is relevant and tailored to their needs, they are more likely to stay engaged and put in the effort required to succeed.
- **Better Academic Performance:** Engaged students are more likely to achieve better academic outcomes. AI-driven engagement strategies, such as personalized learning paths and real-time feedback, help students understand and retain information more effectively, leading to improved performance on assessments and exams.
- **Enhanced Critical Thinking and Problem-Solving Skills:** AI-powered interactive and immersive learning experiences encourage students to think critically and solve problems creatively. By engaging with simulations, gamified activities, and collaborative

projects, students develop essential skills that are crucial for success in the 21st century.

- **Increased Student Retention:** Engaged students are more likely to persist in their studies and complete their educational programs. AI technologies that enhance student engagement can help reduce dropout rates and increase retention, contributing to better long-term educational outcomes.

Challenges and Considerations

- **Access and Equity:** Ensuring equitable access to AI-enhanced learning technologies is a significant challenge. Schools and institutions must address the digital divide by providing necessary resources and support to all students, regardless of their socioeconomic background.
- **Data Privacy and Security:** The use of AI in education involves collecting and analyzing large amounts of student data. Protecting this data and ensuring privacy and security are critical. Schools must implement robust data protection measures and comply with relevant privacy regulations.
- **Teacher Training and Support:** Teachers need adequate training and support to effectively integrate AI technologies into their teaching practices. Professional development programs should focus on building educators' skills and confidence in using AI tools to enhance student engagement.
- **Ethical Considerations:** The use of AI in education raises ethical questions, such as ensuring transparency, avoiding bias, and maintaining the role of human educators. Schools and institutions must consider these ethical implications and develop policies that promote responsible AI use.

AI has the potential to revolutionize student engagement in education. By creating interactive, personalized, and immersive learning experiences, AI can motivate students, improve academic performance, and develop essential skills. However, addressing challenges related to access, data privacy, teacher training, and ethical considerations is crucial to ensuring that AI's benefits are realized equitably and responsibly.

VIRTUAL CLASSROOMS AND AI

The concept of virtual classrooms has gained significant traction, particularly in the wake of global events that have necessitated remote learning. AI plays a crucial role in enhancing the virtual classroom experience, making online education more interactive, engaging, and effective. This section explores how AI is transforming virtual classrooms and the benefits and challenges associated with its integration.

The Role of AI in Virtual Classrooms

- **Personalized Learning Experiences:** AI algorithms analyze student data to tailor learning experiences to individual needs. In a virtual classroom, AI can customize lesson plans, recommend resources, and adjust the difficulty level of assignments in real-time. This personalization ensures that each student receives the appropriate support and challenge, fostering a more effective learning environment.
- **Intelligent Tutoring Systems:** AI-driven intelligent tutoring systems (ITS) provide personalized instruction and feedback in a virtual setting. These systems simulate one-on-one tutoring, guiding students through complex subjects and offering instant feedback on their progress. ITS can identify areas where students struggle and provide targeted interventions, making learning more efficient and engaging.
- **Enhanced Interaction and Engagement:** Virtual classrooms can sometimes lack the interactive elements of traditional classrooms. AI enhances interaction by incorporating features such as interactive quizzes, gamified learning activities, and real-time polls. AI can also facilitate group discussions and collaborative projects, making the virtual learning experience more dynamic and engaging.
- **Real-Time Feedback and Assessment:** AI tools provide real-time feedback on student performance, enabling immediate corrections and improvements. Automated grading systems evaluate assignments and quizzes instantly, giving students timely feedback and helping teachers monitor progress continuously. This real-time assessment helps maintain student engagement and ensures that learning gaps are addressed promptly.
- **Natural Language Processing (NLP):** NLP technologies enable AI to understand and respond to student inquiries in natural language. Virtual teaching assistants powered by NLP can answer questions, provide explanations, and offer study tips, simulating the support students would receive from a human teacher. This capability enhances the accessibility and responsiveness of virtual classrooms.

Benefits of AI-Enhanced Virtual Classrooms

- **Flexibility and Accessibility:** AI-powered virtual classrooms offer flexibility in terms of time and location. Students can access learning materials and participate in classes from anywhere, making education more accessible to those who may have constraints due to geography, health, or other factors. This flexibility also supports diverse learning schedules and paces.
- **Scalability:** Virtual classrooms can accommodate large numbers of students without compromising the quality of education. AI systems can manage and personalize learning experiences for many students simultaneously, making it possible to scale educational programs efficiently.
- **Cost-Effectiveness:** AI-driven virtual classrooms can reduce the costs associated with traditional education, such as physical infrastructure, transportation, and printed materials. Schools can invest these savings into further improving educational technologies and resources, enhancing the overall quality of education.
- **Continuous Learning:** Virtual classrooms supported by AI facilitate continuous learning, even in the face of disruptions such as natural disasters or pandemics. Students can continue their education uninterrupted, ensuring that learning progress is maintained.

Challenges and Considerations

- **Digital Divide:** The digital divide remains a significant challenge in implementing AI-enhanced virtual classrooms. Students from underserved communities may lack access to the necessary technology and internet connectivity. Addressing these disparities is crucial to ensure equitable access to quality education.
- **Data Privacy and Security:** The use of AI in virtual classrooms involves collecting and analyzing large amounts of student data. Ensuring the privacy and security of this data is critical. Schools must implement robust data protection measures and comply with relevant privacy regulations to safeguard student information.
- **Teacher Training and Support:** Teachers need adequate training and support to effectively integrate AI technologies into virtual classrooms. Professional development programs should focus on building educators' skills and confidence in using AI tools and interpreting the data they provide. Ongoing support is essential to help teachers adapt to new technologies and teaching methods.

- **Student Engagement and Motivation:** Maintaining student engagement and motivation in a virtual classroom can be challenging. AI can help by providing interactive and personalized learning experiences, but it is essential to continuously monitor and address student engagement levels. Educators must find innovative ways to keep students motivated and invested in their learning.
- **Ethical Considerations:** The use of AI in education raises important ethical considerations. These include ensuring transparency, avoiding bias, and maintaining the role of human educators. Schools and institutions must consider these ethical implications and develop policies that promote responsible AI use.

Case Studies and Examples

- **ClassIn:** ClassIn is an AI-powered virtual classroom platform that offers interactive teaching tools and real-time analytics. The platform supports features such as virtual whiteboards, breakout rooms, and interactive quizzes, enhancing the online learning experience. AI-driven analytics provide insights into student performance and engagement, helping teachers tailor their instruction to meet individual needs.
- **Vedantu:** Vedantu is an online tutoring platform that uses AI to personalize learning experiences for students. The platform offers live interactive classes, adaptive assessments, and real-time feedback. AI-driven analytics help teachers monitor student progress and provide targeted support, ensuring that each student receives a personalized learning experience.
- **VIPKid:** VIPKid connects students with teachers for one-on-one English language instruction. The platform uses AI to match students with the most suitable teachers based on their learning preferences and performance data. AI also supports personalized lesson plans and real-time feedback, making learning more engaging and effective.

The Future of AI in Virtual Classrooms

The future of AI in virtual classrooms holds exciting possibilities. As AI technologies continue to advance, we can expect even more sophisticated and effective tools that enhance the online learning experience:

- **Augmented Reality (AR) and Virtual Reality (VR) Integration:** The integration of AR and VR with AI will create more immersive and interactive virtual learning environments. These technologies can simulate real-world scenarios and provide hands-on learning experiences, enhancing student engagement and understanding.

- **AI-Powered Peer Learning:** AI can facilitate peer learning by matching students with similar interests and learning goals. AI-driven platforms can support collaborative projects, group discussions, and peer assessments, fostering a sense of community and collective learning in a virtual setting.
- **Advanced Analytics and Insights:** Future AI systems will provide even more detailed and actionable insights into student performance and engagement. Advanced analytics will help educators identify trends, predict learning outcomes, and develop more effective instructional strategies.
- **Adaptive Learning Technologies:** AI-driven adaptive learning technologies will continue to evolve, offering more personalized and responsive learning experiences. These technologies will be able to adjust in real-time to meet the changing needs of students, ensuring that each learner receives the support they need to succeed.

AI is revolutionizing virtual classrooms by providing personalized, interactive, and flexible learning experiences. While challenges such as the digital divide, data privacy, and teacher training must be addressed, the potential benefits of AI-enhanced virtual classrooms are significant. By leveraging AI technologies, educators can create more engaging and effective online learning environments that meet the diverse needs of students.

AI IN SPECIAL EDUCATION

Artificial Intelligence (AI) has the potential to revolutionize special education by providing personalized support and tailored learning experiences to students with diverse needs. AI technologies can assist in identifying learning difficulties, developing individualized education plans (IEPs), and offering adaptive learning tools that cater to each student's unique abilities. This section explores the various applications of AI in special education and the benefits it brings to students, educators, and parents.

Personalized Learning for Diverse Needs

- **Individualized Education Plans (IEPs):** AI can aid in the creation and management of IEPs, ensuring that each student's educational needs are met effectively. By analyzing data on student performance, behavior, and preferences, AI systems can develop comprehensive and personalized IEPs. These plans can be continuously updated based on real-time data, ensuring that they remain relevant and effective.

- **Adaptive Learning Technologies:** Adaptive learning platforms powered by AI can provide personalized educational experiences for students with special needs. These platforms adjust the content, pace, and difficulty of lessons based on each student's progress and learning style. This adaptability helps students engage with the material at their own pace and ensures they receive the appropriate level of support.
- **Assistive Technologies:** AI-driven assistive technologies can support students with physical, cognitive, and sensory disabilities. Examples include speech-to-text and text-to-speech applications, predictive text tools, and AI-powered communication devices. These technologies help students overcome barriers to learning and participate more fully in educational activities.

Enhancing Teacher Capabilities

- **Early Detection and Intervention:** AI can help identify learning disabilities and developmental delays early by analyzing patterns in student behavior and performance. Early detection allows for timely intervention, which is crucial for addressing learning difficulties and supporting student development. AI-driven tools can provide educators with insights and recommendations for interventions tailored to each student's needs.
- **Data-Driven Insights:** AI provides educators with detailed insights into student performance and progress. By analyzing this data, teachers can identify trends, track the effectiveness of interventions, and make informed decisions about instructional strategies. These insights enable educators to provide targeted support and adapt their teaching methods to better meet the needs of their students.
- **Professional Development:** AI can offer personalized professional development resources for teachers working in special education. These resources may include training modules, instructional strategies, and case studies. By providing tailored support, AI helps educators enhance their skills and stay updated with the latest advancements in special education.

Supporting Parents and Caregivers

- **Communication and Collaboration:** AI-powered platforms can facilitate better communication and collaboration between educators, parents, and caregivers. These platforms can provide real-time updates on student progress, share resources, and offer personalized recommendations for supporting learning at home. Enhanced communication helps ensure that everyone involved in the student's education is aligned and working together effectively.

- **Parent Training and Resources:** AI can offer personalized training and resources for parents and caregivers of students with special needs. These resources can include instructional videos, articles, and interactive modules that provide guidance on supporting learning and development. By empowering parents with knowledge and tools, AI helps create a more supportive and effective learning environment at home.

Case Studies and Examples

- **CogniToys:** CogniToys are AI-powered educational toys designed to engage children in interactive learning experiences. These toys use natural language processing to understand and respond to children's questions, providing personalized feedback and support. CogniToys are particularly beneficial for children with learning disabilities, as they offer a fun and engaging way to practice language and cognitive skills.
- **Brainly:** Brainly is an AI-driven platform that provides personalized homework help and tutoring for students. The platform uses AI to analyze student questions and provide relevant answers and resources. Brainly's personalized approach helps students with special needs receive the targeted support they require to understand and complete their assignments.
- **Seeing AI:** Seeing AI is an AI-powered app developed by Microsoft that helps visually impaired students navigate their environment and access educational content. The app uses computer vision to describe the world around the user, read text aloud, and identify objects and people. Seeing AI enhances accessibility and independence for visually impaired students, enabling them to participate more fully in educational activities.

Challenges and Considerations

- **Equity and Access:** Ensuring equitable access to AI-powered special education tools is a significant challenge. Students from underserved communities may lack access to the necessary technology and resources. Schools and policymakers must address these disparities to ensure that all students can benefit from AI advancements in special education.

- **Data Privacy and Security:** The use of AI in special education involves collecting and analyzing sensitive student data. Ensuring the privacy and security of this data is critical. Schools must implement robust data protection measures and comply with relevant privacy regulations to safeguard student information.
- **Bias and Fairness:** AI algorithms can be susceptible to bias, which can impact the fairness and effectiveness of personalized learning experiences. It is essential to develop AI systems that are transparent and free from bias. Regular audits and evaluations of AI tools can help identify and address any biases, ensuring that AI supports equitable educational practices.
- **Teacher Training and Support:** Successful integration of AI into special education requires adequate training and support for educators. Teachers need to understand how to use AI tools effectively and interpret the data they provide. Ongoing professional development and collaboration with AI experts can help teachers harness the full potential of AI in special education.

The Future of AI in Special Education

The future of AI in special education holds exciting possibilities. As AI technologies continue to advance, we can expect even more sophisticated and effective tools that support students with diverse needs:

- **Emotion Recognition and Social Skills Training:** Future AI systems may include emotion recognition capabilities that help identify and respond to students' emotional states. These systems can provide real-time feedback and support for developing social and emotional skills, which are crucial for students with autism and other social communication disorders.
- **Augmented Reality (AR) for Skill Development:** AR technologies, powered by AI, can create immersive learning experiences that support skill development for students with special needs. For example, AR can simulate real-world scenarios to help students practice social interactions, daily living skills, and vocational training in a safe and controlled environment.
- **Enhanced Collaboration Tools:** AI-driven collaboration tools will continue to improve, facilitating better communication and coordination among educators, parents, and caregivers. These tools will support more effective IEP development and implementation, ensuring that all stakeholders are aligned and working together to support student success.

- **Advanced Predictive Analytics:** Predictive analytics will become more advanced, allowing educators to identify potential learning difficulties and developmental delays even earlier. These insights will enable proactive interventions and support, improving educational outcomes for students with special needs.

AI has the potential to transform special education by providing personalized support, enhancing teacher capabilities, and empowering parents and caregivers. While challenges related to equity, data privacy, and bias must be addressed, the benefits of AI in special education are significant. By leveraging AI technologies, we can create more inclusive, effective, and supportive educational environments for students with diverse needs.

PROFESSIONAL DEVELOPMENT AND TRAINING FOR AI INTEGRATION

As Artificial Intelligence (AI) becomes an integral part of educational practices, it is essential to equip educators with the knowledge and skills necessary to effectively integrate AI into their teaching. Professional development and training programs play a crucial role in preparing teachers to leverage AI tools to enhance their instructional capabilities and improve student outcomes. This section explores the importance of professional development for AI integration, key components of effective training programs, and strategies for implementation.

The Importance of Professional Development for AI Integration

- **Building AI Literacy:** Educators need a solid understanding of AI concepts, applications, and implications to effectively integrate AI into their teaching. Professional development programs help build AI literacy, ensuring that teachers are familiar with the basics of AI, its potential uses in education, and the ethical considerations involved.
- **Enhancing Teaching Practices:** AI offers numerous opportunities to enhance teaching practices by providing personalized learning experiences, real-time feedback, and data-driven insights. Professional development equips teachers with the skills to use AI tools effectively, enabling them to create more engaging and impactful learning environments.
- **Supporting Continuous Improvement:** Ongoing professional development fosters a culture of continuous improvement among educators. As AI technologies evolve, teachers need to stay updated with the latest advancements and best practices. Regular training ensures that educators can adapt to new tools and methodologies, maintaining their effectiveness in the classroom.

Key Components of Effective Training Programs

- **Foundational Knowledge of AI:** Training programs should begin with foundational knowledge of AI, covering key concepts such as machine learning, natural language processing, and data analytics. Educators should understand how AI works, its potential applications in education, and the limitations and challenges associated with AI technologies.
- **Practical Applications of AI in Education:** Educators need practical training on how to apply AI tools in their teaching. This includes hands-on workshops and demonstrations of AI-driven platforms for personalized learning, adaptive assessments, and data analysis. Teachers should learn how to integrate these tools into their lesson plans and instructional strategies.
- **Ethical Considerations and Data Privacy:** Addressing ethical considerations and data privacy is essential for responsible AI use. Training programs should cover topics such as algorithmic bias, data protection regulations, and ethical guidelines for AI implementation. Educators should be aware of the potential risks and ethical implications of using AI in the classroom.
- **Collaborative Learning and Peer Support:** Collaborative learning and peer support are crucial for effective professional development. Training programs should facilitate collaboration among educators, allowing them to share experiences, discuss challenges, and co-develop solutions. Peer mentoring and support networks can enhance learning and foster a sense of community.
- **Continuous Professional Development:** Professional development for AI integration should be an ongoing process. Institutions should offer regular training sessions, workshops, and online courses to keep educators updated with the latest AI advancements and best practices. Continuous learning ensures that teachers remain proficient in using AI tools and methodologies.

Strategies for Implementing Professional Development Programs

- **Institutional Support and Commitment:** Successful professional development programs require institutional support and commitment. School leadership should prioritize AI training for educators, allocate resources for professional development, and create a supportive environment for continuous learning.
- **Partnerships with AI Experts and Organizations:** Collaborating with AI experts, technology providers, and educational organizations can enhance the quality of professional development programs.

Partnerships can provide access to cutting-edge AI tools, expert knowledge, and best practices, enriching the training experience for educators.

- **Customized Training Programs:** Professional development programs should be customized to meet the specific needs and contexts of different schools and educators. Tailoring training to address the unique challenges and goals of each institution ensures that the programs are relevant and impactful.
- **Leveraging Online Learning Platforms:** Online learning platforms offer flexible and accessible professional development opportunities. Institutions can use these platforms to deliver AI training courses, webinars, and workshops, allowing educators to learn at their own pace and convenience.
- **Incentives and Recognition:** Providing incentives and recognition for participating in professional development programs can motivate educators to engage in continuous learning. Institutions can offer certificates, professional development credits, and other forms of recognition to acknowledge teachers' commitment to enhancing their AI skills.

Case Studies and Examples

- **ISTE's AI Explorations and Their Practical Use in School Environments:** The International Society for Technology in Education (ISTE) offers a comprehensive professional development program focused on AI integration in K-12 education. The program provides educators with hands-on experience using AI tools, explores ethical considerations, and offers practical strategies for implementing AI in the classroom.
- **Finland's National AI Program for Educators:** Finland has implemented a national AI program aimed at training educators to use AI tools effectively. The program includes online courses, workshops, and collaborative projects, covering topics such as AI literacy, ethical AI use, and practical applications in education. The initiative has successfully enhanced educators' AI skills and improved teaching practices across the country.
- **AI4K12 Initiative:** The AI4K12 Initiative provides resources and professional development for K-12 educators to integrate AI into their curricula. The initiative offers guidelines for teaching AI concepts, hands-on activities, and ethical discussions, helping educators prepare students for an AI-driven future. The AI4K12 Initiative's resources are designed to be accessible and adaptable to different educational contexts.

Challenges and Considerations

- **Resource Constraints:** Limited resources can pose challenges to implementing comprehensive professional development programs. Securing funding, access to AI tools, and expert support are essential for delivering high-quality training. Institutions should explore partnerships and grant opportunities to overcome resource constraints.
- **Diverse Learning Needs:** Educators have diverse learning needs and varying levels of familiarity with AI technologies. Professional development programs must be adaptable and inclusive, accommodating different skill levels and learning styles to ensure that all educators can benefit from the training.
- **Keeping Pace with Technological Advancements:** The rapid pace of AI advancements can make it challenging to keep professional development programs up-to-date. Institutions should establish mechanisms for continuous review and updating of training content to address emerging trends and new developments in AI.
- **Balancing Professional Development with Teaching Responsibilities:** Finding time for professional development can be difficult for educators who are already balancing multiple responsibilities. Institutions should provide flexible and convenient training options, such as online courses and in-person workshops during non-teaching hours, to accommodate educators' schedules.

Conclusion

Professional development and training are essential for preparing educators to effectively integrate AI into their teaching practices. By building AI literacy, enhancing teaching practices, and addressing ethical considerations, professional development programs can empower educators to leverage AI tools to improve student outcomes. Implementing effective training programs requires institutional support, partnerships with AI experts, customized training, and continuous professional development. Addressing challenges such as resource constraints, diverse learning needs, and keeping pace with technological advancements is crucial to ensure the success of professional development initiatives. Through thoughtful and proactive professional development, educators can harness the transformative potential of AI to innovate teaching practices and create more engaging and impactful learning environments.

QUESTIONNAIRE

Question 1: How does AI contribute to curriculum development?

Answer: AI contributes to curriculum development by analyzing vast amounts of educational data to identify effective teaching strategies and content. AI systems can recommend curriculum adjustments based on student performance, learning preferences, and emerging educational trends. This data-driven approach ensures that the curriculum is adaptive, relevant, and aligned with current educational standards, fostering a more personalized and effective learning experience.

Question 2: What are the benefits of AI-driven curriculum development for educators?

Answer: AI-driven curriculum development benefits educators by providing insights into student learning patterns, helping tailor instruction to meet diverse needs. It reduces the time spent on curriculum planning by automating data analysis and content curation. This allows educators to focus more on teaching and engaging with students, ultimately enhancing the overall educational experience.

Question 3: In what ways can AI enhance teacher capabilities?

Answer: AI enhances teacher capabilities by offering tools for personalized instruction, automated grading, and real-time feedback. AI-powered systems can analyze student data to identify learning gaps and suggest targeted interventions. Additionally, AI can assist in creating interactive and engaging lesson plans, freeing teachers from administrative tasks and allowing them to concentrate on direct student interaction and support.

Question 4: How does AI enhance student engagement in the classroom?

Answer: AI enhances student engagement by providing personalized learning experiences and interactive content. AI-driven platforms adapt to individual learning styles and paces, offering tailored resources and activities that keep students motivated and interested. Additionally, AI can create immersive learning environments through gamification and virtual simulations, making the learning process more engaging and enjoyable.

Question 5: What role does AI play in virtual classrooms?

Answer: AI plays a significant role in virtual classrooms by enabling real-time interaction, personalized learning, and efficient management of online education. AI-powered platforms can simulate face-to-face classroom experiences, offering features like virtual whiteboards, breakout rooms, and AI-driven tutoring. These tools ensure that students receive support and engagement similar to traditional classroom settings.

Question 6: How can AI improve the effectiveness of virtual classrooms?

Answer: AI improves the effectiveness of virtual classrooms by providing adaptive learning paths, real-time analytics, and automated administrative tasks. AI systems can track student progress, participation, and engagement, offering personalized feedback and resources. This helps create a more interactive and responsive virtual learning environment, ensuring that students remain engaged and motivated.

Question 7: How can AI be used to support special education?

Answer: AI supports special education by providing personalized learning experiences and adaptive tools tailored to individual needs. AI-driven systems can identify specific learning challenges and offer customized interventions, such as speech recognition software for students with language impairments or AI-powered reading assistants for those with dyslexia. These technologies ensure that students with special needs receive targeted support to enhance their learning outcomes.

Question 8: What are the advantages of using AI in special education?

Answer: The advantages of using AI in special education include personalized learning, real-time feedback, and accessible learning materials. AI can adapt to each student's unique needs, providing tailored interventions and support. This ensures that students with special needs receive individualized attention and resources, promoting inclusivity and improving their educational experiences and outcomes.

Question 9: Why is professional development important for AI integration in education?

Answer: Professional development is crucial for AI integration in education because it equips educators with the necessary skills and knowledge to effectively use AI tools. Training helps teachers understand how to implement AI technologies, interpret data analytics, and integrate AI into their teaching practices. This ensures that AI is used to its full potential, enhancing teaching and learning experiences.

Question 10: What should be included in professional development programs for AI integration?

Answer: Professional development programs for AI integration should include training on AI basics, hands-on experience with AI tools, data analytics, and strategies for incorporating AI into curriculum and instruction. Additionally, programs should cover ethical considerations, data privacy, and ways to address potential biases in AI systems. This comprehensive approach ensures that educators are well-prepared to leverage AI in their teaching practices effectively.

3

Research and Future Directions

AI-DRIVEN EDUCATIONAL RESEARCH

Artificial Intelligence (AI) is revolutionizing educational research by providing new tools and methodologies to analyze data, understand learning processes, and develop innovative educational practices. This section explores the impact of AI on educational research, highlighting key areas where AI is driving advancements and offering insights into future directions.

Key Areas of AI-Driven Educational Research

Learning Analytics: AI-powered learning analytics involve the collection, analysis, and interpretation of data related to student learning. By examining patterns and trends in this data, researchers can gain insights into how students learn, identify factors that influence academic performance, and develop strategies to improve educational outcomes. AI enables the analysis of large datasets, uncovering complex relationships and providing a deeper understanding of the learning process.

- **Predictive Analytics:** Predictive analytics use AI to forecast future educational outcomes based on historical data. By analyzing past student performance and behavior, AI can predict which students are at risk of falling behind, which interventions are likely to be effective, and how changes in instructional strategies may impact learning. These predictions enable educators to make data-driven decisions and implement proactive measures to support student success.
- **Natural Language Processing (NLP):** NLP allows AI systems to understand and interpret human language. In educational research, NLP can analyze written and spoken language to assess student understanding, identify misconceptions, and evaluate the quality of instructional materials. NLP can also facilitate the development of automated feedback systems, providing personalized support to students based on their language use.
- **Adaptive Learning Systems:** Adaptive learning systems use AI to create personalized learning experiences that adjust in real-time based on student performance. Research in this area focuses on developing and refining algorithms that optimize learning paths for individual students. By studying the effectiveness of adaptive learning systems, researchers can identify best practices and improve the design of these technologies.
- **Intelligent Tutoring Systems (ITS):** ITS provide one-on-one instruction and feedback to students using AI. Research on ITS examines how these systems can effectively mimic human tutoring, the impact of personalized feedback on learning, and the ways in which ITS can be integrated into traditional educational settings. This research aims to enhance the capabilities of ITS and maximize their benefits for students.

Benefits of AI-Driven Educational Research

- **Enhanced Data Analysis:** AI enables researchers to analyze large and complex datasets more efficiently and accurately than traditional methods. This capability allows for a more comprehensive understanding of educational phenomena and the identification of subtle patterns that may otherwise go unnoticed.

- **Personalized Insights:** AI-driven research provides personalized insights into student learning, enabling the development of targeted interventions and support strategies. By understanding the unique needs and preferences of individual students, educators can tailor their approaches to optimize learning outcomes.
- **Scalability:** AI technologies can scale to analyze data from large populations of students, providing insights that are generalizable across diverse educational contexts. This scalability makes it possible to conduct research on a broad scale, benefiting a wider range of students and educators.
- **Real-Time Analysis:** AI allows for real-time data analysis, enabling researchers to monitor student progress and assess the impact of interventions as they occur. This real-time feedback supports continuous improvement and helps ensure that educational practices remain effective and responsive to student needs.

Challenges and Considerations

- **Data Privacy and Ethics:** The use of AI in educational research involves collecting and analyzing sensitive student data. Ensuring the privacy and security of this data is critical. Researchers must implement robust data protection measures and adhere to ethical guidelines to safeguard student information and maintain trust.
- **Bias and Fairness:** AI algorithms can be susceptible to bias, which can impact the validity and fairness of research findings. It is essential to develop AI systems that are transparent and free from bias. Regular audits and evaluations of AI tools can help identify and address any biases, ensuring that research outcomes are equitable and reliable.
- **Interpretability:** AI-driven research often involves complex algorithms that can be difficult to interpret. Ensuring that research findings are understandable and actionable for educators and policymakers is crucial. Researchers must strive to make their methods and results accessible and transparent to support informed decision-making.
- **Integration with Traditional Methods:** While AI offers powerful tools for educational research, it is important to integrate these technologies with traditional research methods. Combining AI with qualitative approaches, such as interviews and observations, can provide a more holistic understanding of educational phenomena and enhance the validity of research findings.

Case Studies and Examples

- **EdTech Research with AI:** EdTech companies like Knewton and DreamBox Learning use AI to analyze student data and develop personalized learning experiences. Research conducted by these companies examines the effectiveness of their AI-driven platforms and provides insights into how adaptive learning technologies can improve student outcomes.
- **University Research Initiatives:** Universities around the world are leveraging AI to conduct cutting-edge educational research. For example, the University of Michigan's Learning Analytics and Knowledge (LAK) group uses AI to study student engagement and learning patterns in online courses. Their research informs the design of more effective instructional strategies and support systems.
- **Government and Policy Research:** Governments and educational policy organizations are increasingly using AI to analyze large-scale educational data and inform policy decisions. AI-driven research helps identify trends, evaluate the impact of educational programs, and develop evidence-based policies that promote student success.

The Future of AI-Driven Educational Research

The future of AI-driven educational research holds exciting possibilities. As AI technologies continue to advance, we can expect even more sophisticated tools and methodologies that enhance our understanding of education and improve learning outcomes:

1. **Integration with Wearable Technologies:** The integration of AI with wearable technologies, such as smartwatches and biometric sensors, will provide new data sources for educational research. These technologies can monitor student engagement, stress levels, and other physiological indicators, offering deeper insights into the learning process.
2. **Cross-Disciplinary Research:** AI-driven educational research will increasingly involve collaboration across disciplines, combining insights from psychology, neuroscience, computer science, and education. This interdisciplinary approach will lead to a more comprehensive understanding of how students learn and how to support their development effectively.
3. **Advanced Predictive Modeling:** Advances in AI will enable more accurate and sophisticated predictive modeling, helping researchers forecast educational outcomes and identify the most

effective interventions. These models will support personalized learning and ensure that educational practices are evidence-based and data-driven.

4. **Ethical AI Development:** The development of ethical AI systems will be a key focus in the future of educational research. Ensuring transparency, fairness, and accountability in AI-driven research will be essential to building trust and maximizing the benefits of AI for students and educators.

AI is transforming educational research by providing powerful tools and methodologies that enhance data analysis, personalize insights, and support scalable and real-time research. While challenges related to data privacy, bias, and interpretability must be addressed, the benefits of AI-driven educational research are significant. By leveraging AI technologies, researchers can develop a deeper understanding of education and create innovative strategies that improve learning outcomes for all students.

PREDICTIVE ANALYTICS IN EDUCATION

Predictive analytics is a powerful application of AI that leverages historical data to make predictions about future events. In the context of education, predictive analytics can provide insights into student performance, identify at-risk students, and inform decision-making processes to enhance educational outcomes. This section delves into the role of predictive analytics in education, its benefits, and the challenges associated with its implementation.

How Predictive Analytics Works in Education

- **Data Collection:** Predictive analytics begins with the collection of relevant data. In education, this data can include student demographics, attendance records, grades, test scores, behavioral logs, and engagement metrics from digital learning platforms. The quality and comprehensiveness of the data collected are crucial for accurate predictions.
- **Data Preprocessing:** Once data is collected, it must be cleaned and preprocessed to ensure accuracy and consistency. This involves handling missing values, removing outliers, and normalizing data. Preprocessing is a critical step that ensures the data is suitable for analysis by AI algorithms.
- **Model Development:** AI algorithms are used to develop predictive models based on the preprocessed data. These models can identify patterns and relationships within the data that are indicative of

future outcomes. Common algorithms used in predictive analytics include decision trees, random forests, neural networks, and support vector machines.

- **Model Training and Validation:** The predictive models are trained using historical data and validated to ensure their accuracy. This involves splitting the data into training and testing sets, refining the models, and evaluating their performance using metrics such as accuracy, precision, recall, and F1 score. Validated models are then deployed to make predictions on new data.
- **Implementation and Monitoring:** Once the predictive models are validated, they can be implemented in educational settings. Continuous monitoring and updating of the models are essential to maintain their accuracy and relevance over time. Feedback from educators and students can also be incorporated to improve the models.

Applications of Predictive Analytics in Education

- **Identifying At-Risk Students:** Predictive analytics can identify students who are at risk of academic failure or dropping out. By analyzing factors such as attendance, grades, and engagement levels, AI models can flag students who may need additional support. Early identification allows educators to intervene promptly, providing targeted interventions to help these students succeed.
- **Personalized Learning Paths:** Predictive analytics can help create personalized learning paths for students. By predicting how students will respond to different instructional strategies, AI can recommend tailored learning activities, resources, and pacing. This personalization ensures that each student receives the appropriate level of challenge and support, enhancing their learning experience.
- **Optimizing Resource Allocation:** Educational institutions can use predictive analytics to optimize resource allocation. For example, schools can predict enrollment trends and staffing needs, ensuring that resources are allocated efficiently. Predictive models can also help in planning for future infrastructure and technology investments.
- **Improving Student Engagement:** Predictive analytics can identify patterns in student engagement and suggest strategies to enhance it. By analyzing data from digital learning platforms, AI can predict which students are likely to disengage and recommend interventions to re-engage them. This helps maintain high levels of student participation and motivation.

- **Supporting Curriculum Development:** Predictive analytics can inform curriculum development by identifying which topics or teaching methods are most effective. By analyzing student performance data, AI can highlight areas where the curriculum may need adjustment. This data-driven approach ensures that the curriculum remains relevant and effective in meeting student needs.

Benefits of Predictive Analytics in Education

- **Proactive Interventions:** Predictive analytics enables proactive interventions, allowing educators to address issues before they become critical. Early identification of at-risk students and other challenges helps prevent academic failure and dropout, promoting better educational outcomes.
- **Data-Driven Decision Making:** Predictive analytics provides educators with data-driven insights that inform decision-making processes. By relying on empirical evidence, schools can develop more effective strategies and policies, ensuring that their decisions are grounded in real-world data.
- **Enhanced Personalization:** The ability to predict individual student needs allows for more personalized and adaptive learning experiences. Predictive analytics ensures that each student receives the right level of support and challenge, promoting better engagement and academic performance.
- **Resource Efficiency:** Predictive analytics helps educational institutions allocate resources more efficiently. By anticipating needs and trends, schools can plan effectively, ensuring that resources are used where they are most needed. This efficiency leads to cost savings and improved educational outcomes.

Challenges and Considerations

- **Data Privacy and Security:** The use of predictive analytics in education involves handling sensitive student data. Ensuring the privacy and security of this data is paramount. Schools must implement robust data protection measures and comply with relevant privacy regulations to safeguard student information.
- **Bias and Fairness:** AI algorithms can be susceptible to bias, which can impact the fairness of predictions. It is essential to develop and validate predictive models that are transparent and free from bias. Regular audits and evaluations can help identify and address any biases, ensuring equitable outcomes.

- **Accuracy and Reliability:** The accuracy and reliability of predictive models are critical for their effectiveness. Inaccurate predictions can lead to inappropriate interventions, potentially harming students rather than helping them. Continuous monitoring and updating of models are necessary to maintain their accuracy.
- **Ethical Considerations:** The use of predictive analytics raises ethical considerations, such as the potential for over-reliance on AI and the need to balance data-driven insights with human judgment. Schools must develop ethical guidelines for the use of predictive analytics, ensuring that AI is used responsibly and transparently.

Case Studies and Examples

- **Georgia State University:** Georgia State University uses predictive analytics to improve student retention and graduation rates. By analyzing data on student performance and engagement, the university can identify at-risk students and provide targeted support. This proactive approach has significantly increased retention and graduation rates at the institution.
- **Montgomery County Public Schools:** Montgomery County Public Schools use predictive analytics to identify students at risk of academic failure and dropout. The district's early warning system analyzes data on attendance, behavior, and academic performance to flag students who need additional support. This system allows for timely interventions, improving student outcomes.
- **EdTech Platforms:** Many EdTech platforms, such as Coursera and Khan Academy, use predictive analytics to personalize learning experiences. These platforms analyze user data to recommend tailored learning activities and resources, enhancing engagement and effectiveness. Predictive models help these platforms deliver personalized education at scale.

The Future of Predictive Analytics in Education

The future of predictive analytics in education holds exciting possibilities. As AI technologies continue to advance, we can expect even more sophisticated and effective applications:

- **Integration with Emerging Technologies:** Predictive analytics will increasingly integrate with other emerging technologies, such as IoT and blockchain. IoT devices can provide real-time data on student engagement and learning environments, while blockchain ensures secure and transparent data management.

- **Advanced Behavioral Analytics:** Future predictive models will incorporate more advanced behavioral analytics, providing deeper insights into student behavior and engagement. These models will help educators understand the underlying factors influencing student performance and develop more effective interventions.
- **Real-Time Predictive Models:** The development of real-time predictive models will enable instant analysis and feedback, allowing for immediate interventions. These models will provide continuous insights into student progress, ensuring that support is always timely and relevant.
- **Ethical AI Development:** The development of ethical AI systems will be a key focus in the future of predictive analytics in education. Ensuring transparency, fairness, and accountability in AI-driven predictions will be essential to building trust and maximizing the benefits of predictive analytics for students and educators.

Predictive analytics has the potential to transform education by providing data-driven insights and proactive interventions. While challenges related to data privacy, bias, and accuracy must be addressed, the benefits of predictive analytics are significant. By leveraging AI technologies, educators can create more personalized, effective, and equitable learning experiences for all students.

AI AND LIFELONG LEARNING

Lifelong learning has become increasingly important in today's rapidly changing world, where continuous education and skill development are essential to keep pace with technological advancements and evolving job markets. AI has the potential to transform lifelong learning by providing personalized, flexible, and accessible learning experiences for individuals of all ages. This section explores the role of AI in promoting lifelong learning and the benefits it offers.

The Importance of Lifelong Learning

- **Adapting to Technological Change:** The rapid pace of technological innovation requires individuals to continually update their skills and knowledge. Lifelong learning ensures that people can adapt to new technologies and remain competitive in the job market.
- **Career Advancement:** Continuous education and skill development are critical for career advancement. Lifelong learning helps individuals acquire new competencies, enhance their professional qualifications, and pursue new career opportunities.

- **Personal Growth and Fulfillment:** Lifelong learning contributes to personal growth and fulfillment by allowing individuals to explore new interests, develop new skills, and achieve personal goals. It promotes intellectual curiosity and lifelong engagement with learning.

AI-Driven Lifelong Learning Platforms

- **Personalized Learning Paths:** AI-powered lifelong learning platforms create personalized learning paths for individuals based on their goals, preferences, and learning styles. By analyzing user data, these platforms recommend tailored courses, resources, and activities that align with each learner's needs. Examples include Coursera, Udacity, and LinkedIn Learning, which offer personalized course recommendations and learning experiences.
- **Adaptive Learning Technologies:** Adaptive learning technologies use AI to adjust the content, pace, and difficulty of learning materials in real-time based on user performance. This adaptability ensures that learners receive the appropriate level of challenge and support, promoting effective learning and skill development.
- **AI-Powered Assessment and Feedback:** AI-driven assessment tools provide real-time feedback on learning progress, helping individuals identify their strengths and areas for improvement. These tools can evaluate performance on quizzes, assignments, and projects, offering personalized feedback and recommendations for further study.
- **Virtual Mentors and Tutors:** AI-powered virtual mentors and tutors provide personalized guidance and support to lifelong learners. These virtual assistants can answer questions, provide explanations, and offer study tips, simulating the support individuals would receive from a human mentor. Platforms like IBM's Watson Tutor and Google's Socratic use AI to offer personalized tutoring and support.

Benefits of AI in Lifelong Learning

- **Flexibility and Accessibility:** AI-driven lifelong learning platforms offer flexible and accessible learning experiences, allowing individuals to learn at their own pace and on their own schedule. This flexibility accommodates diverse learning needs and preferences, making education more inclusive and accessible.

- **Personalization:** The ability to personalize learning experiences is a significant advantage of AI in lifelong learning. Personalized learning paths, adaptive technologies, and tailored feedback ensure that each learner receives the appropriate level of support and challenge, promoting effective learning and skill development.
- **Engagement and Motivation:** AI technologies can enhance engagement and motivation by providing interactive and immersive learning experiences. Gamification, virtual reality (VR), and augmented reality (AR) are examples of AI-driven tools that make learning more enjoyable and engaging.
- **Continuous Improvement:** AI-driven lifelong learning platforms continuously collect and analyze data on user performance and behavior, enabling continuous improvement of the learning experience. This data-driven approach ensures that the content and strategies remain relevant and effective.

Challenges and Considerations

- **Equity and Access:** Ensuring equitable access to AI-driven lifelong learning platforms is a significant challenge. Individuals from underserved communities may lack access to the necessary technology and resources. Addressing these disparities is crucial to ensure that all individuals can benefit from AI advancements in lifelong learning.
- **Data Privacy and Security:** The use of AI in lifelong learning involves collecting and analyzing sensitive user data. Ensuring the privacy and security of this data is critical. Lifelong learning platforms must implement robust data protection measures and comply with relevant privacy regulations to safeguard user information.
- **Bias and Fairness:** AI algorithms can be susceptible to bias, which can impact the fairness and effectiveness of personalized learning experiences. It is essential to develop AI systems that are transparent and free from bias. Regular audits and evaluations can help identify and address any biases, ensuring equitable outcomes.
- **Quality of Content:** The quality of the content provided by AI-driven lifelong learning platforms is crucial for effective learning. Ensuring that the content is accurate, up-to-date, and relevant to the learner's goals is essential. Platforms must work with experts and educators to curate high-quality content.

Case Studies and Examples

- **Coursera:** Coursera is an online learning platform that offers a wide range of courses, specializations, and degrees from top universities and organizations. The platform uses AI to recommend courses based on user interests and learning history, providing a personalized learning experience. Coursera's AI-driven features include adaptive learning technologies, personalized feedback, and tailored course recommendations.
- **LinkedIn Learning:** LinkedIn Learning is a professional development platform that offers courses on various topics, including business, technology, and creative skills. The platform uses AI to analyze user data and recommend personalized learning paths. LinkedIn Learning also provides real-time feedback and assessment tools to help users track their progress and achieve their learning goals.
- **IBM Watson Tutor:** IBM Watson Tutor is an AI-powered virtual tutor that provides personalized support and guidance to learners. The platform uses natural language processing (NLP) and machine learning algorithms to understand and respond to user inquiries. Watson Tutor offers personalized explanations, study tips, and recommendations, simulating the support of a human tutor.

The Future of AI in Lifelong Learning

The future of AI in lifelong learning holds exciting possibilities. As AI technologies continue to advance, we can expect even more sophisticated and effective tools that support continuous education and skill development:

- **Integration with Emerging Technologies:** The integration of AI with emerging technologies such as IoT, blockchain, and 5G will enhance the capabilities of lifelong learning platforms. IoT devices can provide real-time data on learning environments, while blockchain ensures secure and transparent data management. 5G will enable faster and more reliable connectivity, supporting seamless learning experiences.
- **Advanced Personalization:** Future AI systems will offer even more advanced personalization, providing highly tailored learning experiences based on detailed user profiles. These systems will analyze a wide range of data, including behavioral and biometric data, to create comprehensive and personalized learning paths.
- **Immersive Learning Experiences:** The use of immersive technologies such as VR and AR will become more prevalent in lifelong learning. These technologies can create realistic and

interactive learning environments, enhancing engagement and understanding. AI will play a crucial role in personalizing and optimizing these immersive experiences.

- **Lifelong Learning Ecosystems:** The future of lifelong learning will involve the development of comprehensive ecosystems that integrate various learning platforms, tools, and resources. AI will facilitate the seamless integration of these components, creating cohesive and interconnected learning experiences. These ecosystems will support continuous education and skill development throughout an individual's life.

AI has the potential to transform lifelong learning by providing personalized, flexible, and accessible learning experiences. While challenges related to equity, data privacy, and bias must be addressed, the benefits of AI-driven lifelong learning are significant. By leveraging AI technologies, individuals can engage in continuous education and skill development, ensuring they remain competitive in the job market and achieve personal growth and fulfillment.

AI IN HIGHER EDUCATION

Higher education institutions are increasingly adopting AI technologies to enhance teaching, learning, and administrative processes. AI has the potential to revolutionize higher education by providing personalized learning experiences, improving operational efficiency, and supporting innovative research. This section explores the various applications of AI in higher education and the benefits and challenges associated with its implementation.

Applications of AI in Higher Education

- **Personalized Learning:** AI-powered platforms in higher education can create personalized learning experiences for students by analyzing their performance, learning styles, and preferences. These platforms use adaptive learning technologies to adjust the content, pace, and difficulty of lessons in real-time, ensuring that each student receives the appropriate level of support and challenge. Examples include platforms like Coursera and EdX, which offer personalized course recommendations and adaptive learning paths.
- **Intelligent Tutoring Systems (ITS):** ITS in higher education provide personalized instruction and feedback to students, simulating the one-on-one interaction with a human tutor. These systems can help students understand complex concepts, offer targeted support, and provide instant feedback on assignments

and assessments. ITS can be particularly beneficial in large classes where individual attention from instructors is limited.

- **AI-Powered Research: Tools** AI technologies support research in higher education by providing advanced data analysis, natural language processing (NLP), and machine learning capabilities. AI can analyze large datasets, identify patterns and trends, and generate insights that inform research outcomes. These tools enhance the efficiency and accuracy of research processes, enabling scholars to make groundbreaking discoveries.
- **Administrative Efficiency:** AI can streamline administrative processes in higher education, improving efficiency and reducing costs. Applications include automated grading, attendance tracking, scheduling, and resource allocation. AI-powered chatbots and virtual assistants can handle routine administrative tasks, answer student inquiries, and provide support services, freeing up staff to focus on more complex issues.
- **Predictive Analytics:** Predictive analytics in higher education can forecast student performance, retention, and graduation rates. By analyzing historical data, AI models can identify at-risk students and recommend interventions to support their success. Predictive analytics can also inform enrollment management, curriculum planning, and resource allocation, helping institutions optimize their operations.

Benefits of AI in Higher Education

- **Enhanced Student Engagement:** AI technologies can create more engaging and interactive learning experiences, promoting student motivation and participation. Personalized learning paths, interactive simulations, and gamified activities make learning more enjoyable and effective.
- **Improved Academic Outcomes:** By providing personalized support and adaptive learning experiences, AI can improve academic outcomes for students. Real-time feedback and targeted interventions help students master concepts more effectively, leading to better grades and higher retention rates.
- **Increased Operational Efficiency:** AI can automate routine administrative tasks, improving operational efficiency and reducing costs. This efficiency allows institutions to allocate resources more effectively and focus on strategic priorities.
- **Support for Research and Innovation:** AI-powered research tools enhance the capabilities of scholars, enabling them to analyze

data more efficiently and generate new insights. These tools support innovative research and contribute to the advancement of knowledge across various disciplines.

Challenges and Considerations

- **Data Privacy and Security:** The use of AI in higher education involves collecting and analyzing sensitive student data. Ensuring the privacy and security of this data is critical. Institutions must implement robust data protection measures and comply with relevant privacy regulations to safeguard student information.
- **Bias and Fairness:** AI algorithms can be susceptible to bias, which can impact the fairness and accuracy of predictions and recommendations. It is essential to develop AI systems that are transparent and free from bias. Regular audits and evaluations can help identify and address any biases, ensuring equitable outcomes for all students.
- **Teacher Training and Support:** Successful integration of AI into higher education requires adequate training and support for educators. Instructors need to understand how to use AI tools effectively and interpret the data they provide. Ongoing professional development and collaboration with AI experts can help educators harness the full potential of AI in teaching and research.
- **Ethical Considerations:** The use of AI in higher education raises important ethical considerations, such as ensuring transparency, avoiding over-reliance on technology, and maintaining the role of human educators. Institutions must develop ethical guidelines for the use of AI, ensuring that it is used responsibly and transparently.

Case Studies and Examples

- **Georgia Institute of Technology:** Georgia Tech has implemented an AI-powered virtual teaching assistant named Jill Watson. Developed using IBM's Watson platform, Jill Watson assists students in an online master's program by answering questions, providing feedback, and facilitating discussions. The virtual assistant has improved student engagement and satisfaction by providing timely and personalized support.
- **University of California, Irvine:** The University of California, Irvine, uses predictive analytics to improve student retention and graduation rates. By analyzing data on student performance, behavior, and engagement, the university can identify at-risk students and provide targeted interventions. This proactive

approach has led to significant improvements in student success metrics.

- **Harvard University:** Harvard University employs AI-powered research tools to support its scholars. The tools analyze large datasets, identify patterns, and generate insights that inform research across various disciplines. AI has enhanced the efficiency and accuracy of research processes, enabling Harvard scholars to make groundbreaking discoveries.

The Future of AI in Higher Education

The future of AI in higher education holds exciting possibilities. As AI technologies continue to advance, we can expect even more sophisticated and effective applications:

- **Integration with Emerging Technologies:** The integration of AI with emerging technologies such as IoT, blockchain, and 5G will enhance the capabilities of higher education institutions. IoT devices can provide real-time data on learning environments, blockchain can ensure secure and transparent data management, and 5G will enable faster and more reliable connectivity.
- **Advanced Personalization:** Future AI systems will offer even more advanced personalization, providing highly tailored learning experiences based on detailed student profiles. These systems will analyze a wide range of data, including behavioral and biometric data, to create comprehensive and personalized learning paths.
- **Immersive Learning Experiences:** The use of immersive technologies such as VR and AR will become more prevalent in higher education. These technologies can create realistic and interactive learning environments, enhancing engagement and understanding. AI will play a crucial role in personalizing and optimizing these immersive experiences.
- **Lifelong Learning and Micro-Credentials:** AI will support the development of lifelong learning and micro-credentialing programs in higher education. These programs will offer flexible and personalized learning experiences that enable individuals to acquire new skills and qualifications throughout their careers. AI will help institutions design and deliver these programs effectively.

AI has the potential to transform higher education by providing personalized learning experiences, improving operational efficiency, and supporting innovative research. While challenges related to data privacy, bias, and ethical considerations must be addressed, the benefits of AI in higher education are significant. By leveraging AI technologies, institutions can enhance teaching and learning, support student success, and drive research and innovation.

AI AND GLOBAL EDUCATION TRENDS

Artificial Intelligence (AI) is not only transforming education at the local and national levels but also influencing global education trends. As educational institutions worldwide adopt AI technologies, new patterns and practices emerge that shape the future of education on a global scale. This section explores how AI is impacting global education trends and the potential benefits and challenges associated with these developments.

Global Adoption of AI in Education

- **Widespread Implementation:** AI technologies are being implemented in educational systems across the globe. Countries with advanced technological infrastructures, such as the United States, China, and European nations, are leading the way in integrating AI into their educational practices. These countries are investing in AI-powered tools and platforms to enhance teaching, learning, and administration.
- **Digital Learning Platforms:** AI-driven digital learning platforms, such as Khan Academy, Coursera, and EdX, are accessible to students worldwide. These platforms offer a vast array of courses and resources, enabling learners from diverse backgrounds to access high-quality education. AI enhances these platforms by providing personalized learning experiences and adaptive content.
- **International Collaboration:** AI is fostering international collaboration among educational institutions, researchers, and policymakers. Collaborative projects and initiatives are leveraging AI to address common challenges, share best practices, and develop innovative solutions. Global conferences and forums on AI in education facilitate the exchange of knowledge and ideas, promoting a more interconnected and cooperative global education landscape.

Key Global Education Trends Influenced by AI

- **Personalized Learning:** Personalized learning, powered by AI, is becoming a key trend in global education. AI technologies enable educators to tailor learning experiences to individual students' needs, preferences, and abilities. This approach is gaining traction worldwide as it promotes student engagement and improves academic outcomes.

- **Blended and Hybrid Learning:** Blended and hybrid learning models, which combine online and in-person instruction, are increasingly popular. AI supports these models by providing personalized content, real-time feedback, and adaptive assessments. This flexibility allows institutions to offer more accessible and inclusive education, catering to diverse learning needs.
- **Lifelong Learning and Skills Development:** The demand for lifelong learning and continuous skills development is rising globally. AI facilitates lifelong learning by offering personalized learning paths, micro-credentials, and flexible learning opportunities. This trend is particularly important in a rapidly changing job market, where individuals need to continuously update their skills and knowledge.
- **Data-Driven Decision Making:** AI-driven data analytics is transforming how educational institutions make decisions. By analyzing vast amounts of data, AI provides insights into student performance, resource allocation, and institutional effectiveness. This data-driven approach enables more informed and strategic decision-making, improving educational outcomes and operational efficiency.
- **Equity and Inclusion:** AI has the potential to promote equity and inclusion in education by providing personalized support to underserved and marginalized students. AI-powered tools can identify learning gaps, offer targeted interventions, and ensure that all students have access to high-quality education. This trend is gaining momentum as countries strive to achieve more equitable and inclusive educational systems.

Benefits of AI in Global Education

- **Access to Quality Education:** AI-driven digital learning platforms and tools provide access to high-quality education for students worldwide, regardless of their geographical location or socioeconomic status. This accessibility helps bridge educational gaps and promotes global equity.
- **Scalability:** AI technologies can scale to serve large numbers of students, making it possible to implement personalized learning at a global level. This scalability ensures that educational innovations can reach a broader audience and have a more significant impact.
- **Collaboration and Knowledge Sharing:** AI fosters international collaboration and knowledge sharing among educators, researchers, and policymakers. By working together, countries can address

common educational challenges, share best practices, and develop innovative solutions that benefit the global education community.

- **Continuous Improvement:** AI enables continuous improvement of educational practices by providing real-time data and feedback. Institutions can use this information to refine their strategies, optimize resource allocation, and enhance the quality of education.

Challenges and Considerations

- **Digital Divide:** The digital divide remains a significant challenge in global education. While AI technologies offer many benefits, they are not equally accessible to all students and institutions. Addressing disparities in technology access and infrastructure is crucial to ensure that the benefits of AI are distributed equitably.
- **Data Privacy and Security:** The use of AI in education involves collecting and analyzing sensitive student data. Ensuring the privacy and security of this data is essential. Institutions must implement robust data protection measures and comply with international privacy regulations to safeguard student information.
- **Cultural and Contextual Differences:** AI-driven educational tools and platforms must be adapted to different cultural and contextual settings to be effective. Educators and developers need to consider local languages, cultural norms, and educational practices when implementing AI technologies in diverse environments.
- **Ethical Considerations:** The use of AI in global education raises important ethical considerations, such as ensuring transparency, avoiding bias, and maintaining the role of human educators. Developing ethical guidelines and standards for AI in education is essential to promote responsible and fair use of these technologies.

Case Studies and Examples

- **China's AI Education Initiatives:** China is at the forefront of AI integration in education. The country has implemented AI-driven tools and platforms in schools across the nation, enhancing personalized learning, student assessment, and administrative efficiency. China's AI education initiatives aim to improve educational outcomes and prepare students for the future job market.
- **Estonia's Digital Education Transformation:** Estonia has embraced digital education and AI to create a modern, inclusive, and efficient educational system. The country uses AI-powered platforms to provide personalized learning experiences, support

teacher professional development, and streamline administrative processes. Estonia's digital education transformation serves as a model for other countries seeking to leverage AI in education.

- **UNESCO's AI in Education Programs:** UNESCO is promoting the use of AI in education through various programs and initiatives. The organization collaborates with member states to develop AI policies, share best practices, and implement AI-driven educational tools. UNESCO's efforts aim to ensure that AI benefits all students and contributes to global educational equity and inclusion.

The Future of AI in Global Education

The future of AI in global education holds exciting possibilities. As AI technologies continue to advance, we can expect even more innovative applications and transformative impacts:

- **Global AI-Powered Learning Networks:** The development of global AI-powered learning networks will enable students, educators, and institutions to connect and collaborate on a global scale. These networks will facilitate knowledge sharing, peer learning, and international partnerships, promoting a more interconnected and collaborative global education system.
- **AI for Multilingual and Multicultural Education:** AI will play a crucial role in supporting multilingual and multicultural education. AI-powered language translation and interpretation tools will enable students to access educational content in their native languages, promoting inclusivity and understanding across cultures.
- **Advanced AI-Driven Educational Research:** AI will enhance educational research by providing advanced data analysis and predictive modeling capabilities. Researchers will be able to analyze large-scale data from diverse contexts, generating insights that inform global educational policies and practices.
- **Sustainable and Inclusive AI Solutions:** The development of sustainable and inclusive AI solutions will ensure that the benefits of AI in education are distributed equitably. Efforts to bridge the digital divide, address ethical concerns, and promote cultural relevance will be essential to creating a fair and just global education system.

AI is transforming global education by providing personalized learning experiences, improving operational efficiency, and fostering international collaboration. While challenges related to the digital divide, data privacy, and ethical considerations must be addressed, the benefits of AI in global education are significant. By leveraging AI technologies, the global education community can enhance teaching and learning, promote equity and inclusion, and support continuous improvement and innovation.

AI AND THE TRANSFORMATION OF EDUCATIONAL RESEARCH METHODS

Artificial Intelligence (AI) is revolutionizing educational research by introducing advanced methodologies and tools that enable deeper insights and more precise data analysis. The integration of AI in research is transforming how studies are conducted, how data is interpreted, and how findings are applied to improve educational outcomes. This section explores the impact of AI on educational research methods, highlighting key advancements, benefits, challenges, and future directions.

Key Advancements in AI-Driven Educational Research

- **Enhanced Data Collection and Analysis:** AI technologies facilitate the collection and analysis of vast amounts of educational data. Machine learning algorithms can process large datasets quickly and accurately, identifying patterns and trends that would be impossible to detect manually. This capability allows researchers to gain deeper insights into student behavior, learning outcomes, and educational practices.
- **Natural Language Processing (NLP):** NLP enables researchers to analyze textual data, such as student essays, discussion forums, and social media posts, to understand student sentiment, engagement, and comprehension. AI-driven text analysis can uncover subtle nuances in language use and provide a richer understanding of student experiences.
- **Predictive Analytics:** Predictive analytics, powered by AI, allows researchers to forecast educational outcomes based on historical data. By identifying at-risk students and predicting future performance, educators can implement targeted interventions to improve student success. Predictive models can also inform policy decisions and resource allocation.
- **Learning Analytics:** Learning analytics involves the use of AI to analyze data generated by students' interactions with digital learning environments. This analysis helps researchers understand how students learn, identify effective teaching strategies, and develop personalized learning experiences. Learning analytics can also provide real-time feedback to educators and students.
- **Automated Assessment and Feedback:** AI-driven tools for automated assessment and feedback streamline the evaluation

process and provide immediate, objective feedback to students. These tools can assess various types of assignments, including essays, quizzes, and projects, with high accuracy. Automated feedback helps students understand their strengths and areas for improvement, supporting continuous learning.

Benefits of AI-Driven Educational Research

- **Increased Precision and Accuracy:** AI technologies enhance the precision and accuracy of educational research by minimizing human error and bias. Machine learning algorithms can analyze complex datasets with high reliability, ensuring that research findings are robust and dependable.
- **Scalability:** AI enables researchers to scale their studies to include larger and more diverse populations. This scalability ensures that research findings are generalizable and applicable to a wide range of educational contexts. Large-scale studies can provide more comprehensive insights into educational practices and outcomes.
- **Timely and Actionable Insights:** AI-driven research methods provide timely and actionable insights that can inform educational practices and policies. Real-time data analysis and predictive models enable educators to respond quickly to emerging trends and challenges, enhancing their ability to support student success.
- **Personalized Learning:** AI-driven research supports the development of personalized learning experiences tailored to individual student needs. By understanding how students learn and what factors influence their success, researchers can design interventions that optimize learning outcomes for each student.
- **Cost-Effectiveness:** AI technologies can reduce the cost of conducting educational research by automating data collection, analysis, and assessment processes. This cost-effectiveness allows researchers to allocate resources more efficiently and focus on high-impact areas of study.

Challenges and Ethical Considerations

5. **Data Privacy and Security:** The use of AI in educational research raises concerns about data privacy and security. Researchers must implement robust data protection measures to ensure that student information is handled responsibly and ethically. Compliance with data privacy regulations, such as GDPR and FERPA, is essential.
6. **Algorithmic Bias:** AI algorithms can perpetuate biases present in the training data, leading to skewed research findings. Researchers

must be vigilant in identifying and mitigating algorithmic bias to ensure that their studies are fair and inclusive. This involves using diverse and representative datasets and regularly auditing AI systems for bias.

7. **Interpretability and Transparency:** The complexity of AI algorithms can make it challenging to interpret and explain research findings. Researchers must strive for transparency in their methods and ensure that their AI models are interpretable and understandable to stakeholders. Clear communication of research processes and results is crucial for building trust.
8. **Ethical Use of AI:** Researchers must adhere to ethical guidelines for the use of AI in educational research. This includes obtaining informed consent from participants, ensuring the confidentiality of data, and considering the potential impact of their findings on educational practices and policies.

Future Directions for AI-Driven Educational Research

- **Interdisciplinary Collaboration:** The future of AI-driven educational research lies in interdisciplinary collaboration. By bringing together experts from education, computer science, psychology, sociology, and other fields, researchers can develop more comprehensive and innovative approaches to studying education. Interdisciplinary teams can leverage diverse perspectives and expertise to address complex educational challenges.
- **Real-Time Data and Adaptive Research:** The integration of real-time data and adaptive research methods will enhance the responsiveness of educational research. AI-driven tools can continuously collect and analyze data, allowing researchers to adjust their studies dynamically based on emerging insights. This adaptability ensures that research remains relevant and impactful.
- **Focus on Equity and Inclusion:** Future research should prioritize equity and inclusion, ensuring that AI-driven studies address the needs of diverse student populations. Researchers must focus on identifying and mitigating disparities in educational outcomes and developing interventions that promote equity. This includes studying the impact of AI on underrepresented and marginalized groups.
- **Longitudinal Studies:** Longitudinal studies that track students over extended periods will provide deeper insights into the long-term impact of AI on education. By following cohorts of students throughout their educational journeys, researchers can understand

how AI-driven interventions influence academic and personal development over time.

- **Policy Impact and Advocacy:** AI-driven educational research should inform policy decisions and advocate for evidence-based practices. Researchers must engage with policymakers, educators, and other stakeholders to translate their findings into actionable recommendations. By influencing policy, research can drive systemic changes that improve educational outcomes.
- **Global Collaboration:** Global collaboration in AI-driven educational research will foster the exchange of knowledge, resources, and best practices. Researchers from different countries and regions can work together to address shared challenges and leverage AI technologies to enhance education worldwide. International partnerships can also promote cultural understanding and inclusivity.

Conclusion

AI is transforming educational research methods, enabling deeper insights, greater precision, and more impactful findings. By leveraging AI technologies, researchers can enhance data collection and analysis, develop personalized learning experiences, and inform evidence-based practices and policies. However, addressing challenges such as data privacy, algorithmic bias, and ethical considerations is crucial to ensuring the responsible use of AI in research. Future directions for AI-driven educational research include interdisciplinary collaboration, real-time data and adaptive methods, a focus on equity and inclusion, longitudinal studies, policy impact, and global collaboration. Through thoughtful and innovative research, AI has the potential to significantly advance our understanding of education and drive meaningful improvements in educational outcomes.

QUESTIONNAIRE

Question 1: How is AI being utilized in educational research?

Answer: AI is utilized in educational research to analyze large datasets, identify patterns, and generate insights that inform educational practices and policies. AI-driven tools can process and interpret complex data from various sources, including student performance, engagement metrics, and behavioral data. This helps researchers understand learning processes, evaluate the effectiveness of educational interventions, and develop evidence-based strategies to enhance teaching and learning outcomes.

Question 2: How can predictive analytics improve educational outcomes?

Answer: Predictive analytics can improve educational outcomes by identifying students who may need additional support, predicting future performance trends, and informing instructional strategies. This allows educators to intervene early, tailor their teaching methods, and provide targeted resources to address individual student needs. Ultimately, predictive analytics helps create a more responsive and effective educational environment.

Question 3: How does AI support lifelong learning?

Answer: AI supports lifelong learning by providing personalized learning experiences, continuous skill development, and access to a wide range of educational resources. AI-driven platforms can adapt to individual learning needs, offering customized content and recommendations based on users' goals and progress. This ensures that learners can continuously update their skills and knowledge throughout their lives, staying relevant in an ever-changing job market.

Question 4: What are the key benefits of AI in lifelong learning?

Answer: Key benefits of AI in lifelong learning include personalized learning paths, flexibility, and accessibility. AI can tailor educational content to individual needs, making learning more efficient and engaging. Additionally, AI-driven platforms can be accessed anytime and anywhere, providing opportunities for continuous learning. This helps individuals stay current with industry trends and enhances their career prospects.

Question 5: What role does AI play in higher education?

Answer: AI plays a significant role in higher education by enhancing administrative efficiency, personalizing learning experiences, and supporting research initiatives. AI-driven tools can automate administrative tasks, such as enrollment and grading, freeing up faculty time for teaching and research. Additionally, AI can provide personalized tutoring and adaptive learning resources, helping students succeed in their academic pursuits.

Question 6: How can AI improve the quality of education in universities?

Answer: AI can improve the quality of education in universities by offering personalized learning support, streamlining administrative processes, and facilitating advanced research. AI-powered tutoring systems provide students with tailored assistance, while predictive analytics help identify students at risk of falling behind. Furthermore, AI can enhance research capabilities by analyzing large datasets and identifying novel insights, contributing to academic excellence.

Question 7: What are some global education trends influenced by AI?

Answer: Global education trends influenced by AI include the rise of personalized learning, the expansion of online and remote education, and the integration of AI in educational policy and decision-making. AI-driven technologies are transforming how education is delivered, making it more accessible and customized. Additionally, AI is informing policy decisions by providing data-driven insights into educational systems and outcomes worldwide.

Question 8: How is AI shaping the future of global education?

Answer: AI is shaping the future of global education by democratizing access to quality education, enabling personalized learning, and driving innovation in teaching and learning practices. AI technologies facilitate remote and online learning, breaking down geographical barriers and providing educational opportunities to diverse populations. Additionally, AI-driven insights help educators and policymakers develop effective strategies to address educational challenges and improve learning outcomes globally.

Question 9: How is AI transforming educational research methods?

Answer: AI is transforming educational research methods by enabling more efficient data collection, analysis, and interpretation. AI-powered tools can process large volumes of data quickly, uncovering patterns and trends that might be missed by traditional methods. This allows researchers to conduct more comprehensive and in-depth studies, leading to a better understanding of educational processes and outcomes.

Question 10: What are the advantages of using AI in educational research?

Answer: Advantages of using AI in educational research include increased accuracy, efficiency, and the ability to handle complex data sets. AI algorithms can analyze diverse data sources, providing insights that inform educational practices and policies. This leads to more effective interventions, better resource allocation, and ultimately, improved educational outcomes. Additionally, AI can automate repetitive tasks, allowing researchers to focus on higher-level analysis and interpretation.

4

Ethical and Social Considerations

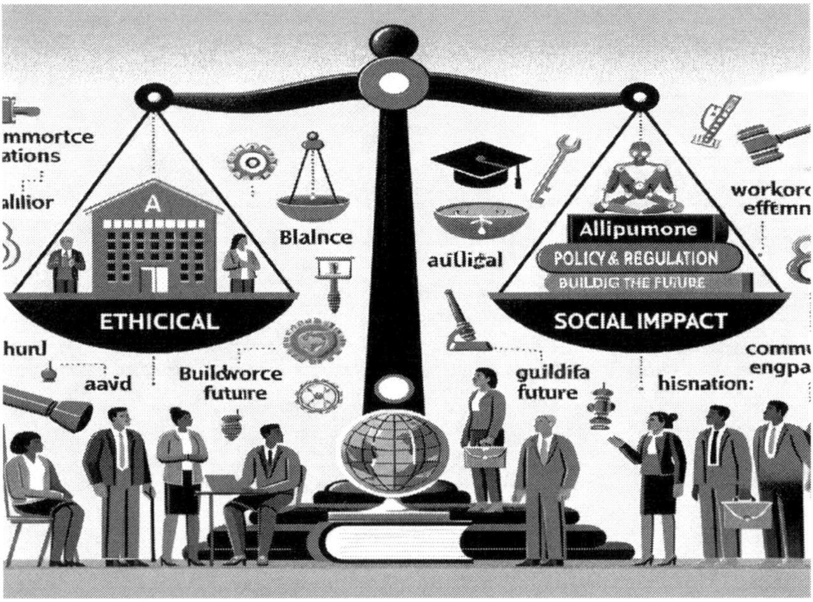

ETHICAL IMPLICATIONS OF AI IN EDUCATION

The integration of Artificial Intelligence (AI) into education offers numerous benefits, including personalized learning, enhanced student engagement, and improved administrative efficiency. However, the adoption of AI also raises significant ethical concerns that must be addressed to ensure that its use is fair, transparent, and beneficial for all stakeholders. This section explores the ethical implications of AI in education and provides guidelines for addressing these challenges.

Key Ethical Considerations

- **Data Privacy and Security:** AI systems in education rely on vast amounts of data, including sensitive information about students, teachers, and educational institutions. Protecting this data from unauthorized access, breaches, and misuse is paramount. Schools and educational platforms must implement robust data protection measures and comply with relevant privacy regulations to safeguard student information.
- **Algorithmic Bias and Fairness:** AI algorithms can inadvertently perpetuate or exacerbate existing biases if they are trained on biased data or developed without considering diverse perspectives. This can lead to unfair outcomes, such as discriminatory practices in admissions, grading, or disciplinary actions. It is essential to develop AI systems that are transparent, unbiased, and regularly audited for fairness.
- **Transparency and Accountability:** The decision-making processes of AI systems should be transparent and understandable to all stakeholders. This includes providing clear explanations of how AI algorithms work, the data they use, and the rationale behind their decisions. Additionally, there must be mechanisms for accountability, ensuring that individuals and institutions can challenge and appeal AI-driven decisions.
- **Human Oversight:** While AI can enhance educational practices, it should not replace human judgment and expertise. Educators and administrators must retain oversight and control over AI systems, ensuring that they complement rather than replace human decision-making. Human oversight is crucial for interpreting AI insights within the broader context of education and providing the necessary emotional and pedagogical support to students.
- **Equity and Access:** Ensuring equitable access to AI technologies in education is a significant ethical concern. The digital divide can exacerbate existing inequalities, with underserved communities lacking access to the necessary technology and resources. Efforts must be made to bridge this gap and ensure that all students, regardless of their socioeconomic background, can benefit from AI advancements.

Guidelines for Ethical AI in Education

- **Develop Ethical Frameworks:** Educational institutions and policymakers should develop comprehensive ethical frameworks that guide the use of AI in education. These frameworks should address key ethical considerations, including data privacy, fairness, transparency, and accountability. They should also provide guidelines for the responsible development, deployment, and monitoring of AI systems.

- **Implement Data Protection Measures:** Schools and educational platforms must implement robust data protection measures to safeguard student information. This includes encrypting data, using secure storage solutions, and ensuring compliance with privacy regulations such as the General Data Protection Regulation (GDPR) and the Family Educational Rights and Privacy Act (FERPA).
- **Ensure Algorithmic Fairness:** AI developers should prioritize fairness and inclusivity in the design and training of algorithms. This involves using diverse and representative datasets, regularly auditing AI systems for bias, and involving stakeholders from various backgrounds in the development process. Transparency in algorithm design and decision-making processes is also crucial to ensure fairness.
- **Promote Transparency and Accountability:** Educational institutions should promote transparency in the use of AI by providing clear explanations of how AI systems work and the decisions they make. Mechanisms for accountability should be established, allowing stakeholders to challenge and appeal AI-driven decisions. This includes setting up oversight committees and ensuring that there are channels for feedback and complaints.
- **Maintain Human Oversight:** Educators and administrators must retain oversight and control over AI systems. AI should be used as a tool to augment human decision-making, not replace it. Training programs should be developed to help educators understand how to use AI tools effectively and interpret the data they provide.
- **Address Equity and Access:** Efforts must be made to bridge the digital divide and ensure that all students have access to AI technologies. This includes providing the necessary infrastructure, devices, and internet connectivity, as well as offering training and support to students and teachers. Policies should be implemented to promote inclusive access to AI-driven educational resources.

Case Studies and Examples

- **Proctorio and Exam Surveillance:** Proctorio is an AI-driven remote proctoring system used to monitor students during online exams. While it offers benefits such as preventing cheating and ensuring exam integrity, it has raised ethical concerns about privacy, surveillance, and bias. Students and advocacy groups have criticized the lack of transparency in Proctorio's algorithms and the potential for discriminatory practices. This case highlights the need for transparency, fairness, and accountability in AI-driven educational tools.

- **AI in College Admissions:** Several universities have experimented with using AI to support college admissions processes. AI can analyze large volumes of data to identify patterns and predict student success. However, concerns about bias and fairness have emerged, particularly if the algorithms reinforce existing inequalities. Ensuring that AI systems used in admissions are transparent, unbiased, and regularly audited is essential to address these ethical challenges.
- **AI-Powered Personalized Learning:** AI-driven personalized learning platforms, such as Knewton and DreamBox, offer tailored learning experiences based on individual student needs. These platforms use data to adjust content, pace, and difficulty, enhancing student engagement and outcomes. While personalized learning has significant benefits, it also raises concerns about data privacy and the potential for algorithmic bias. Ensuring ethical practices in data collection, algorithm design, and transparency is crucial to maximize the benefits of personalized learning.

The Future of Ethical AI in Education

The future of AI in education will depend on our ability to address ethical considerations and develop responsible practices. As AI technologies continue to evolve, it is essential to prioritize ethics and ensure that AI serves as a force for good in education. Key areas of focus for the future include:

- **Developing Global Ethical Standards:** Establishing global ethical standards for AI in education will promote consistency and accountability across different regions and institutions. International collaboration and cooperation will be crucial to developing and implementing these standards.
- **Advancing Ethical AI Research:** Continued research into the ethical implications of AI in education is essential. This includes exploring ways to mitigate bias, enhance transparency, and ensure fairness. Research should also focus on developing innovative solutions to address ethical challenges and promote responsible AI use.

- **Empowering Educators and Students:** Empowering educators and students with the knowledge and skills to use AI responsibly is critical. This includes providing training programs, resources, and support to help stakeholders understand the ethical considerations of AI and how to navigate them effectively.
- **Promoting Inclusive and Equitable AI:** Ensuring that AI technologies are inclusive and equitable is a key priority. Efforts to bridge the digital divide, promote diverse representation in AI development, and ensure equitable access to AI-driven educational resources will be essential to creating a fair and just education system.

The integration of AI into education offers significant benefits but also raises important ethical considerations. By addressing these challenges and developing responsible practices, we can ensure that AI serves as a force for good in education. Prioritizing data privacy, fairness, transparency, accountability, and equity will be essential to harnessing the full potential of AI while safeguarding the interests of all stakeholders.

SOCIAL IMPACT OF AI IN EDUCATION

The introduction of Artificial Intelligence (AI) into the educational sector is reshaping the landscape of learning, teaching, and administration. While AI brings numerous benefits, it also has significant social implications that must be carefully considered. This section explores the social impact of AI in education, highlighting both the positive outcomes and the challenges that arise with its integration.

Positive Social Impacts

- **Increased Accessibility and Inclusion:** AI has the potential to make education more accessible and inclusive. AI-driven tools and platforms can cater to diverse learning needs, providing support for students with disabilities, language barriers, and varying learning paces. For example, speech-to-text and text-to-speech technologies help students with visual or auditory impairments, while language translation tools enable non-native speakers to access educational content.
- **Personalized Learning:** Personalized learning is one of the most significant benefits of AI in education. AI systems can analyze individual student data to create customized learning experiences, ensuring that each student receives the appropriate level of support and challenge. This personalization can lead to better academic

outcomes and increased student engagement, particularly for those who struggle in traditional learning environments.

- **Enhanced Teacher Support:** AI can assist teachers by automating administrative tasks, providing real-time feedback, and offering data-driven insights into student performance. This support allows teachers to focus more on instruction and student interaction, improving the overall quality of education. AI can also recommend professional development resources, helping educators enhance their skills and adapt to new teaching methodologies.
- **Lifelong Learning Opportunities:** AI-powered platforms offer flexible and accessible lifelong learning opportunities. These platforms provide a wide range of courses and resources that individuals can access at any time, allowing them to continue their education and develop new skills throughout their lives. This flexibility supports career advancement and personal growth, contributing to a more educated and skilled workforce.
- **Global Collaboration and Knowledge Sharing:** AI facilitates global collaboration and knowledge sharing among educators, researchers, and students. Online platforms and AI-driven tools enable individuals from different parts of the world to connect, share resources, and collaborate on projects. This interconnectedness promotes a more inclusive and diverse educational community, fostering innovation and mutual understanding.

Challenges and Negative Social Impacts

- **Digital Divide:** The digital divide is a significant challenge in the adoption of AI in education. While AI technologies offer numerous benefits, they are not equally accessible to all students and institutions. Students from low-income families or underserved communities may lack access to the necessary technology and internet connectivity, exacerbating existing inequalities. Addressing the digital divide is crucial to ensuring that all students can benefit from AI advancements.
- **Data Privacy and Security:** The use of AI in education involves collecting and analyzing large amounts of student data. Ensuring the privacy and security of this data is critical to maintaining trust and protecting student rights. Breaches of data privacy can have serious consequences, including identity theft and the misuse of sensitive information. Schools and institutions must implement robust data protection measures and comply with privacy regulations to safeguard student data.

- **Algorithmic Bias and Fairness:** AI systems can inadvertently perpetuate or exacerbate existing biases if they are trained on biased data or developed without considering diverse perspectives. This can lead to unfair outcomes, such as discriminatory practices in admissions, grading, or disciplinary actions. Ensuring that AI systems are transparent, unbiased, and regularly audited for fairness is essential to promoting equity in education.
- **Impact on Employment:** The automation of administrative tasks and other functions through AI can lead to job displacement in the education sector. While AI can enhance efficiency and reduce costs, it may also result in the reduction of certain roles, particularly those involving routine tasks. Institutions must consider the social implications of AI-driven automation and provide support for employees affected by these changes, such as retraining and upskilling opportunities.
- **Over-Reliance on Technology:** Over-reliance on AI and technology in education can have negative consequences, such as reduced human interaction and the devaluation of traditional teaching methods. While AI can enhance education, it should not replace the essential role of human educators. Maintaining a balance between AI-driven and human-led instruction is crucial to preserving the quality and integrity of education.

Strategies for Mitigating Negative Social Impacts

- **Bridging the Digital Divide:** Addressing the digital divide requires coordinated efforts from governments, educational institutions, and private organizations. Initiatives to provide affordable internet access, distribute devices to underserved students, and offer training and support for digital literacy are essential to ensuring equitable access to AI-driven educational resources.
- **Implementing Strong Data Protection Measures:** Ensuring the privacy and security of student data is critical to maintaining trust and protecting student rights. Schools and institutions must implement robust data protection measures, such as encryption, secure storage solutions, and regular security audits. Compliance with privacy regulations, such as the General Data Protection Regulation (GDPR) and the Family Educational Rights and Privacy Act (FERPA), is essential.
- **Promoting Algorithmic Fairness and Transparency:** Developing fair and transparent AI systems requires diverse and representative datasets, regular audits for bias, and clear

explanations of how algorithms work and make decisions. Involving stakeholders from various backgrounds in the development process can help ensure that AI systems are inclusive and equitable.

- **Supporting Employees Affected by AI Automation:** Institutions should provide support for employees affected by AI-driven automation, such as retraining and upskilling opportunities. This support can help individuals transition to new roles and continue to contribute to the educational sector. Additionally, involving employees in discussions about AI implementation and its potential impact can help build trust and ensure a smoother transition.
- **Maintaining a Balanced Approach to AI Integration:** While AI can enhance education, it is important to maintain a balanced approach that values human interaction and traditional teaching methods. AI should complement, not replace, the essential role of educators. Institutions should prioritize human oversight and ensure that AI-driven tools are used to support and enhance human-led instruction.

Case Studies and Examples

- **Bridge International Academies:** Bridge International Academies, operating in Kenya and other countries, uses AI to deliver personalized learning experiences to students in underserved communities. The organization provides affordable education through AI-driven platforms that offer tailored content and real-time feedback. This approach helps bridge the digital divide and promote educational equity.
- **ProFuturo Digital Education Program:** The ProFuturo Digital Education Program, supported by the Telefónica Foundation and "la Caixa" Foundation, aims to provide quality education to children in vulnerable communities worldwide. The program uses AI-driven tools to offer personalized learning experiences and support teachers with data-driven insights. ProFuturo's initiatives help address educational inequalities and promote inclusion.
- **Khan Academy:** Khan Academy is an online learning platform that provides free, high-quality educational resources to students worldwide. The platform uses AI to personalize learning experiences and offer real-time feedback. Khan Academy's mission to provide accessible education aligns with efforts to bridge the digital divide and promote global equity.

The Future of AI and Its Social Impact on Education

The future of AI in education holds promise for addressing social challenges and promoting positive outcomes. Key areas of focus for the future include:

- **Advancing Inclusive AI Technologies:** Developing AI technologies that are inclusive and accessible to all students is a priority. Efforts to bridge the digital divide, promote diverse representation in AI development, and ensure equitable access to AI-driven educational resources will be essential to creating a fair and just education system.
- **Enhancing Human-AI Collaboration:** The future of education will involve greater collaboration between humans and AI. Educators, students, and AI systems will work together to create personalized and effective learning experiences. Maintaining a balance between AI-driven and human-led instruction will be crucial to preserving the quality and integrity of education.
- **Fostering Global Collaboration:** AI will continue to facilitate global collaboration and knowledge sharing among educators, researchers, and students. International partnerships and initiatives will promote the exchange of ideas and best practices, contributing to a more interconnected and innovative global education community.
- **Addressing Ethical and Social Challenges:** As AI technologies evolve, it will be essential to address ethical and social challenges proactively. Developing and implementing ethical guidelines, promoting transparency and accountability, and ensuring fairness and equity will be critical to maximizing the benefits of AI while minimizing its negative impacts.

AI has the potential to significantly impact the social landscape of education, offering increased accessibility, personalized learning, and enhanced support for teachers and lifelong learners. However, addressing challenges such as the digital divide, data privacy, algorithmic bias, and the impact on employment is essential to ensure that AI serves as a force for good in education. By adopting responsible practices and prioritizing equity and inclusion, we can harness the full potential of AI to create a more just and effective global education system.

POLICY AND REGULATION OF AI IN EDUCATION

As Artificial Intelligence (AI) becomes increasingly integrated into education, the development of comprehensive policies and regulations is essential to ensure its ethical and effective use. Governments, educational institutions, and organizations must collaborate to create frameworks that address the ethical, legal, and social implications of AI in education. This section explores the key aspects of policy and regulation in AI-driven education and provides recommendations for developing robust regulatory frameworks.

Key Areas of Policy and Regulation

- **Data Privacy and Security:** Protecting student data is a critical concern in AI-driven education. Policies must ensure that educational institutions and technology providers implement robust data protection measures. This includes encryption, secure storage solutions, and compliance with privacy regulations such as the General Data Protection Regulation (GDPR) and the Family Educational Rights and Privacy Act (FERPA). Regulations should also mandate transparent data usage practices and obtain informed consent from students and parents.
- **Algorithmic Transparency and Accountability:** Policies should promote transparency in AI algorithms used in education. This includes clear documentation of how algorithms are developed, the data they use, and the decision-making processes they follow. Regulatory frameworks should require regular audits and evaluations of AI systems to ensure fairness and accuracy. Mechanisms for accountability should be established, allowing stakeholders to challenge and appeal AI-driven decisions.
- **Bias and Fairness:** Addressing algorithmic bias is crucial to ensure that AI systems in education are fair and equitable. Policies should mandate the use of diverse and representative datasets in AI development and require regular audits to identify and mitigate biases. Inclusive development practices should involve stakeholders from various backgrounds to ensure that AI systems cater to the needs of all students.
- **Ethical Use of AI:** The ethical use of AI in education should be a cornerstone of policy and regulation. This includes guidelines for responsible AI development, deployment, and monitoring. Ethical frameworks should emphasize the importance of human oversight, the avoidance of over-reliance on technology, and the preservation of the essential role of educators. Policies should also address the broader societal implications of AI in education, promoting transparency, fairness, and accountability.
- **Equitable Access to AI Technologies:** Ensuring equitable access to AI technologies is essential to prevent exacerbating existing inequalities. Policies should address the digital divide by providing

funding and resources to underserved communities, ensuring that all students have access to the necessary technology and internet connectivity. Initiatives to promote digital literacy and provide training and support for educators and students are also crucial.

Developing Robust Regulatory Frameworks

- **Collaboration and Stakeholder Engagement:** Developing effective policies and regulations for AI in education requires collaboration among governments, educational institutions, technology providers, and other stakeholders. Inclusive policymaking processes should involve input from educators, students, parents, and experts in AI, ethics, and education. This collaborative approach ensures that policies address diverse perspectives and needs.
- **International Standards and Guidelines:** Establishing international standards and guidelines for AI in education can promote consistency and accountability across different regions and institutions. International organizations, such as UNESCO and the International Telecommunication Union (ITU), can play a key role in developing and promoting these standards. Collaboration among countries can facilitate the exchange of best practices and the development of global regulatory frameworks.
- **Ongoing Monitoring and Evaluation:** Policies and regulations for AI in education should include provisions for ongoing monitoring and evaluation. This ensures that regulatory frameworks remain relevant and effective in addressing emerging challenges and technological advancements. Regular assessments can identify areas for improvement and ensure that policies continue to promote ethical and equitable AI use.
- **Public Awareness and Education:** Raising public awareness about the ethical and social implications of AI in education is essential for informed policymaking and regulation. Educational campaigns and public consultations can engage stakeholders and promote understanding of AI technologies and their impact. This awareness can drive demand for responsible AI practices and support the development of effective policies.

Case Studies and Examples

- **European Union AI Policy:** The European Union (EU) has been proactive in developing policies and regulations for AI. The EU's General Data Protection Regulation (GDPR) sets stringent standards for data privacy and security, applicable to AI systems in education. The EU's proposed AI Act aims to establish a comprehensive regulatory framework for AI, emphasizing transparency, accountability, and fairness. These initiatives provide valuable lessons for developing robust AI policies in education.

- **Singapore's AI Governance Framework:** Singapore has developed a national AI strategy that includes a robust governance framework for AI. The framework emphasizes ethical AI development, transparency, and accountability. Singapore's AI Governance Framework provides guidelines for responsible AI use, including in the education sector. The country's approach highlights the importance of balancing innovation with ethical considerations.
- **UNESCO's AI in Education Initiatives:** UNESCO has been actively involved in promoting ethical AI use in education. The organization has developed guidelines and policy recommendations for integrating AI into educational systems. UNESCO's initiatives emphasize the importance of equitable access, data privacy, and algorithmic fairness. These efforts aim to ensure that AI technologies contribute to inclusive and quality education for all.

Recommendations for Policy and Regulation

- **Establish Comprehensive Data Protection Standards:** Develop and enforce comprehensive data protection standards that safeguard student data and ensure privacy and security. Policies should require educational institutions and technology providers to implement robust data protection measures and comply with relevant regulations.
- **Promote Transparency and Accountability in AI Systems:** Mandate transparency in AI algorithms and decision-making processes. Require regular audits and evaluations of AI systems to ensure fairness and accuracy. Establish mechanisms for accountability, allowing stakeholders to challenge and appeal AI-driven decisions.
- **Address Algorithmic Bias and Promote Fairness:** Develop policies that address algorithmic bias and promote fairness in AI systems. Require the use of diverse and representative datasets in AI development and involve stakeholders from various backgrounds in the development process. Conduct regular audits to identify and mitigate biases.
- **Ensure Ethical AI Development and Use:** Create ethical frameworks for AI development, deployment, and monitoring. Emphasize the importance of human oversight, the avoidance of

over-reliance on technology, and the preservation of the essential role of educators. Address broader societal implications of AI in education.

- **Bridge the Digital Divide and Promote Equitable Access:** Implement initiatives to bridge the digital divide and ensure equitable access to AI technologies. Provide funding and resources to underserved communities, promote digital literacy, and offer training and support for educators and students.

The integration of AI into education presents significant opportunities and challenges. Developing comprehensive policies and regulations is essential to ensure the ethical and effective use of AI in education. By addressing data privacy, algorithmic fairness, transparency, accountability, and equitable access, policymakers can create frameworks that promote the responsible use of AI. Collaboration among stakeholders, ongoing monitoring and evaluation, and public awareness are crucial to the success of these efforts. By adopting robust regulatory frameworks, we can harness the potential of AI to enhance education while safeguarding the interests of all stakeholders.

AI AND WORKFORCE DEVELOPMENT

The integration of Artificial Intelligence (AI) into education not only enhances learning outcomes but also plays a crucial role in workforce development. As industries evolve and new technologies emerge, there is a growing need for workers to continuously update their skills and knowledge. AI-driven education can bridge the gap between educational outcomes and workforce demands, ensuring that students and professionals are well-equipped for the future job market. This section explores the impact of AI on workforce development and the strategies to maximize its benefits.

Key Areas of AI in Workforce Development

- **Skills Gap Analysis:** AI can analyze labor market data to identify skills gaps and emerging trends. By examining job postings, industry reports, and economic indicators, AI systems can pinpoint the skills that are in high demand and forecast future workforce needs. This analysis helps educational institutions design curricula that align with market requirements, ensuring that graduates possess the skills needed by employers.
- **Personalized Learning Pathways:** AI-powered platforms can create personalized learning pathways that align with individual career goals and industry demands. These platforms assess learners' skills, interests, and career aspirations to recommend

tailored courses, certifications, and training programs. Personalized learning ensures that individuals acquire the competencies necessary for their desired career paths, enhancing employability and job satisfaction.

- **Continuous Learning and Upskilling:** The rapid pace of technological change necessitates continuous learning and upskilling throughout one's career. AI-driven education platforms offer flexible and accessible learning opportunities, enabling professionals to update their skills and stay competitive in the job market. Micro-credentials, online courses, and AI-powered training programs provide targeted learning experiences that fit into busy schedules.
- **Job Matching and Career Guidance:** AI can enhance job matching and career guidance by analyzing data on job seekers and employers. AI systems can recommend job opportunities that align with an individual's skills and preferences, improving the efficiency of the job search process. Additionally, AI-driven career guidance tools can provide personalized advice on career development, helping individuals navigate their career paths effectively.
- **Industry Collaboration and Partnerships:** Collaboration between educational institutions and industries is essential for effective workforce development. AI can facilitate these partnerships by providing data-driven insights into industry needs and educational outcomes. By working together, educational institutions and employers can develop training programs, internships, and apprenticeships that prepare students for the workforce and ensure a smooth transition from education to employment.

Benefits of AI in Workforce Development

- **Alignment with Industry Needs:** AI-driven education ensures that curricula and training programs are aligned with current and future industry needs. This alignment helps bridge the skills gap, ensuring that graduates possess the competencies required by employers. As a result, individuals are better prepared for the job market, and employers can find the talent they need.
- **Enhanced Employability:** Personalized learning pathways and continuous upskilling opportunities enhance employability by providing individuals with the skills and knowledge needed to succeed in their careers. AI-driven education supports lifelong learning, enabling individuals to adapt to changing job market demands and pursue new career opportunities.

- **Increased Workforce Flexibility:** AI-powered education promotes workforce flexibility by offering accessible and flexible learning opportunities. Professionals can acquire new skills and credentials at their own pace, enabling them to adapt to new roles and responsibilities. This flexibility supports career advancement and helps individuals navigate career transitions more effectively.
- **Improved Job Matching:** AI enhances job matching by analyzing data on job seekers and employers to recommend suitable job opportunities. This data-driven approach improves the efficiency of the job search process, reducing the time and effort required to find the right job. AI-driven career guidance also provides personalized advice on career development, helping individuals make informed decisions about their career paths.

Challenges and Considerations

- **Access and Equity:** Ensuring equitable access to AI-driven education and training programs is a significant challenge. Individuals from underserved communities may lack access to the necessary technology and resources, limiting their opportunities for workforce development. Addressing the digital divide is essential to ensure that all individuals can benefit from AI advancements.
- **Data Privacy and Security:** The use of AI in workforce development involves collecting and analyzing sensitive data on individuals' skills, career aspirations, and job performance. Ensuring the privacy and security of this data is critical. Educational institutions and employers must implement robust data protection measures and comply with relevant privacy regulations to safeguard personal information.
- **Bias and Fairness:** AI algorithms can be susceptible to bias, which can impact the fairness and accuracy of job matching and career guidance. It is essential to develop AI systems that are transparent, unbiased, and regularly audited for fairness. Ensuring diverse representation in AI development and using inclusive datasets can help mitigate biases.
- **Integration with Existing Systems:** Integrating AI-driven education and training programs with existing systems and practices can be challenging. Educational institutions and employers must collaborate to ensure seamless integration and alignment with organizational goals. Effective communication and collaboration are essential to maximize the benefits of AI-driven workforce development.

Case Studies and Examples

- **IBM SkillsBuild:** IBM SkillsBuild is an AI-powered platform that offers personalized learning pathways and career guidance for students and professionals. The platform provides courses, certifications, and training programs that align with industry needs. AI-driven career guidance tools help users identify suitable job opportunities and develop their career paths. IBM SkillsBuild supports continuous learning and upskilling, enhancing employability and workforce flexibility.
- **LinkedIn Learning:** LinkedIn Learning uses AI to provide personalized course recommendations and career development resources. The platform analyzes user data to recommend courses that align with individual career goals and industry trends. LinkedIn Learning's AI-driven tools also provide insights into job market demands and skills gaps, helping users stay competitive in the job market.
- **Coursera for Business:** Coursera for Business offers AI-powered training programs and certifications for organizations. The platform provides personalized learning pathways that align with organizational goals and industry needs. AI-driven analytics help employers identify skills gaps and develop targeted training programs. Coursera for Business supports workforce development by providing flexible and accessible learning opportunities for employees.

The Future of AI in Workforce Development

The future of AI in workforce development holds exciting possibilities. As AI technologies continue to advance, we can expect even more innovative applications and transformative impacts:

- **Advanced Skills Gap Analysis:** AI will provide more sophisticated skills gap analysis, offering detailed insights into current and future workforce needs. Advanced predictive modeling and real-time data analysis will enable educational institutions and employers to develop proactive strategies for workforce development.
- **Integration with Emerging Technologies:** The integration of AI with emerging technologies such as blockchain, IoT, and 5G will enhance the capabilities of workforce development platforms. Blockchain can ensure secure and transparent credentialing, IoT can provide real-time data on job performance, and 5G will enable faster and more reliable connectivity for remote learning and training.

- **Lifelong Learning Ecosystems:** The future of workforce development will involve the creation of lifelong learning ecosystems that integrate various learning platforms, tools, and resources. AI will facilitate the seamless integration of these components, creating cohesive and interconnected learning experiences that support continuous education and skill development throughout an individual's career.
- **Ethical AI Development:** Ensuring ethical AI development will be a key focus in the future of workforce development. Transparent, fair, and accountable AI systems will be essential to building trust and maximizing the benefits of AI for workforce development. Developing ethical guidelines and standards for AI in education and workforce development will promote responsible and equitable AI use.

AI has the potential to transform workforce development by providing personalized learning pathways, continuous upskilling opportunities, and enhanced job matching and career guidance. While challenges related to access, data privacy, bias, and integration must be addressed, the benefits of AI-driven workforce development are significant. By leveraging AI technologies, educational institutions and employers can ensure that individuals are well-equipped for the future job market, enhancing employability and supporting career advancement.

BUILDING THE FUTURE WITH AI EDUCATION

The integration of Artificial Intelligence (AI) in education is a transformative force that has the potential to revolutionize how we learn, teach, and manage educational institutions. As we look to the future, it is crucial to harness the power of AI responsibly and effectively to build a more inclusive, equitable, and innovative educational landscape. This section explores the strategies for building the future with AI in education, focusing on innovation, collaboration, and ethical considerations.

Innovative Approaches to AI in Education

- **Personalized Learning at Scale:** AI can provide personalized learning experiences for students at scale, catering to individual learning styles, paces, and preferences. By leveraging adaptive learning technologies, AI can create customized learning paths that ensure each student receives the appropriate level of challenge and support. This approach can significantly enhance student engagement, motivation, and academic outcomes.

- **Immersive Learning Environments:** The use of AI-powered immersive technologies such as Virtual Reality (VR) and Augmented Reality (AR) can create interactive and engaging learning environments. These technologies can simulate real-world scenarios, allowing students to explore, experiment, and learn in a safe and controlled setting. Immersive learning experiences can deepen understanding and retention of complex concepts.
- **AI-Driven Research and Innovation:** AI can accelerate educational research and innovation by providing advanced data analysis, predictive modeling, and natural language processing capabilities. Researchers can leverage AI to analyze large datasets, identify patterns and trends, and generate insights that inform educational practices and policies. This can lead to the development of new teaching methodologies, learning tools, and educational technologies.
- **Enhanced Teacher Support:** AI can support teachers by automating administrative tasks, providing real-time feedback on student performance, and offering data-driven insights into instructional effectiveness. AI-powered professional development resources can help educators enhance their skills and adapt to new teaching strategies. By reducing administrative burdens, AI enables teachers to focus more on instruction and student interaction.
- **Global Collaboration and Knowledge Sharing:** AI can facilitate global collaboration and knowledge sharing among educators, researchers, and policymakers. Online platforms and AI-driven tools enable individuals from different parts of the world to connect, share resources, and collaborate on projects. This interconnectedness promotes a more inclusive and diverse educational community, fostering innovation and mutual understanding.

Strategies for Building the Future with AI in Education

- **Developing Robust Ethical Frameworks:** Ensuring the ethical use of AI in education is paramount. Educational institutions, governments, and technology providers must collaborate to develop comprehensive ethical frameworks that address data privacy, algorithmic fairness, transparency, and accountability. These frameworks should guide the responsible development, deployment, and monitoring of AI systems.
- **Promoting Digital Literacy and Skills:** To fully leverage the benefits of AI in education, it is essential to promote digital literacy and skills among students, educators, and administrators.

This includes providing training and resources to help individuals understand and effectively use AI technologies. Digital literacy initiatives can empower stakeholders to navigate the digital landscape confidently and responsibly.

- **Ensuring Equitable Access to AI Technologies:** Bridging the digital divide is crucial to ensuring that all students can benefit from AI advancements. Efforts to provide affordable internet access, distribute devices to underserved communities, and offer training and support are essential. Policies should promote inclusive access to AI-driven educational resources, ensuring that no student is left behind.
- **Fostering Public-Private Partnerships:** Public-private partnerships can play a key role in advancing AI in education. Collaboration between governments, educational institutions, technology providers, and other stakeholders can drive innovation, fund research, and develop scalable solutions. These partnerships can also facilitate the sharing of best practices and resources, promoting a more integrated and effective educational ecosystem.
- **Implementing Continuous Monitoring and Evaluation:** Continuous monitoring and evaluation of AI systems are essential to ensure their effectiveness and ethical use. Regular assessments can identify areas for improvement, address emerging challenges, and ensure that AI technologies remain aligned with educational goals. Feedback from educators, students, and other stakeholders should inform ongoing refinements and updates.

Case Studies and Examples

- **Finland's AI in Education Strategy:** Finland has implemented a comprehensive AI in education strategy that emphasizes ethical considerations, digital literacy, and equitable access. The country's approach includes integrating AI into the curriculum, providing training for educators, and fostering public-private partnerships. Finland's strategy serves as a model for other countries seeking to leverage AI in education responsibly.
- **OpenAI's Education Initiatives:** OpenAI is involved in several education initiatives that aim to promote the ethical use of AI and enhance educational outcomes. The organization collaborates with educational institutions to develop AI-driven learning tools and resources. OpenAI also emphasizes transparency and accountability in AI development, ensuring that its technologies align with ethical standards.

- **India's Digital Education Transformation:** India is leveraging AI to transform its education system, focusing on increasing access, improving quality, and promoting digital literacy. The government's initiatives include deploying AI-driven learning platforms, providing training for educators, and addressing the digital divide. India's efforts highlight the potential of AI to enhance education in diverse and large-scale contexts.

The Future of AI in Education

The future of AI in education holds immense potential for innovation, inclusivity, and growth. As AI technologies continue to advance, key areas of focus for the future include:

- **Expanding Personalized Learning:** The expansion of personalized learning will ensure that AI-driven educational experiences cater to the diverse needs of all students. Advanced algorithms and adaptive technologies will provide even more tailored learning paths, enhancing engagement and academic success.
- **Integrating AI with Emerging Technologies:** The integration of AI with emerging technologies such as blockchain, IoT, and 5G will create more connected and efficient educational ecosystems. These technologies will enhance data security, real-time monitoring, and connectivity, supporting seamless and effective learning experiences.
- **Enhancing Lifelong Learning and Workforce Development:** AI will play a critical role in promoting lifelong learning and workforce development. Personalized learning pathways, continuous upskilling opportunities, and AI-driven career guidance will ensure that individuals remain competitive in the job market and capable of navigating career transitions.
- **Promoting Global Collaboration:** AI will continue to facilitate global collaboration and knowledge sharing among educators, researchers, and policymakers. International partnerships and initiatives will promote the exchange of ideas and best practices, contributing to a more interconnected and innovative global education community.

Building the future with AI in education requires a strategic and responsible approach that prioritizes innovation, collaboration, and ethical considerations. By developing robust ethical frameworks, promoting digital literacy, ensuring equitable access, fostering public-private partnerships, and implementing continuous monitoring and evaluation, we can harness the full potential of AI to transform education. Through these efforts, we can create a more inclusive, equitable, and innovative educational landscape that prepares students and professionals for the challenges and opportunities of the future.

COMMUNITY AND STAKEHOLDER ENGAGEMENT IN AI EDUCATION

As Artificial Intelligence (AI) continues to influence education, engaging communities and stakeholders is crucial for ensuring ethical and socially responsible implementation. Community and stakeholder engagement involves collaboration, transparency, and inclusive decision-making, which are essential for building trust and ensuring that AI technologies benefit all members of society. This section explores the importance of community and stakeholder engagement in AI education, effective strategies for fostering collaboration, and the long-term benefits of inclusive practices.

The Importance of Community and Stakeholder Engagement

- **Building Trust and Transparency:** Engaging communities and stakeholders fosters trust and transparency in AI-driven educational initiatives. When stakeholders are involved in the decision-making process and understand how AI technologies are used, they are more likely to support and trust these initiatives. Transparent communication about AI's benefits, risks, and ethical considerations builds a foundation of trust.
- **Ensuring Inclusivity and Equity:** Inclusive engagement ensures that diverse perspectives and needs are considered in the development and implementation of AI technologies. By involving stakeholders from various backgrounds, including underrepresented and marginalized groups, educational institutions can address equity issues and create AI solutions that are fair and accessible to all students.
- **Enhancing Relevance and Effectiveness:** Community and stakeholder input helps ensure that AI technologies address real-world educational challenges and meet the needs of students, educators, and parents. Engaging stakeholders in the design and evaluation of AI tools enhances their relevance and effectiveness, leading to better educational outcomes.
- **Ethical Decision-Making:** Stakeholder engagement promotes ethical decision-making by incorporating diverse viewpoints and values into the development process. This collaborative approach helps identify potential ethical issues and develop strategies to

mitigate them, ensuring that AI technologies are used responsibly and ethically.

Effective Strategies for Fostering Collaboration

- **Establishing Stakeholder Advisory Committees:** Creating stakeholder advisory committees that include representatives from various groups, such as educators, parents, students, community leaders, and AI experts, ensures that diverse perspectives are considered. These committees can provide guidance, feedback, and recommendations on AI initiatives, promoting inclusive decision-making.
- **Conducting Public Consultations and Workshops:** Public consultations and workshops provide opportunities for stakeholders to learn about AI technologies, share their views, and contribute to the development process. These events can be held in-person or virtually, ensuring broad participation and engagement. Facilitating open discussions and interactive sessions helps stakeholders feel heard and valued.
- **Implementing Feedback Mechanisms:** Establishing feedback mechanisms, such as surveys, suggestion boxes, and online forums, allows stakeholders to share their opinions and concerns continuously. Regularly reviewing and addressing this feedback demonstrates a commitment to transparency and responsiveness, fostering trust and collaboration.
- **Co-Designing AI Solutions:** Involving stakeholders in the co-design of AI solutions ensures that their needs and preferences are integrated into the development process. Co-design workshops and collaborative projects enable stakeholders to contribute ideas, test prototypes, and provide input on the usability and functionality of AI tools.
- **Providing Education and Resources:** Educating stakeholders about AI technologies, their potential impact, and ethical considerations is essential for informed engagement. Providing resources, such as informational materials, webinars, and training sessions, empowers stakeholders to participate meaningfully in discussions and decision-making processes.

Long-Term Benefits of Inclusive Practices

- **Sustainable and Ethical AI Implementation:** Inclusive practices contribute to the sustainable and ethical implementation of AI technologies in education. By addressing diverse needs and perspectives, institutions can develop AI solutions that are more widely accepted and supported, ensuring long-term success and positive impact.

- **Empowered Communities:** Engaging communities and stakeholders empowers them to take an active role in shaping AI-driven educational initiatives. This empowerment fosters a sense of ownership and responsibility, encouraging ongoing collaboration and support for educational advancements.
- **Enhanced Social Cohesion:** Inclusive engagement practices promote social cohesion by fostering mutual understanding and respect among different groups. Collaborative efforts to develop and implement AI technologies can strengthen community bonds and create a shared commitment to improving education for all.
- **Continuous Improvement and Innovation:** Ongoing stakeholder engagement facilitates continuous improvement and innovation in AI-driven education. Regular feedback and collaborative problem-solving help identify areas for enhancement and drive the development of new and innovative solutions that address evolving educational challenges.

Case Studies and Examples

- **Barcelona's Education Innovation Program:** Barcelona's Education Innovation Program involves educators, students, parents, and community members in the development and implementation of AI-driven educational initiatives. Stakeholder advisory committees and public workshops ensure that diverse perspectives are considered, leading to more inclusive and effective AI solutions.
- **New York City Department of Education's AI Ethics Initiative:** The New York City Department of Education has established an AI Ethics Initiative that engages stakeholders in discussions about the ethical implications of AI in education. The initiative includes public consultations, advisory committees, and educational resources to promote transparency, trust, and ethical decision-making.
- **UNESCO's Global Education Coalition:** UNESCO's Global Education Coalition brings together governments, educational institutions, technology providers, and community organizations to collaboratively address educational challenges using AI technologies.

The coalition promotes inclusive engagement, ensuring that AI-driven solutions are equitable and culturally relevant.

Challenges and Considerations

- **Balancing Diverse Interests:** Balancing the diverse interests and priorities of different stakeholder groups can be challenging. Effective engagement requires careful facilitation, active listening, and a commitment to finding common ground and mutually beneficial solutions.
- **Overcoming Resistance to Change:** Resistance to change can be a barrier to stakeholder engagement. Institutions must communicate the benefits of AI technologies clearly and address concerns and misconceptions to foster acceptance and support.
- **Ensuring Accessibility:** Ensuring that engagement opportunities are accessible to all stakeholders, including those with disabilities and those from underserved communities, is essential for inclusive participation. Providing multiple channels for engagement and accommodating diverse needs enhances accessibility.
- **Maintaining Engagement Over Time:** Sustaining stakeholder engagement over the long term requires ongoing effort and commitment. Institutions should establish regular communication, provide updates on progress, and continuously seek input to maintain stakeholder interest and involvement.

Conclusion

Community and stakeholder engagement is crucial for the ethical and socially responsible implementation of AI in education. By fostering collaboration, transparency, and inclusivity, educational institutions can build trust, ensure equity, and develop AI solutions that meet the diverse needs of students, educators, and communities. Effective strategies for engagement include establishing advisory committees, conducting public consultations, implementing feedback mechanisms, co-designing AI solutions, and providing education and resources. The long-term benefits of inclusive practices include sustainable and ethical AI implementation, empowered communities, enhanced social cohesion, and continuous improvement and innovation. Through thoughtful and proactive engagement, we can harness the transformative potential of AI to create a more inclusive, equitable, and effective educational landscape.

QUESTIONNAIRE

Question 1: How can educational institutions address ethical issues related to AI?

Answer: Educational institutions can address ethical issues related to AI by implementing robust data privacy policies, ensuring transparency in AI algorithms, and promoting ethical AI use. Regular audits and assessments can help identify and mitigate biases in AI systems. Institutions should also engage stakeholders, including students, parents, and educators, in discussions about AI implementation and its ethical implications, fostering a collaborative approach to ethical AI use.

Question 2: How can AI help bridge educational gaps in underserved communities?

Answer: AI can help bridge educational gaps in underserved communities by providing affordable and accessible learning resources, personalized tutoring, and real-time feedback. AI-driven platforms can offer customized content and support, addressing individual learning needs and overcoming barriers such as lack of qualified teachers or educational materials. This ensures that students in underserved areas receive quality education and opportunities for academic success.

Question 3: Why is policy and regulation important for AI in education?

Answer: Policy and regulation are important for AI in education to ensure the ethical, equitable, and effective use of AI technologies. Regulations can establish standards for data privacy, algorithmic transparency, and accountability, protecting students' rights and promoting trust in AI systems. Policies can guide the implementation of AI in a way that maximizes its benefits while minimizing potential risks, ensuring a balanced and responsible approach.

Question 4: What should be included in policies regulating AI in education?

Answer: Policies regulating AI in education should include guidelines on data privacy and security, measures to prevent and address algorithmic bias, standards for transparency and accountability, and protocols for ethical AI use. They should also outline requirements for stakeholder engagement, including input from students, parents, educators, and policymakers. Additionally, policies should promote ongoing research and evaluation to ensure AI technologies are continually improving and aligning with educational goals.

Question 5: How does AI influence workforce development in education?

Answer: AI influences workforce development in education by automating administrative tasks, providing personalized professional development, and identifying skill gaps. AI-driven tools can streamline routine processes, allowing educators to focus on teaching and mentoring. AI can also offer tailored training programs, helping educators enhance their skills and stay current with technological advancements. This prepares the workforce for the evolving demands of the education sector.

Question 6: What skills are essential for educators to effectively integrate AI into their teaching?

Answer: Essential skills for educators to effectively integrate AI into their teaching include digital literacy, data analysis, and a strong understanding of AI technologies. Educators should be proficient in using AI-driven tools and interpreting data insights to inform instructional strategies. Additionally, they should be knowledgeable about the ethical implications of AI and equipped to address students' concerns about AI use in education. Continuous professional development is crucial to keeping these skills up-to-date.

Question 7: How can AI education prepare students for the future?

Answer: AI education can prepare students for the future by equipping them with critical thinking, problem-solving, and digital literacy skills. Understanding AI technologies and their applications helps students navigate an increasingly tech-driven world. AI education also fosters adaptability and lifelong learning, essential traits in a rapidly changing job market. By integrating AI into the curriculum, schools can prepare students for careers in emerging fields and ensure they are informed and responsible digital citizens.

Question 8: What role do educators play in building the future with AI education?

Answer: Educators play a crucial role in building the future with AI education by integrating AI into their teaching practices, fostering a culture of innovation, and guiding students in ethical AI use. They act as facilitators, helping students understand and navigate AI technologies. Educators also advocate for equitable access to AI resources and continuous learning opportunities. Their involvement ensures that AI education is comprehensive, inclusive, and aligned with the needs and aspirations of students.

Question 9: Why is community and stakeholder engagement important in AI education?

Answer: Community and stakeholder engagement is important in AI education to ensure that AI implementation meets the needs and values of all parties involved. Engaging students, parents, educators, policymakers, and technologists fosters a collaborative approach to AI integration, promoting transparency, trust, and ethical use. It also helps address concerns, gather diverse perspectives, and ensure that AI technologies are developed and used in ways that benefit the entire educational community.

Question 10: How can schools effectively engage stakeholders in AI education initiatives?

Answer: Schools can effectively engage stakeholders in AI education initiatives by organizing informational sessions, workshops, and forums to discuss AI's benefits, challenges, and ethical implications. Involving stakeholders in decision-making processes, soliciting feedback, and maintaining open communication channels are crucial. Collaborative projects and partnerships with tech companies, universities, and community organizations can also enhance stakeholder involvement and support for AI education initiatives.

5

Practical Applications and Case Studies

IMPLEMENTING AI IN K-12 EDUCATION

Artificial Intelligence (AI) is increasingly being integrated into K-12 education, transforming how students learn and how teachers instruct. From personalized learning to administrative efficiency, AI offers numerous benefits that can enhance the educational experience for students and educators alike. This section explores practical applications of AI in K-12 education, provides examples of successful implementations, and discusses strategies for effective integration.

Practical Applications of AI in K-12 Education

- **Personalized Learning:** AI-driven personalized learning platforms adjust the content, pace, and difficulty of lessons based on individual student performance and learning styles. These platforms can identify areas where students need additional support and offer tailored resources to help them master concepts. Examples include DreamBox for mathematics and Smart Sparrow for interactive science lessons.
- **Intelligent Tutoring Systems (ITS):** Intelligent Tutoring Systems provide one-on-one instruction to students, simulating the personalized attention of a human tutor. These systems use AI to analyze student responses and provide immediate feedback, hints, and explanations. ITS can be particularly effective for subjects like math and science, where step-by-step problem-solving is crucial. Examples include Carnegie Learning's MATHia and the ASSISTments platform.
- **Automated Grading and Feedback:** AI can automate the grading of assignments and exams, providing instant feedback to students. This not only saves teachers time but also ensures consistent and objective evaluation. AI-powered grading systems can handle multiple-choice tests, short answers, and even essays by using natural language processing (NLP) to assess content and structure. Platforms like Gradescope and Turnitin use AI to assist with grading and plagiarism detection.
- **Classroom Management Tools:** AI-driven classroom management tools help teachers monitor student engagement and participation. These tools can track attendance, analyze classroom behavior, and provide insights into student interactions. AI can also support teachers in creating dynamic seating arrangements and managing classroom activities more efficiently. Examples include Classcraft and GoGuardian.
- **Educational Content Creation:** AI can assist in creating educational content, such as quizzes, flashcards, and interactive exercises. By analyzing curricular standards and student performance data, AI systems can generate customized content that aligns with learning objectives. This can help teachers supplement their instruction with high-quality, personalized materials. Tools like Quizlet and Knewton leverage AI to create adaptive learning resources.

Case Studies and Examples

- **New York City Public Schools:** New York City Public Schools have implemented AI-driven tools to support personalized learning and improve student outcomes. The district uses platforms like DreamBox and ST Math to provide adaptive math instruction, allowing students to progress at their own pace and receive targeted support. These tools have been shown to enhance student engagement and achievement in mathematics.
- **Baltimore County Public Schools:** Baltimore County Public Schools use AI-powered classroom management tools to monitor student behavior and engagement. The district has implemented Classcraft, a gamified classroom management platform that uses AI to track student participation and reward positive behavior. This approach has improved classroom dynamics and fostered a more positive learning environment.
- **Los Angeles Unified School District:** The Los Angeles Unified School District (LAUSD) has adopted AI-driven automated grading systems to streamline the assessment process. Using platforms like Gradescope, teachers can quickly grade assignments and provide timely feedback to students. This has reduced the administrative burden on teachers and allowed them to focus more on instruction.
- **Montgomery County Public Schools:** Montgomery County Public Schools in Maryland have integrated AI into their curriculum development process. Using AI-powered tools, the district can analyze student performance data and align instructional materials with curricular standards. This data-driven approach ensures that the curriculum remains relevant and effective in meeting student needs.

Strategies for Effective Integration of AI in K-12 Education

- **Professional Development and Training:** Providing teachers with the necessary training and support is crucial for the successful integration of AI in K-12 education. Professional development programs should focus on building educators' skills and confidence in using AI tools and interpreting the data they provide. Ongoing training and support can help teachers stay updated with the latest AI advancements and best practices.
- **Involving Stakeholders:** Involving stakeholders, including students, parents, and educators, in the decision-making process is

essential for successful AI integration. Gathering input from these groups can help identify the needs and preferences of the school community and ensure that AI implementations align with their goals. Transparent communication and collaboration can build trust and support for AI initiatives.

- **Ensuring Data Privacy and Security:** Protecting student data is critical when implementing AI in education. Schools must ensure that AI systems comply with data privacy regulations, such as the Family Educational Rights and Privacy Act (FERPA). Implementing robust data protection measures, such as encryption and secure storage solutions, is essential to safeguard student information.
- **Monitoring and Evaluation:** Continuous monitoring and evaluation of AI implementations are crucial to ensure their effectiveness and address any emerging challenges. Schools should regularly assess the impact of AI tools on student learning and engagement, gather feedback from educators and students, and make data-driven adjustments as needed. This iterative process can help optimize the use of AI in education.
- **Fostering a Culture of Innovation:** Promoting a culture of innovation and experimentation can facilitate the successful integration of AI in K-12 education. Encouraging educators to explore new AI tools and methodologies, share best practices, and collaborate on innovative projects can drive continuous improvement and enhance the overall educational experience.

Challenges and Considerations

- **Access and Equity:** Ensuring equitable access to AI technologies is a significant challenge. Schools in underserved communities may lack the necessary infrastructure, devices, and internet connectivity to implement AI-driven education effectively. Addressing these disparities is crucial to ensure that all students can benefit from AI advancements.
- **Ethical Considerations:** The use of AI in K-12 education raises ethical considerations, such as ensuring transparency in AI decision-making processes, avoiding bias, and maintaining human oversight. Schools must develop ethical guidelines for AI use, emphasizing the importance of fairness, accountability, and the role of educators in the learning process.
- **Teacher Acceptance and Buy-In:** Gaining teacher acceptance and buy-in is essential for the successful implementation of AI in education. Educators may have concerns about the impact of AI on

their roles and the quality of education. Addressing these concerns through transparent communication, professional development, and demonstrating the benefits of AI can help build support for AI initiatives.

- **Integration with Existing Systems:** Integrating AI tools with existing educational systems and practices can be challenging. Schools must ensure that AI implementations align with curricular standards, instructional goals, and administrative processes. Effective integration requires careful planning, collaboration, and ongoing support.

Implementing AI in K-12 education offers significant opportunities to enhance personalized learning, improve teacher support, and streamline administrative processes. By leveraging AI technologies, schools can create more engaging and effective learning environments for students. However, addressing challenges related to access, equity, data privacy, and ethical considerations is essential to ensure the responsible and effective use of AI in education. Through careful planning, collaboration, and continuous improvement, we can harness the full potential of AI to transform K-12 education and prepare students for the future.

AI AND EDUCATIONAL CONTENT CREATION

Artificial Intelligence (AI) is revolutionizing the creation of educational content by enabling the development of dynamic, personalized, and engaging learning materials. AI-driven content creation tools can analyze curricular standards, student performance data, and learning preferences to generate customized educational resources. This section explores the various applications of AI in educational content creation, provides examples of successful implementations, and discusses strategies for effective integration.

Practical Applications of AI in Educational Content Creation

- **Adaptive Learning Materials:** AI-powered platforms can create adaptive learning materials that adjust in real-time to meet the needs of individual students. These materials include interactive exercises, quizzes, and assessments that vary in difficulty based on student performance. By personalizing content, AI ensures that each student receives the appropriate level of challenge and support, enhancing engagement and learning outcomes.
- **Intelligent Textbooks:** Intelligent textbooks use AI to provide a more interactive and personalized reading experience. These digital textbooks can highlight key concepts, offer multimedia resources

such as videos and simulations, and provide instant feedback on comprehension checks. AI can also generate summaries and suggest additional resources based on student progress and interests.

- **Automated Content Generation:** AI can assist in the automated generation of educational content, such as lesson plans, practice problems, and instructional videos. By analyzing curricular standards and educational goals, AI systems can create high-quality content that aligns with learning objectives. This automation can save educators time and ensure consistency in content quality.
- **Language Translation and Localization:** AI-driven language translation tools can make educational content accessible to students who speak different languages. These tools can translate text, audio, and video content, allowing students to learn in their native language. AI can also localize content to align with cultural and regional contexts, making learning more relevant and inclusive.
- **Virtual Labs and Simulations:** AI can create virtual labs and simulations that provide hands-on learning experiences in a safe and controlled environment. These virtual environments can simulate real-world scenarios, allowing students to experiment, explore, and learn by doing. AI-driven simulations can enhance understanding and retention of complex concepts, particularly in STEM (Science, Technology, Engineering, and Mathematics) subjects.

Case Studies and Examples

- **Knewton:** Knewton is an AI-powered adaptive learning platform that creates personalized educational content for students. By analyzing student performance data, Knewton adjusts the content and pace of learning materials to meet individual needs. The platform's adaptive technology ensures that students receive the right level of challenge and support, improving engagement and learning outcomes.
- **Pearson's REVEL:** REVEL is a digital learning platform by Pearson that uses AI to enhance the educational experience. The platform offers interactive textbooks with multimedia resources, real-time assessments, and personalized feedback. AI-driven analytics help educators track student progress and adjust instruction accordingly, ensuring that learning objectives are met.
- **Content Technologies, Inc. (CTI):** CTI uses AI to generate customized educational content, including textbooks and study guides. The company's AI-driven platform analyzes curricular standards and educational goals to create high-quality, personalized

learning materials. CTI's automated content generation saves educators time and ensures that students have access to relevant and engaging resources.

- **Labster:** Labster is a platform that provides AI-driven virtual labs and simulations for science education. The platform offers a range of interactive simulations that allow students to conduct experiments and explore scientific concepts in a virtual environment. AI enhances the learning experience by providing real-time feedback and personalized guidance, helping students develop critical thinking and problem-solving skills.

Strategies for Effective Integration of AI in Educational Content Creation

- **Aligning with Curricular Standards:** Ensuring that AI-generated content aligns with curricular standards and learning objectives is crucial for effective integration. Educational institutions and technology providers should collaborate to develop content that meets educational requirements and supports student learning goals.
- **Providing Professional Development for Educators:** Training and support for educators are essential to maximize the benefits of AI-driven content creation tools. Professional development programs should focus on building educators' skills in using AI tools, understanding AI-generated content, and integrating these resources into their teaching practices.
- **Ensuring Quality and Consistency:** Maintaining high quality and consistency in AI-generated content is critical. Regular reviews and updates of content are necessary to ensure accuracy and relevance. Involving educators and subject matter experts in the content creation process can help maintain standards and ensure that content meets educational needs.
- **Addressing Data Privacy and Security:** Protecting student data used in AI-driven content creation is essential. Educational institutions must implement robust data protection measures and comply with privacy regulations to safeguard student information. Transparent data usage practices and informed consent from students and parents are also crucial.
- **Encouraging Collaboration and Feedback:** Collaboration among educators, students, and technology providers can enhance the effectiveness of AI-driven content creation. Gathering feedback from users can help identify areas for improvement and ensure that content meets the needs of learners. Open communication and

collaboration can foster a culture of continuous improvement and innovation.

Challenges and Considerations

- **Access and Equity:** Ensuring equitable access to AI-driven content creation tools is a significant challenge. Schools in underserved communities may lack the necessary technology and resources to implement these tools effectively. Addressing these disparities is crucial to ensure that all students can benefit from AI advancements.
- **Bias and Fairness:** AI algorithms can be susceptible to bias, which can impact the fairness and inclusivity of educational content. Ensuring that AI systems are trained on diverse and representative datasets, regularly audited for bias, and designed with inclusivity in mind is essential to promote fairness.
- **Integration with Existing Systems:** Integrating AI-generated content with existing educational systems and practices can be challenging. Schools must ensure that new tools and content align with curricular standards, instructional goals, and classroom dynamics. Effective integration requires careful planning, collaboration, and ongoing support.
- **Ethical Considerations:** The use of AI in educational content creation raises ethical considerations, such as ensuring transparency in AI decision-making processes, maintaining human oversight, and avoiding over-reliance on technology. Schools must develop ethical guidelines for AI use, emphasizing the importance of fairness, accountability, and the role of educators.

AI-driven educational content creation offers significant opportunities to enhance personalized learning, improve engagement, and streamline the development of high-quality learning materials. By leveraging AI technologies, educational institutions can create dynamic and relevant content that meets the diverse needs of students. However, addressing challenges related to access, equity, bias, and ethical considerations is essential to ensure the responsible and effective use of AI in content creation. Through careful planning, collaboration, and continuous improvement, we can harness the full potential of AI to transform educational content and support student success.

AI IN CLASSROOM MANAGEMENT

Classroom management is a critical aspect of effective teaching, and AI can play a significant role in enhancing classroom dynamics and administrative efficiency. AI-driven tools can help teachers monitor student behavior, track attendance, manage classroom activities, and provide personalized support. This section explores the various applications of AI in classroom management, provides examples of successful implementations, and discusses strategies for effective integration.

Practical Applications of AI in Classroom Management

- **Behavior Monitoring and Analysis:** AI-powered tools can monitor and analyze student behavior in real-time, providing insights into classroom dynamics. These tools can detect patterns of disruptive behavior, identify students who may need additional support, and suggest interventions to improve classroom climate. AI can also track individual student behavior over time, helping teachers understand the root causes of issues and address them effectively.
- **Attendance Tracking:** AI can automate attendance tracking, reducing the administrative burden on teachers. Facial recognition technology and smart sensors can automatically record student attendance, ensuring accuracy and saving time. AI systems can also generate attendance reports and alert teachers to patterns of absenteeism, enabling timely interventions.
- **Classroom Layout and Seating Arrangements:** AI-driven classroom management tools can optimize seating arrangements based on student needs and classroom dynamics. These tools can consider factors such as student behavior, learning styles, and social interactions to create seating plans that enhance learning and reduce disruptions. AI can also suggest changes to the classroom layout to improve accessibility and engagement.
- **Personalized Support and Interventions:** AI can provide personalized support to students by analyzing their behavior, performance, and engagement. AI-driven tools can suggest targeted interventions and resources to help students succeed. For example, AI can recommend additional practice exercises for students who struggle with specific concepts or suggest strategies to improve focus and concentration for students with attention difficulties.
- **Gamification and Engagement:** AI can enhance student engagement through gamification, incorporating game-like elements into classroom activities. AI-driven platforms can create interactive and competitive learning experiences, motivating students to participate and perform better. Gamification can also promote positive behavior by rewarding students for meeting specific goals and displaying desired behaviors.

Case Studies and Examples

- **Classcraft:** Classcraft is an AI-powered classroom management platform that gamifies the classroom experience. Teachers can use Classcraft to create interactive and engaging activities, track student behavior, and provide real-time feedback. The platform uses AI to analyze student data and suggest interventions to improve classroom dynamics. Classcraft's gamification elements, such as rewards and challenges, enhance student motivation and engagement.
- **GoGuardian:** GoGuardian is an AI-driven classroom management tool that helps teachers monitor student behavior and online activity. The platform provides real-time insights into student engagement, enabling teachers to identify and address issues quickly. GoGuardian also offers features such as web filtering, screen monitoring, and activity reports, helping teachers create a safe and focused learning environment.
- **Lightspeed Systems:** Lightspeed Systems uses AI to provide comprehensive classroom management solutions. The platform offers tools for behavior monitoring, attendance tracking, and content filtering. Lightspeed Systems' AI-driven analytics provide actionable insights into student behavior and engagement, helping teachers make data-driven decisions to enhance classroom management.
- **NetSupport School:** NetSupport School is an AI-powered classroom management software that offers a range of features to support teachers. The platform includes tools for behavior monitoring, real-time assessment, and personalized feedback. AI-driven analytics help teachers understand classroom dynamics and identify students who need additional support. NetSupport School also provides tools for interactive learning and collaboration, enhancing student engagement.

Strategies for Effective Integration of AI in Classroom Management

- **Providing Professional Development for Educators:** Training and support for educators are essential to maximize the benefits of AI-driven classroom management tools. Professional development programs should focus on building teachers' skills in using AI tools, interpreting data, and implementing interventions. Ongoing training and support can help educators stay updated with the latest AI advancements and best practices.

- **Involving Stakeholders in Decision-Making:** Involving stakeholders, including students, parents, and educators, in the decision-making process is crucial for successful AI integration. Gathering input from these groups can help identify the needs and preferences of the school community and ensure that AI implementations align with their goals. Transparent communication and collaboration can build trust and support for AI initiatives.
- **Ensuring Data Privacy and Security:** Protecting student data is critical when implementing AI in classroom management. Schools must ensure that AI systems comply with data privacy regulations, such as the Family Educational Rights and Privacy Act (FERPA). Implementing robust data protection measures, such as encryption and secure storage solutions, is essential to safeguard student information.
- **Monitoring and Evaluation:** Continuous monitoring and evaluation of AI implementations are crucial to ensure their effectiveness and address any emerging challenges. Schools should regularly assess the impact of AI tools on classroom management, gather feedback from educators and students, and make data-driven adjustments as needed. This iterative process can help optimize the use of AI in classroom management.
- **Fostering a Culture of Innovation:** Promoting a culture of innovation and experimentation can facilitate the successful integration of AI in classroom management. Encouraging educators to explore new AI tools and methodologies, share best practices, and collaborate on innovative projects can drive continuous improvement and enhance the overall educational experience.

Challenges and Considerations

- **Access and Equity:** Ensuring equitable access to AI-driven classroom management tools is a significant challenge. Schools in underserved communities may lack the necessary infrastructure, devices, and internet connectivity to implement AI-driven education effectively. Addressing these disparities is crucial to ensure that all students can benefit from AI advancements.
- **Bias and Fairness:** AI algorithms can be susceptible to bias, which can impact the fairness and inclusivity of classroom management practices. Ensuring that AI systems are trained on diverse and representative datasets, regularly audited for bias, and designed with inclusivity in mind is essential to promote fairness.

- **Teacher Acceptance and Buy-In:** Gaining teacher acceptance and buy-in is essential for the successful implementation of AI in classroom management. Educators may have concerns about the impact of AI on their roles and the quality of education. Addressing these concerns through transparent communication, professional development, and demonstrating the benefits of AI can help build support for AI initiatives.
- **Ethical Considerations:** The use of AI in classroom management raises ethical considerations, such as ensuring transparency in AI decision-making processes, maintaining human oversight, and avoiding over-reliance on technology. Schools must develop ethical guidelines for AI use, emphasizing the importance of fairness, accountability, and the role of educators.

AI-driven classroom management tools offer significant opportunities to enhance student behavior monitoring, attendance tracking, personalized support, and engagement. By leveraging AI technologies, schools can create more efficient and effective classroom environments that support student learning and development. However, addressing challenges related to access, equity, bias, and ethical considerations is essential to ensure the responsible and effective use of AI in classroom management. Through careful planning, collaboration, and continuous improvement, we can harness the full potential of AI to transform classroom management and support student success.

AI IN LANGUAGE LEARNING

Language learning is an area where Artificial Intelligence (AI) has made significant strides, offering innovative solutions that enhance the learning experience. AI-driven tools and platforms provide personalized, interactive, and engaging methods to learn new languages, catering to diverse learning styles and needs. This section explores the various applications of AI in language learning, provides examples of successful implementations, and discusses strategies for effective integration.

Practical Applications of AI in Language Learning

- **Personalized Learning Paths:** AI-driven language learning platforms can create personalized learning paths based on individual learner profiles, including their proficiency levels, learning styles, and goals. These platforms use adaptive algorithms to tailor content, pace, and difficulty, ensuring that learners receive the appropriate level of challenge and support. Examples include Duolingo and Babbel, which offer customized lessons and exercises.

- **Real-Time Feedback and Correction:** AI-powered tools provide real-time feedback and correction on language use, pronunciation, grammar, and vocabulary. These tools can analyze spoken and written input, offering instant suggestions for improvement. This immediate feedback helps learners practice more effectively and reinforces correct language use. Examples include Rosetta Stone and Elsa Speak, which offer real-time pronunciation feedback.
- **Conversational AI and Chatbots:** Conversational AI and chatbots enable learners to practice language skills through interactive dialogues. These AI-driven tools simulate real-life conversations, helping learners develop their speaking and listening abilities. Chatbots can adapt to the learner's proficiency level and provide contextually relevant responses, making language practice more engaging and realistic. Examples include Replika and Google Assistant's language learning features.
- **Language Translation and Transcription:** AI-powered language translation and transcription tools can assist learners in understanding and producing content in different languages. These tools can translate text, audio, and video content, making it easier for learners to access and comprehend material in their target language. AI-driven transcription tools can convert spoken language into text, helping learners improve their listening and writing skills. Examples include Google Translate and Microsoft Translator.
- **Gamification and Interactive Exercises:** AI-driven gamification elements and interactive exercises make language learning more enjoyable and motivating. These tools use game-like features, such as points, badges, and leaderboards, to encourage learners to complete tasks and achieve goals. Interactive exercises, such as quizzes, puzzles, and simulations, provide engaging ways to practice language skills. Examples include Memrise and Lingodeer, which incorporate gamification into their language learning platforms.

Case Studies and Examples

- **Duolingo:** Duolingo is an AI-powered language learning platform that offers personalized lessons and exercises. The platform uses adaptive algorithms to tailor content to each learner's proficiency level and learning style. Duolingo provides real-time feedback on language use and includes gamification elements to motivate learners. The platform's success demonstrates the effectiveness of AI in creating engaging and personalized language learning experiences.

- **Rosetta Stone:** Rosetta Stone leverages AI to provide real-time feedback on pronunciation and language use. The platform's speech recognition technology analyzes spoken input and offers instant corrections, helping learners improve their pronunciation and speaking skills. Rosetta Stone's AI-driven features enhance the language learning process by providing immediate and personalized feedback.
- **Elsa Speak:** Elsa Speak is an AI-powered app focused on improving English pronunciation. The app uses advanced speech recognition and analysis to provide real-time feedback on pronunciation accuracy. Elsa Speak's AI-driven technology helps learners identify and correct their pronunciation errors, making it an effective tool for language learners looking to improve their speaking skills.
- **Replika:** Replika is an AI-driven chatbot that enables users to practice language skills through interactive conversations. The chatbot adapts to the user's proficiency level and provides contextually relevant responses, making language practice more realistic and engaging. Replika's conversational AI technology helps learners develop their speaking and listening abilities in a natural and interactive manner.

Strategies for Effective Integration of AI in Language Learning

- **Aligning with Learning Objectives:** Ensuring that AI-driven language learning tools align with educational goals and learning objectives is crucial for effective integration. Language instructors and institutions should collaborate with technology providers to develop content that supports language acquisition and proficiency development.
- **Providing Professional Development for Educators:** Training and support for language educators are essential to maximize the benefits of AI-driven tools. Professional development programs should focus on building teachers' skills in using AI tools, understanding AI-generated feedback, and integrating these resources into their teaching practices. Ongoing training and support can help educators stay updated with the latest AI advancements and best practices.
- **Ensuring Data Privacy and Security:** Protecting learner data used in AI-driven language learning tools is essential. Educational institutions and technology providers must implement robust data protection measures and comply with privacy regulations to safeguard learner information. Transparent data usage practices and informed consent from learners are also crucial.

- **Monitoring and Evaluation:** Continuous monitoring and evaluation of AI-driven language learning tools are crucial to ensure their effectiveness and address any emerging challenges. Institutions should regularly assess the impact of AI tools on language learning outcomes, gather feedback from learners and educators, and make data-driven adjustments as needed. This iterative process can help optimize the use of AI in language learning.
- **Promoting Learner Engagement:** Encouraging learner engagement with AI-driven language learning tools is essential for their success. Instructors can promote engagement by incorporating interactive exercises, gamification elements, and real-life conversational practice into language learning activities. Creating a supportive and motivating learning environment can enhance learner motivation and participation.

Challenges and Considerations

- **Access and Equity:** Ensuring equitable access to AI-driven language learning tools is a significant challenge. Learners in underserved communities may lack the necessary technology and resources to implement these tools effectively. Addressing these disparities is crucial to ensure that all learners can benefit from AI advancements.
- **Bias and Fairness:** AI algorithms can be susceptible to bias, which can impact the fairness and inclusivity of language learning tools. Ensuring that AI systems are trained on diverse and representative datasets, regularly audited for bias, and designed with inclusivity in mind is essential to promote fairness.
- **Teacher Acceptance and Buy-In:** Gaining teacher acceptance and buy-in is essential for the successful implementation of AI in language learning. Educators may have concerns about the impact of AI on their roles and the quality of education. Addressing these concerns through transparent communication, professional development, and demonstrating the benefits of AI can help build support for AI initiatives.
- **Integration with Existing Systems:** Integrating AI-driven language learning tools with existing educational systems and practices can be challenging. Institutions must ensure that new tools and content align with curricular standards, instructional goals, and classroom dynamics. Effective integration requires careful planning, collaboration, and ongoing support.

AI-driven language learning tools offer significant opportunities to enhance personalized learning, provide real-time feedback, and create engaging and interactive learning experiences. By leveraging AI technologies, educational institutions can create dynamic and relevant language learning environments that meet the diverse needs of learners. However, addressing challenges related to access, equity, bias, and ethical considerations is essential to ensure the responsible and effective use of AI in language learning. Through careful planning, collaboration, and continuous improvement, we can harness the full potential of AI to transform language learning and support learner success.

AI AND GAMIFICATION IN EDUCATION

Gamification, the application of game-design elements in non-game contexts, has become a powerful tool in education, and Artificial Intelligence (AI) is enhancing its effectiveness. AI-driven gamification strategies can create personalized, engaging, and motivating learning experiences. This section explores the applications of AI in gamification for education, provides examples of successful implementations, and discusses strategies for effective integration.

Practical Applications of AI in Gamification

- **Personalized Learning Experiences:** AI can tailor gamified learning experiences to meet the needs and preferences of individual students. By analyzing data on student performance, behavior, and engagement, AI systems can adjust game difficulty, provide personalized challenges, and offer tailored rewards. This personalization enhances motivation and ensures that learning activities are appropriately challenging for each student.
- **Real-Time Feedback and Adaptation:** AI-powered gamification tools provide real-time feedback and adapt to student progress. These tools can offer instant feedback on tasks, quizzes, and activities, helping students understand their strengths and areas for improvement. AI systems can also dynamically adjust the game's difficulty and content based on student performance, ensuring a continuous and engaging learning experience.
- **Achievement and Rewards Systems:** AI can enhance traditional achievement and rewards systems by making them more personalized and adaptive. AI-driven platforms can analyze student data to create customized reward structures that align with individual goals and preferences. These systems can include

badges, points, leaderboards, and other incentives that motivate students to achieve their learning objectives.

- **Collaborative Learning and Social Interaction:** AI can facilitate collaborative learning and social interaction through gamification. AI-driven platforms can create team-based challenges, collaborative projects, and social learning activities that encourage students to work together and support each other. These interactions help develop social skills, teamwork, and a sense of community among learners.
- **Engagement Analytics:** AI can provide detailed analytics on student engagement and learning outcomes. By tracking interactions, progress, and engagement levels, AI systems can generate insights that help educators understand the effectiveness of gamified learning activities. These analytics can inform instructional strategies and help educators make data-driven decisions to enhance learning experiences.

Case Studies and Examples

- **Kahoot!:** Kahoot! is an AI-powered gamification platform that offers interactive quizzes and learning games. The platform uses AI to analyze student responses and adjust the difficulty of questions in real-time. Kahoot! provides instant feedback and rewards, such as points and badges, to motivate students. The platform's collaborative features enable students to participate in team-based challenges, enhancing engagement and social interaction.
- **Classcraft:** Classcraft is a gamification platform that uses AI to create personalized and engaging learning experiences. The platform gamifies classroom management and learning activities by incorporating game-like elements such as avatars, quests, and rewards. AI-driven analytics provide insights into student behavior and engagement, helping educators tailor their instructional strategies. Classcraft's social learning features promote collaboration and teamwork among students.
- **DreamBox Learning:** DreamBox Learning is an adaptive math platform that uses AI-driven gamification to personalize learning experiences. The platform provides interactive math games and activities that adjust in real-time based on student performance. AI algorithms analyze student data to offer personalized challenges and rewards, ensuring that each learner progresses at their own pace. DreamBox's gamified approach enhances motivation and supports mastery of math concepts.

- **Quizizz:** Quizizz is an AI-powered platform that gamifies quizzes and assessments. The platform uses AI to create personalized quizzes that adapt to student performance. Quizizz offers real-time feedback and rewards, such as points and leaderboards, to motivate students. The platform's collaborative features enable students to participate in group activities and competitions, fostering a sense of community and engagement.

Strategies for Effective Integration of AI in Gamification

- **Aligning with Educational Goals:** Ensuring that AI-driven gamification aligns with educational goals and learning objectives is crucial for effective integration. Educators and institutions should collaborate with technology providers to design gamified activities that support curriculum standards and promote meaningful learning outcomes.
- **Providing Professional Development for Educators:** Training and support for educators are essential to maximize the benefits of AI-driven gamification. Professional development programs should focus on building teachers' skills in using gamification tools, interpreting engagement analytics, and integrating these resources into their teaching practices. Ongoing training and support can help educators stay updated with the latest gamification strategies and best practices.
- **Ensuring Data Privacy and Security:** Protecting student data used in AI-driven gamification tools is essential. Educational institutions and technology providers must implement robust data protection measures and comply with privacy regulations to safeguard student information. Transparent data usage practices and informed consent from students and parents are also crucial.
- **Monitoring and Evaluation:** Continuous monitoring and evaluation of AI-driven gamification tools are crucial to ensure their effectiveness and address any emerging challenges. Schools should regularly assess the impact of gamification on student engagement and learning outcomes, gather feedback from educators and students, and make data-driven adjustments as needed. This iterative process can help optimize the use of gamification in education.
- **Promoting Student Engagement:** Encouraging student engagement with AI-driven gamification tools is essential for their success. Educators can promote engagement by incorporating

diverse game elements, offering meaningful rewards, and creating a supportive and motivating learning environment. Involving students in the design and selection of gamified activities can also enhance their investment and participation.

Challenges and Considerations

- **Access and Equity:** Ensuring equitable access to AI-driven gamification tools is a significant challenge. Students in underserved communities may lack the necessary technology and resources to participate in gamified learning activities effectively. Addressing these disparities is crucial to ensure that all students can benefit from AI advancements.
- **Bias and Fairness:** AI algorithms can be susceptible to bias, which can impact the fairness and inclusivity of gamified learning activities. Ensuring that AI systems are trained on diverse and representative datasets, regularly audited for bias, and designed with inclusivity in mind is essential to promote fairness.
- **Teacher Acceptance and Buy-In:** Gaining teacher acceptance and buy-in is essential for the successful implementation of AI in gamification. Educators may have concerns about the impact of AI on their roles and the quality of education. Addressing these concerns through transparent communication, professional development, and demonstrating the benefits of AI can help build support for gamification initiatives.
- **Ethical Considerations:** The use of AI in gamification raises ethical considerations, such as ensuring transparency in AI decision-making processes, maintaining human oversight, and avoiding over-reliance on technology. Schools must develop ethical guidelines for AI use, emphasizing the importance of fairness, accountability, and the role of educators.

AI-driven gamification offers significant opportunities to enhance personalized learning, provide real-time feedback, and create engaging and interactive learning experiences. By leveraging AI technologies, educational institutions can create dynamic and relevant gamified environments that meet the diverse needs of students. However, addressing challenges related to access, equity, bias, and ethical considerations is essential to ensure the responsible and effective use of AI in gamification. Through careful planning, collaboration, and continuous improvement, we can harness the full potential of AI to transform gamification in education and support student success.

AI IN SPECIAL EDUCATION: TRANSFORMING LEARNING FOR DIVERSE NEEDS

Artificial Intelligence (AI) holds significant promise for enhancing special education by providing personalized learning experiences, tailored support, and innovative tools that address the diverse needs of students with disabilities. This section explores how AI is being applied in special education, highlighting key benefits, case studies, and challenges. AI-driven solutions can create more inclusive learning environments, ensuring that all students have the opportunity to succeed.

Key Benefits of AI in Special Education

- **Personalized Learning Plans:** AI can develop personalized learning plans for students with special needs by analyzing their strengths, weaknesses, learning preferences, and progress. Adaptive learning technologies adjust the pace and content of instruction to meet individual needs, ensuring that students receive appropriate challenges and support.
- **Assistive Technologies:** AI-powered assistive technologies, such as speech-to-text, text-to-speech, and augmented reality (AR) tools, help students with disabilities access and engage with educational content. These technologies support various learning disabilities, including dyslexia, visual and hearing impairments, and mobility challenges, enhancing students' independence and participation in the classroom.
- **Behavioral and Emotional Support:** AI-driven tools can monitor and analyze students' behavioral and emotional states, providing real-time feedback and interventions. For example, wearable devices and emotion recognition software can detect signs of anxiety or stress, allowing educators to respond promptly and effectively. These tools help create a supportive learning environment that addresses students' emotional well-being.
- **Improved Communication:** AI technologies facilitate communication for students with speech and language impairments. AI-powered communication devices and apps enable students to express themselves using alternative communication methods, such as symbol-based communication boards or predictive text systems. These tools empower students to participate more fully in classroom activities and social interactions.
- **Data-Driven Decision Making:** AI provides educators with valuable data insights that inform decision-making and instructional

strategies. By analyzing student performance, engagement, and behavior data, AI can identify patterns and trends that help educators develop targeted interventions and monitor progress. Data-driven approaches ensure that support is tailored to each student's unique needs.

Case Studies and Examples

- **IBM Watson and Pearson for Special Education:** IBM Watson and Pearson have collaborated to create AI-driven tools that support personalized learning for students with special needs. Watson's natural language processing capabilities analyze student data to provide tailored recommendations and resources. These tools help educators create customized learning plans and track student progress.
- **Cognii's Virtual Learning Assistant:** Cognii's AI-powered Virtual Learning Assistant offers personalized tutoring and assessment for students with disabilities. The assistant uses natural language processing to engage students in interactive dialogues, providing instant feedback and customized learning pathways. This technology supports differentiated instruction and enhances learning outcomes for students with diverse needs.
- **Speechify: Text-to-Speech Technology:** Speechify is an AI-driven text-to-speech tool that helps students with reading disabilities, such as dyslexia, access written content. The tool converts text into natural-sounding speech, allowing students to listen to textbooks, articles, and other educational materials. Speechify supports various languages and offers customizable settings to accommodate individual preferences.
- **TouchChat: Augmentative and Alternative Communication (AAC):** TouchChat is an AI-powered AAC app that assists students with speech and language impairments. The app features a range of communication options, including symbol-based communication boards and predictive text. TouchChat's AI algorithms learn from user interactions to provide personalized word suggestions, enhancing communication efficiency and effectiveness.

Challenges and Considerations

- **Ensuring Accessibility:** While AI technologies offer significant benefits for special education, ensuring accessibility is crucial. Developers must design AI tools that accommodate various disabilities and provide customizable features to meet individual needs. Ensuring compatibility with existing assistive technologies is also essential for seamless integration.

- **Data Privacy and Security:** Protecting the privacy and security of student data is a critical concern in AI-driven special education. Institutions must implement robust data protection measures and comply with relevant privacy regulations to safeguard sensitive information. Transparency about data collection, usage, and storage practices builds trust among students, parents, and educators.
- **Addressing Bias in AI Algorithms:** AI algorithms can perpetuate biases present in the training data, leading to unfair outcomes for students with disabilities. Ensuring that AI systems are trained on diverse and representative datasets is essential for mitigating bias. Regular audits and evaluations of AI tools can help identify and address any biases that may arise.
- **Training and Professional Development:** Educators need adequate training and professional development to effectively use AI tools in special education. Institutions should provide ongoing support and resources to help teachers integrate AI technologies into their instructional practices. Professional development programs should cover both technical skills and ethical considerations related to AI use.
- **Collaborative Approach:** Implementing AI in special education requires a collaborative approach that involves educators, students, parents, and AI experts. Engaging stakeholders in the development and evaluation of AI tools ensures that the technologies meet the needs of students with disabilities and align with educational goals. Collaboration fosters a shared commitment to creating inclusive and effective learning environments.

Future Directions

- **Advancements in AI-Driven Assistive Technologies:** Future advancements in AI-driven assistive technologies hold promise for further enhancing special education. Innovations in areas such as brain-computer interfaces, advanced robotics, and personalized learning algorithms will continue to improve accessibility and support for students with disabilities.
- **Integration with Universal Design for Learning (UDL):** Integrating AI technologies with the principles of Universal Design for Learning (UDL) can create more inclusive educational environments. UDL emphasizes flexible learning approaches that accommodate diverse learners. AI can support UDL by providing

personalized and adaptable learning experiences that meet the needs of all students.

- **Longitudinal Research and Impact Assessment:** Conducting longitudinal research on the impact of AI in special education is essential for understanding its long-term benefits and challenges. Ongoing studies can provide insights into how AI technologies influence student outcomes, engagement, and well-being over time. This research can inform the development of best practices and guide future innovations.

Conclusion

AI has the potential to transform special education by providing personalized learning experiences, assistive technologies, and data-driven insights that address the diverse needs of students with disabilities. Case studies and examples demonstrate the significant benefits of AI-driven tools, including improved communication, behavioral support, and customized learning plans. However, challenges such as ensuring accessibility, protecting data privacy, addressing algorithmic bias, and providing adequate training must be addressed to maximize the potential of AI in special education. A collaborative approach that involves educators, students, parents, and AI experts is essential for creating inclusive and effective learning environments. As AI technologies continue to advance, they offer promising opportunities for enhancing special education and ensuring that all students have the opportunity to succeed.

QUESTIONNAIRE

Question 1: How is AI being implemented in K-12 education?

Answer: AI is being implemented in K-12 education through personalized learning platforms, intelligent tutoring systems, and automated administrative tasks. AI-driven tools can analyze student performance data to tailor educational content to individual needs, provide real-time feedback, and recommend learning activities. In classrooms, AI supports teachers by automating tasks such as grading and attendance tracking, allowing more time for direct student interaction and instruction.

Question 2: What are the benefits of using AI in K-12 education?

Answer: The benefits of using AI in K-12 education include personalized learning experiences, improved student engagement, and enhanced efficiency in administrative tasks. AI can adapt to individual learning styles, providing customized support and resources. This helps address diverse learning needs and promotes student success. Additionally, AI tools free up teachers from routine tasks, enabling them to focus more on teaching and fostering a supportive learning environment.

Question 3: How does AI contribute to educational content creation?

Answer: AI contributes to educational content creation by generating personalized and adaptive learning materials. AI algorithms can analyze educational standards and student data to create tailored lesson plans, quizzes, and interactive activities. This ensures that content is relevant, engaging, and aligned with curriculum goals. AI can also update and refine content based on real-time feedback and evolving educational needs, maintaining the material's effectiveness and relevance.

Question 4: What role does AI play in classroom management?

Answer: AI plays a significant role in classroom management by automating administrative tasks, monitoring student behavior, and providing data-driven insights. AI systems can track attendance, manage classroom schedules, and handle routine communications. Additionally, AI can analyze student interactions and engagement, identifying potential issues and suggesting interventions. This helps create a more organized, efficient, and supportive classroom environment.

Question 5: How can AI improve the efficiency of classroom management?

Answer: AI improves the efficiency of classroom management by automating tasks such as grading, attendance tracking, and lesson planning. AI-driven tools can provide real-time analytics on student participation and performance, helping teachers identify areas that need attention. By reducing the administrative burden on educators, AI allows them to focus more on teaching and interacting with students, ultimately enhancing the overall classroom experience.

Question 6: How is AI transforming language learning?

Answer: AI is transforming language learning by offering personalized and interactive learning experiences. AI-driven language learning apps, such as Duolingo and Babbel, use natural language processing and machine learning algorithms to adapt lessons to individual progress and preferences. These apps provide instant feedback, speech recognition, and adaptive challenges, making language learning more engaging and effective.

Question 7: What are the advantages of using AI in language learning?

Answer: The advantages of using AI in language learning include personalized instruction, real-time feedback, and increased accessibility. AI-driven platforms can tailor lessons to individual needs, ensuring that learners receive the right level of challenge and support. Real-time feedback helps learners correct mistakes immediately and improve their language skills more efficiently. Additionally, AI-powered tools can be accessed anytime and anywhere, making language learning more flexible and convenient.

Question 8: How does AI enhance gamification in education?

Answer: AI enhances gamification in education by creating personalized, adaptive learning experiences that keep students engaged and motivated. AI algorithms can analyze student performance and preferences to tailor game-based learning activities to individual needs. This ensures that challenges are appropriately matched to skill levels, promoting continuous improvement. AI also provides real-time feedback and rewards, further motivating students and making learning enjoyable.

Question 9: How is AI transforming special education?

Answer: AI is transforming special education by providing personalized support and adaptive learning tools for students with diverse needs. AI-driven technologies can analyze individual learning patterns and customize content to suit specific requirements. Tools such as speech recognition software, AI-powered reading assistants, and personalized learning apps help students with disabilities overcome challenges and improve their academic performance.

Question 10: What are the benefits of using AI in special education?

Answer: The benefits of using AI in special education include personalized learning experiences, enhanced accessibility, and improved student outcomes. AI can adapt content to individual learning styles and needs, providing customized support that helps students with disabilities succeed. AI-powered tools also offer real-time feedback and progress monitoring, enabling educators to make data-driven decisions and tailor interventions effectively. This promotes inclusivity and ensures that all students have access to quality education.

6

Future Prospects and Innovations

AI AND STEAM EDUCATION

The integration of Artificial Intelligence (AI) into STEAM (Science, Technology, Engineering, Arts, and Mathematics) education is transforming how these subjects are taught and learned. AI technologies offer innovative tools and approaches that enhance engagement, personalize learning, and support the development of critical skills needed for the future workforce. This section explores the impact of AI on STEAM education, provides examples of successful implementations, and discusses strategies for effective integration.

Practical Applications of AI in STEAM Education

- **Personalized Learning and Adaptive Content:** AI-driven platforms can personalize STEAM education by tailoring content to individual student needs and learning styles. Adaptive learning technologies analyze student performance data to adjust the difficulty and pace of lessons, ensuring that each student receives the appropriate level of challenge and support. Examples include Khan Academy and ALEKS, which offer personalized math and science instruction.
- **Interactive Simulations and Virtual Labs:** AI-powered simulations and virtual labs provide hands-on learning experiences that are essential for STEAM education. These tools allow students to conduct experiments, explore scientific concepts, and visualize complex phenomena in a virtual environment. AI enhances these simulations by providing real-time feedback and adaptive challenges. Examples include Labster and PhET Interactive Simulations.
- **AI-Driven Creativity and Design Tools:** AI can support the creative aspects of STEAM education by providing tools for design, art, and music. AI-driven software can assist students in creating digital art, composing music, and designing engineering projects. These tools can analyze student work, offer suggestions for improvement, and inspire creativity. Examples include Adobe Creative Cloud's AI-powered features and Google's Magenta project for music creation.
- **Robotics and Coding Education:** AI plays a significant role in robotics and coding education, teaching students essential skills for the future workforce. AI-driven platforms and tools provide interactive coding lessons, simulate robotics challenges, and offer real-time feedback on programming tasks. These tools help students develop problem-solving skills, logical thinking, and technical proficiency. Examples include LEGO Mindstorms and Code.org.
- **Data Analytics and Visualization:** AI can enhance data analytics and visualization in STEAM education, helping students understand and interpret complex data sets. AI-driven tools can analyze data, identify patterns, and generate visual representations that make data more accessible and comprehensible. These tools support inquiry-based learning and critical thinking. Examples include Tableau and IBM Watson Analytics.

Case Studies and Examples

- **Khan Academy:** Khan Academy uses AI to provide personalized math and science instruction. The platform's adaptive learning technology analyzes student performance data to adjust the difficulty and pace of lessons, ensuring that each student receives tailored support. Khan Academy's AI-driven approach enhances engagement and supports mastery of STEAM concepts.
- **Labster:** Labster offers AI-powered virtual labs that provide interactive and immersive science education experiences. The platform's simulations allow students to conduct experiments and explore scientific concepts in a virtual environment. AI enhances these simulations by providing real-time feedback and adaptive challenges, making science education more engaging and effective.
- **Adobe Creative Cloud:** Adobe Creative Cloud integrates AI-powered features that support creativity in art and design education. Tools such as Adobe Sensei offer suggestions for improving digital art, automate repetitive tasks, and inspire creative projects. Adobe's AI-driven tools enhance the creative process and support the development of artistic skills in STEAM education.
- **Code.org:** Code.org uses AI to teach coding and computer science to students of all ages. The platform provides interactive coding lessons, real-time feedback, and adaptive challenges that help students develop programming skills. Code.org's AI-driven approach makes coding education more accessible and engaging, preparing students for future careers in technology.

Strategies for Effective Integration of AI in STEAM Education

- **Aligning with Educational Goals:** Ensuring that AI-driven tools and approaches align with educational goals and STEAM curriculum standards is crucial for effective integration. Educators and institutions should collaborate with technology providers to design AI-enhanced activities that support learning objectives and promote mastery of STEAM concepts.
- **Providing Professional Development for Educators:** Training and support for educators are essential to maximize the benefits of AI in STEAM education. Professional development programs should focus on building teachers' skills in using AI tools, understanding AI-generated data, and integrating these resources into their teaching practices. Ongoing training and support can help educators stay updated with the latest AI advancements and best practices.

- **Ensuring Data Privacy and Security:** Protecting student data used in AI-driven STEAM tools is essential. Educational institutions and technology providers must implement robust data protection measures and comply with privacy regulations to safeguard student information. Transparent data usage practices and informed consent from students and parents are also crucial.
- **Monitoring and Evaluation:** Continuous monitoring and evaluation of AI-driven STEAM tools are crucial to ensure their effectiveness and address any emerging challenges. Schools should regularly assess the impact of AI tools on student engagement and learning outcomes, gather feedback from educators and students, and make data-driven adjustments as needed. This iterative process can help optimize the use of AI in STEAM education.
- **Promoting Student Engagement:** Encouraging student engagement with AI-driven STEAM tools is essential for their success. Educators can promote engagement by incorporating interactive simulations, hands-on projects, and real-world applications into STEAM activities. Creating a supportive and motivating learning environment can enhance student interest and participation.

Challenges and Considerations

- **Access and Equity:** Ensuring equitable access to AI-driven STEAM tools is a significant challenge. Students in underserved communities may lack the necessary technology and resources to participate in AI-enhanced STEAM education effectively. Addressing these disparities is crucial to ensure that all students can benefit from AI advancements.
- **Bias and Fairness:** AI algorithms can be susceptible to bias, which can impact the fairness and inclusivity of STEAM education tools. Ensuring that AI systems are trained on diverse and representative datasets, regularly audited for bias, and designed with inclusivity in mind is essential to promote fairness.
- **Teacher Acceptance and Buy-In:** Gaining teacher acceptance and buy-in is essential for the successful implementation of AI in STEAM education. Educators may have concerns about the impact of AI on their roles and the quality of education. Addressing these concerns through transparent communication, professional development, and demonstrating the benefits of AI can help build support for AI initiatives.

- **Ethical Considerations:** The use of AI in STEAM education raises ethical considerations, such as ensuring transparency in AI decision-making processes, maintaining human oversight, and avoiding over-reliance on technology. Schools must develop ethical guidelines for AI use, emphasizing the importance of fairness, accountability, and the role of educators.

AI-driven tools and approaches offer significant opportunities to enhance personalized learning, provide interactive simulations, and support creativity and innovation in STEAM education. By leveraging AI technologies, educational institutions can create dynamic and relevant STEAM learning environments that meet the diverse needs of students. However, addressing challenges related to access, equity, bias, and ethical considerations is essential to ensure the responsible and effective use of AI in STEAM education. Through careful planning, collaboration, and continuous improvement, we can harness the full potential of AI to transform STEAM education and support student success.

AI AND COLLABORATIVE LEARNING

Collaborative learning, an educational approach where students work together to solve problems and complete tasks, can be significantly enhanced by Artificial Intelligence (AI). AI technologies facilitate collaboration by providing tools that support communication, coordination, and feedback among students. This section explores the impact of AI on collaborative learning, provides examples of successful implementations, and discusses strategies for effective integration.

Practical Applications of AI in Collaborative Learning

- **AI-Powered Collaboration Platforms:** AI-driven collaboration platforms provide a suite of tools that enable students to work together seamlessly. These platforms offer features such as real-time chat, video conferencing, shared workspaces, and collaborative document editing. AI can enhance these platforms by providing real-time translation, summarization, and recommendation features. Examples include Google Workspace for Education and Microsoft Teams.
- **Intelligent Tutoring Systems (ITS):** ITS can facilitate collaborative learning by providing group-based learning activities and feedback. AI-driven ITS can form groups based on students' skills and learning preferences, assign collaborative tasks, and monitor group dynamics. These systems offer real-time feedback

and support, helping students work together effectively. Examples include Carnegie Learning's MATHia and the ASSISTments platform.

- **Adaptive Learning Environments:** AI can create adaptive learning environments that support collaborative learning by adjusting content and activities based on group performance. These environments can provide personalized challenges and resources tailored to the needs of each group, ensuring that all students are engaged and supported. AI can also track group progress and provide insights to educators. Examples include Knewton and Smart Sparrow.
- **Virtual and Augmented Reality (VR/AR):** AI-powered VR and AR technologies can create immersive collaborative learning experiences. These technologies allow students to explore virtual environments, conduct experiments, and work on projects together, regardless of their physical location. AI enhances these experiences by providing real-time feedback and adaptive challenges. Examples include ClassVR and zSpace.
- **Peer Assessment and Feedback:** AI can facilitate peer assessment and feedback in collaborative learning environments. AI-driven tools can analyze student submissions, provide initial feedback, and guide peer review processes. These tools help students develop critical thinking and self-assessment skills while ensuring fair and consistent evaluations. Examples include Peergrade and Turnitin's Feedback Studio.

Case Studies and Examples

- **Google Workspace for Education:** Google Workspace for Education is an AI-powered collaboration platform that provides tools for real-time communication and collaboration. Features such as Google Docs, Sheets, and Slides enable students to work together on projects, while AI-driven tools like Google Translate and Smart Compose enhance communication and productivity. Google Classroom integrates with these tools to facilitate collaborative learning and streamline classroom management.
- **Microsoft Teams:** Microsoft Teams is an AI-driven collaboration platform that supports real-time chat, video conferencing, and collaborative document editing. The platform's AI features include real-time translation, meeting transcription, and smart recommendations. Microsoft Teams integrates with other Microsoft Office applications, providing a comprehensive suite of tools for collaborative learning.

- **Carnegie Learning's MATHia:** MATHia is an intelligent tutoring system that supports collaborative learning in math education. The platform forms groups based on students' skills and learning preferences, assigns collaborative tasks, and provides real-time feedback. MATHia's AI-driven approach enhances group dynamics and supports effective teamwork in math problem-solving.
- **ClassVR:** ClassVR is an AI-powered VR platform that creates immersive collaborative learning experiences. The platform allows students to explore virtual environments and work on projects together, providing real-time feedback and adaptive challenges. ClassVR's AI-driven features enhance engagement and support collaborative learning in various subjects.

Strategies for Effective Integration of AI in Collaborative Learning

- **Aligning with Educational Goals:** Ensuring that AI-driven collaborative learning tools align with educational goals and curriculum standards is crucial for effective integration. Educators and institutions should collaborate with technology providers to design activities that support learning objectives and promote meaningful collaboration.
- **Providing Professional Development for Educators:** Training and support for educators are essential to maximize the benefits of AI in collaborative learning. Professional development programs should focus on building teachers' skills in using AI tools, facilitating collaborative activities, and interpreting collaboration analytics. Ongoing training and support can help educators stay updated with the latest AI advancements and best practices.
- **Ensuring Data Privacy and Security:** Protecting student data used in AI-driven collaborative learning tools is essential. Educational institutions and technology providers must implement robust data protection measures and comply with privacy regulations to safeguard student information. Transparent data usage practices and informed consent from students and parents are also crucial.
- **Monitoring and Evaluation:** Continuous monitoring and evaluation of AI-driven collaborative learning tools are crucial to ensure their effectiveness and address any emerging challenges. Schools should regularly assess the impact of AI tools on student collaboration and learning outcomes, gather feedback from educators and students, and make data-driven adjustments as needed. This iterative process can help optimize the use of AI in collaborative learning.

- **Promoting Student Engagement:** Encouraging student engagement with AI-driven collaborative learning tools is essential for their success. Educators can promote engagement by incorporating interactive activities, real-world applications, and opportunities for peer interaction into collaborative learning projects. Creating a supportive and motivating learning environment can enhance student interest and participation.

Challenges and Considerations

- **Access and Equity:** Ensuring equitable access to AI-driven collaborative learning tools is a significant challenge. Students in underserved communities may lack the necessary technology and resources to participate in AI-enhanced collaborative learning effectively. Addressing these disparities is crucial to ensure that all students can benefit from AI advancements.
- **Bias and Fairness:** AI algorithms can be susceptible to bias, which can impact the fairness and inclusivity of collaborative learning tools. Ensuring that AI systems are trained on diverse and representative datasets, regularly audited for bias, and designed with inclusivity in mind is essential to promote fairness.
- **Teacher Acceptance and Buy-In:** Gaining teacher acceptance and buy-in is essential for the successful implementation of AI in collaborative learning. Educators may have concerns about the impact of AI on their roles and the quality of education. Addressing these concerns through transparent communication, professional development, and demonstrating the benefits of AI can help build support for AI initiatives.
- **Ethical Considerations:** The use of AI in collaborative learning raises ethical considerations, such as ensuring transparency in AI decision-making processes, maintaining human oversight, and avoiding over-reliance on technology. Schools must develop ethical guidelines for AI use, emphasizing the importance of fairness, accountability, and the role of educators.

AI-driven tools and approaches offer significant opportunities to enhance collaborative learning by providing real-time communication, personalized support, and interactive experiences. By leveraging AI technologies, educational institutions can create dynamic and engaging collaborative learning environments that meet the diverse needs of students. However, addressing challenges related to access, equity, bias, and ethical considerations is essential to ensure the responsible and effective use of AI in collaborative learning. Through careful planning, collaboration, and continuous improvement, we can harness the full potential of AI to transform collaborative learning and support student success.

AI AND LEARNING ANALYTICS

Artificial Intelligence (AI) is revolutionizing learning analytics by providing powerful tools to analyze educational data, generate insights, and inform decision-making. AI-driven learning analytics can enhance teaching and learning by identifying patterns, predicting outcomes, and providing personalized recommendations. This section explores the impact of AI on learning analytics, provides examples of successful implementations, and discusses strategies for effective integration.

Practical Applications of AI in Learning Analytics

- **Predictive Analytics:** AI-driven predictive analytics can forecast student performance, identify at-risk students, and recommend interventions to support their success. By analyzing historical and real-time data, AI models can predict academic outcomes and provide actionable insights to educators. This proactive approach helps in timely intervention and improves student retention and achievement. Examples include Civitas Learning and IBM Watson Education.
- **Personalized Learning Recommendations:** AI-powered learning analytics systems can generate personalized learning recommendations based on individual student data. These recommendations can include tailored learning activities, resources, and pacing to meet each student's unique needs. AI can continuously refine these recommendations by analyzing ongoing student performance and engagement. Examples include Knewton and DreamBox Learning.
- **Student Engagement Analysis:** AI can analyze student engagement data to provide insights into learning behaviors and identify factors that influence engagement. By monitoring interactions with digital learning platforms, AI systems can detect patterns of disengagement and suggest strategies to re-engage students. This analysis helps educators understand how to create more engaging learning environments. Examples include Classcraft and GoGuardian.
- **Curriculum and Instructional Design:** AI-driven learning analytics can inform curriculum and instructional design by identifying effective teaching practices and areas for improvement. By analyzing data on student performance and feedback, AI

can highlight successful instructional strategies and suggest adjustments to the curriculum. This data-driven approach ensures that educational content remains relevant and effective. Examples include Edmentum and Blackboard Analytics.

- **Real-Time Feedback and Assessment:** AI can provide real-time feedback and assessment to students and educators. By analyzing student responses and performance data, AI systems can offer instant feedback on assignments, quizzes, and exams. This immediate feedback helps students understand their strengths and areas for improvement and supports formative assessment practices. Examples include Gradescope and Turnitin.

Case Studies and Examples

- **Civitas Learning:** Civitas Learning uses AI-driven predictive analytics to help educational institutions improve student outcomes. The platform analyzes data on student performance, engagement, and behavior to predict academic success and identify at-risk students. Civitas Learning provides actionable insights and recommendations to educators, enabling timely interventions that support student retention and achievement.
- **IBM Watson Education:** IBM Watson Education leverages AI to provide personalized learning recommendations and predictive analytics. The platform analyzes student data to offer tailored learning activities and resources, enhancing personalized learning experiences. IBM Watson Education also provides predictive insights to educators, helping them identify and support at-risk students.
- **Edmentum:** Edmentum offers AI-driven learning analytics tools that inform curriculum and instructional design. The platform analyzes student performance data to identify effective teaching practices and suggest adjustments to the curriculum. Edmentum's AI-driven approach ensures that educational content aligns with student needs and promotes successful learning outcomes.
- **Gradescope:** Gradescope is an AI-powered assessment platform that provides real-time feedback and grading for assignments and exams. The platform uses AI to analyze student responses and offer instant feedback, supporting formative assessment practices. Gradescope's AI-driven features enhance the efficiency and accuracy of grading, providing valuable insights to both students and educators.

Strategies for Effective Integration of AI in Learning Analytics

- **Aligning with Educational Goals:** Ensuring that AI-driven learning analytics tools align with educational goals and curriculum standards is crucial for effective integration. Educators and institutions should collaborate with technology providers to design analytics systems that support learning objectives and promote meaningful insights.
- **Providing Professional Development for Educators:** Training and support for educators are essential to maximize the benefits of AI in learning analytics. Professional development programs should focus on building teachers' skills in using analytics tools, interpreting data, and implementing data-driven interventions. Ongoing training and support can help educators stay updated with the latest AI advancements and best practices.
- **Ensuring Data Privacy and Security:** Protecting student data used in AI-driven learning analytics tools is essential. Educational institutions and technology providers must implement robust data protection measures and comply with privacy regulations to safeguard student information. Transparent data usage practices and informed consent from students and parents are also crucial.
- **Monitoring and Evaluation:** Continuous monitoring and evaluation of AI-driven learning analytics tools are crucial to ensure their effectiveness and address any emerging challenges. Schools should regularly assess the impact of analytics tools on student outcomes, gather feedback from educators and students, and make data-driven adjustments as needed. This iterative process can help optimize the use of AI in learning analytics.
- **Promoting Data-Driven Decision Making:** Encouraging data-driven decision-making practices among educators and administrators is essential for the successful integration of AI in learning analytics. Institutions should promote a culture of using data to inform instructional strategies, curriculum design, and student support services. Providing access to analytics tools and resources can empower educators to make informed decisions that enhance student learning.

Challenges and Considerations

- **Access and Equity:** Ensuring equitable access to AI-driven learning analytics tools is a significant challenge. Students in underserved communities may lack the necessary technology and resources to benefit from these tools effectively. Addressing these disparities is crucial to ensure that all students can benefit from AI advancements.

- **Bias and Fairness:** AI algorithms can be susceptible to bias, which can impact the fairness and inclusivity of learning analytics tools. Ensuring that AI systems are trained on diverse and representative datasets, regularly audited for bias, and designed with inclusivity in mind is essential to promote fairness.
- **Teacher Acceptance and Buy-In:** Gaining teacher acceptance and buy-in is essential for the successful implementation of AI in learning analytics. Educators may have concerns about the impact of AI on their roles and the quality of education. Addressing these concerns through transparent communication, professional development, and demonstrating the benefits of AI can help build support for analytics initiatives.
- **Ethical Considerations:** The use of AI in learning analytics raises ethical considerations, such as ensuring transparency in AI decision-making processes, maintaining human oversight, and avoiding over-reliance on technology. Schools must develop ethical guidelines for AI use, emphasizing the importance of fairness, accountability, and the role of educators.

AI-driven learning analytics offer significant opportunities to enhance teaching and learning by providing powerful tools to analyze educational data, generate insights, and inform decision-making. By leveraging AI technologies, educational institutions can create data-driven learning environments that support personalized learning, predictive analytics, and real-time feedback. However, addressing challenges related to access, equity, bias, and ethical considerations is essential to ensure the responsible and effective use of AI in learning analytics. Through careful planning, collaboration, and continuous improvement, we can harness the full potential of AI to transform learning analytics and support student success.

AI AND CREATIVE ARTS EDUCATION

Artificial Intelligence (AI) is transforming creative arts education by offering innovative tools that enhance creativity, provide personalized feedback, and support the development of artistic skills. AI-driven technologies enable students to explore new artistic possibilities, receive real-time feedback, and collaborate in ways that were previously unimaginable. This section explores the impact of AI on creative arts education, provides examples of successful implementations, and discusses strategies for effective integration.

Practical Applications of AI in Creative Arts Education

- **AI-Enhanced Artistic Creation:** AI-driven tools can assist students in creating digital art, music, and other forms of creative expression. These tools use algorithms to generate ideas, suggest improvements, and automate repetitive tasks, allowing students to focus on the creative aspects of their work. Examples include DeepArt for digital painting and Amper Music for music composition.
- **Personalized Feedback and Assessment:** AI-powered platforms provide personalized feedback on artistic work, helping students refine their skills and improve their creations. These platforms analyze student work, identify areas for improvement, and offer constructive suggestions. This real-time feedback enhances the learning process and supports skill development. Examples include Artomatix for digital art and Humtap for music composition.
- **Interactive Learning Experiences:** AI can create interactive and immersive learning experiences in the creative arts. Virtual reality (VR) and augmented reality (AR) technologies allow students to explore virtual galleries, participate in interactive performances, and engage with artistic content in new ways. AI enhances these experiences by providing real-time feedback and adaptive challenges. Examples include Tilt Brush for VR painting and AR Music Kit for augmented reality music creation.
- **Collaborative Artistic Projects:** AI-driven platforms facilitate collaboration among students on artistic projects. These platforms provide tools for real-time collaboration, shared workspaces, and communication, enabling students to work together regardless of their physical location. AI can also assist in coordinating collaborative efforts and providing feedback on group work. Examples include Adobe Creative Cloud for collaborative design and Soundation for collaborative music production.
- **Creative Arts Analytics:** AI can analyze artistic work and provide insights into creative processes and outcomes. These analytics help educators understand student progress, identify effective teaching strategies, and tailor instruction to meet individual needs. AI-driven analytics can also support students in developing their artistic skills by highlighting strengths and areas for improvement. Examples include The Infinite Drum Machine for music analysis and Google's Art Project for visual art exploration.

Case Studies and Examples

- **DeepArt:** DeepArt is an AI-powered platform that transforms photos into digital artworks using neural networks. The platform analyzes images and applies artistic styles inspired by famous artists. DeepArt allows students to experiment with different styles and techniques, enhancing their creativity and understanding of digital art.
- **Amper Music:** Amper Music is an AI-driven music composition tool that enables users to create original music tracks. The platform uses AI algorithms to compose music based on user inputs, such as mood, genre, and instrumentation. Amper Music provides real-time feedback and suggestions, helping students develop their music composition skills.
- **Tilt Brush:** Tilt Brush by Google is a VR painting application that allows users to create 3D art in a virtual environment. The platform offers a range of brushes and tools for creating immersive artworks. Tilt Brush's AI-driven features enhance the creative process by providing real-time feedback and adaptive challenges.
- **Adobe Creative Cloud:** Adobe Creative Cloud is a suite of AI-powered design and creativity tools that support collaboration among students. The platform includes tools for graphic design, video editing, web development, and more. Adobe's AI-driven features, such as Adobe Sensei, offer personalized suggestions and automate repetitive tasks, enhancing the creative process.
- **Soundation:** Soundation is an AI-powered platform for collaborative music production. The platform provides tools for creating, recording, and editing music tracks in real-time. Soundation's AI-driven features facilitate collaboration by enabling students to work together on music projects, regardless of their physical location.

Strategies for Effective Integration of AI in Creative Arts Education

- **Aligning with Educational Goals:** Ensuring that AI-driven tools and approaches align with educational goals and creative arts curriculum standards is crucial for effective integration. Educators and institutions should collaborate with technology providers to design activities that support learning objectives and promote artistic development.
- **Providing Professional Development for Educators:** Training and support for educators are essential to maximize the benefits of AI in creative arts education. Professional development

programs should focus on building teachers' skills in using AI tools, facilitating creative activities, and interpreting artistic analytics. Ongoing training and support can help educators stay updated with the latest AI advancements and best practices.

- **Ensuring Data Privacy and Security:** Protecting student data used in AI-driven creative arts tools is essential. Educational institutions and technology providers must implement robust data protection measures and comply with privacy regulations to safeguard student information. Transparent data usage practices and informed consent from students and parents are also crucial.
- **Monitoring and Evaluation:** Continuous monitoring and evaluation of AI-driven creative arts tools are crucial to ensure their effectiveness and address any emerging challenges. Schools should regularly assess the impact of AI tools on student creativity and learning outcomes, gather feedback from educators and students, and make data-driven adjustments as needed. This iterative process can help optimize the use of AI in creative arts education.
- **Promoting Student Engagement:** Encouraging student engagement with AI-driven creative arts tools is essential for their success. Educators can promote engagement by incorporating interactive activities, real-world applications, and opportunities for artistic exploration into creative arts projects. Creating a supportive and motivating learning environment can enhance student interest and participation.

Challenges and Considerations

- **Access and Equity:** Ensuring equitable access to AI-driven creative arts tools is a significant challenge. Students in underserved communities may lack the necessary technology and resources to participate in AI-enhanced creative arts education effectively. Addressing these disparities is crucial to ensure that all students can benefit from AI advancements.
- **Bias and Fairness:** AI algorithms can be susceptible to bias, which can impact the fairness and inclusivity of creative arts tools. Ensuring that AI systems are trained on diverse and representative datasets, regularly audited for bias, and designed with inclusivity in mind is essential to promote fairness.
- **Teacher Acceptance and Buy-In:** Gaining teacher acceptance and buy-in is essential for the successful implementation of AI in creative arts education. Educators may have concerns about the impact of AI on their roles and the quality of education. Addressing

these concerns through transparent communication, professional development, and demonstrating the benefits of AI can help build support for AI initiatives.

- **Ethical Considerations:** The use of AI in creative arts education raises ethical considerations, such as ensuring transparency in AI decision-making processes, maintaining human oversight, and avoiding over-reliance on technology. Schools must develop ethical guidelines for AI use, emphasizing the importance of fairness, accountability, and the role of educators.

AI-driven tools and approaches offer significant opportunities to enhance creativity, provide personalized feedback, and support artistic skill development in creative arts education. By leveraging AI technologies, educational institutions can create dynamic and engaging learning environments that meet the diverse needs of students. However, addressing challenges related to access, equity, bias, and ethical considerations is essential to ensure the responsible and effective use of AI in creative arts education. Through careful planning, collaboration, and continuous improvement, we can harness the full potential of AI to transform creative arts education and support student success.

AI AND EDUCATION FOR SUSTAINABLE DEVELOPMENT

Artificial Intelligence (AI) can play a pivotal role in advancing education for sustainable development (ESD). By integrating AI technologies into ESD initiatives, educational institutions can create more effective and engaging learning experiences that promote sustainability literacy and empower students to address global challenges. This section explores the impact of AI on education for sustainable development, provides examples of successful implementations, and discusses strategies for effective integration.

Practical Applications of AI in Education for Sustainable Development

- **Interactive Simulations and Virtual Labs:** AI-driven simulations and virtual labs can provide students with hands-on experiences in sustainability-related topics. These tools allow students to explore complex systems, conduct experiments, and visualize the impacts of various actions on the environment. AI enhances these simulations by providing real-time feedback and adaptive challenges, making learning more engaging and effective. Examples include SimCityEDU for urban planning and EcoMUVE for ecosystem education.

- **Personalized Learning Paths:** AI-powered platforms can create personalized learning paths that cater to individual student needs and interests in sustainability. By analyzing student data, AI systems can recommend tailored resources, activities, and projects that align with each student's learning goals. Personalized learning ensures that students receive the appropriate level of challenge and support, enhancing their engagement and understanding of sustainability concepts. Examples include Knewton and DreamBox Learning.
- **Data-Driven Decision Making:** AI can support data-driven decision making in ESD by analyzing large datasets and generating insights into sustainability practices. These insights can inform curriculum development, instructional strategies, and school policies that promote sustainable practices. AI-driven analytics can also help educators track student progress and assess the effectiveness of ESD initiatives. Examples include Tableau and IBM Watson Analytics.
- **Collaborative Learning Platforms:** AI-driven collaborative learning platforms facilitate teamwork and knowledge sharing among students on sustainability projects. These platforms provide tools for real-time communication, shared workspaces, and collaborative document editing, enabling students to work together on projects regardless of their physical location. AI can assist in coordinating collaborative efforts and providing feedback on group work. Examples include Google Workspace for Education and Microsoft Teams.
- **AI-Powered Educational Content Creation:** AI can assist in creating high-quality educational content related to sustainability. AI-driven tools can generate lesson plans, quizzes, and interactive activities that align with sustainability goals. These tools can also analyze curricular standards and student performance data to ensure that content is relevant and effective. Examples include Articulate 360 and Content Technologies, Inc. (CTI).

Case Studies and Examples

- **SimCityEDU:** SimCityEDU is an AI-powered educational game that teaches students about urban planning and sustainability. The game allows students to build and manage virtual cities, making decisions that impact the environment and community well-being. AI-driven simulations provide real-time feedback and adaptive challenges, helping students understand the complexities of sustainable urban development.
- **EcoMUVE:** EcoMUVE is an AI-driven virtual ecosystem simulation that helps students learn about ecology and environmental science.

The platform provides immersive learning experiences where students can explore ecosystems, conduct experiments, and observe the impacts of various actions on the environment. AI enhances these simulations by providing real-time feedback and personalized learning paths.

- **Knewton:** Knewton is an AI-powered adaptive learning platform that personalizes educational content based on student needs and interests. The platform's adaptive technology can be applied to ESD, providing tailored resources and activities that align with sustainability goals. Knewton's AI-driven approach ensures that students receive personalized support and challenge, enhancing their understanding of sustainability concepts.
- **Articulate 360:** Articulate 360 is an AI-driven content creation tool that assists educators in developing interactive and engaging educational materials. The platform can be used to create lessons, quizzes, and activities related to sustainability. Articulate 360's AI-driven features ensure that content is high-quality, relevant, and effective in promoting sustainability literacy.

Strategies for Effective Integration of AI in Education for Sustainable Development

- **Aligning with Sustainability Goals:** Ensuring that AI-driven tools and approaches align with sustainability goals and ESD curriculum standards is crucial for effective integration. Educators and institutions should collaborate with technology providers to design activities that support learning objectives and promote sustainability literacy.
- **Providing Professional Development for Educators:** Training and support for educators are essential to maximize the benefits of AI in ESD. Professional development programs should focus on building teachers' skills in using AI tools, facilitating sustainability projects, and interpreting data-driven insights. Ongoing training and support can help educators stay updated with the latest AI advancements and best practices.
- **Ensuring Data Privacy and Security:** Protecting student data used in AI-driven ESD tools is essential. Educational institutions and technology providers must implement robust data protection measures and comply with privacy regulations to safeguard student information. Transparent data usage practices and informed consent from students and parents are also crucial.

- **Monitoring and Evaluation:** Continuous monitoring and evaluation of AI-driven ESD tools are crucial to ensure their effectiveness and address any emerging challenges. Schools should regularly assess the impact of AI tools on student engagement and learning outcomes, gather feedback from educators and students, and make data-driven adjustments as needed. This iterative process can help optimize the use of AI in ESD.
- **Promoting Student Engagement:** Encouraging student engagement with AI-driven ESD tools is essential for their success. Educators can promote engagement by incorporating interactive activities, real-world applications, and opportunities for hands-on exploration into ESD projects. Creating a supportive and motivating learning environment can enhance student interest and participation.

Challenges and Considerations

- **Access and Equity:** Ensuring equitable access to AI-driven ESD tools is a significant challenge. Students in underserved communities may lack the necessary technology and resources to participate in AI-enhanced ESD effectively. Addressing these disparities is crucial to ensure that all students can benefit from AI advancements.
- **Bias and Fairness:** AI algorithms can be susceptible to bias, which can impact the fairness and inclusivity of ESD tools. Ensuring that AI systems are trained on diverse and representative datasets, regularly audited for bias, and designed with inclusivity in mind is essential to promote fairness.
- **Teacher Acceptance and Buy-In:** Gaining teacher acceptance and buy-in is essential for the successful implementation of AI in ESD. Educators may have concerns about the impact of AI on their roles and the quality of education. Addressing these concerns through transparent communication, professional development, and demonstrating the benefits of AI can help build support for AI initiatives.
- **Ethical Considerations:** The use of AI in ESD raises ethical considerations, such as ensuring transparency in AI decision-making processes, maintaining human oversight, and avoiding over-reliance on technology. Schools must develop ethical guidelines for AI use, emphasizing the importance of fairness, accountability, and the role of educators.

AI-driven tools and approaches offer significant opportunities to enhance education for sustainable development by providing interactive simulations, personalized learning paths, and data-driven insights. By leveraging AI technologies, educational institutions can create dynamic and engaging learning environments that promote sustainability literacy and empower students to address global challenges. However, addressing challenges related to access, equity, bias, and ethical considerations is essential to ensure the responsible and effective use of AI in ESD. Through careful planning, collaboration, and continuous improvement, we can harness the full potential of AI to transform education for sustainable development and support student success.

AI IN EDUCATIONAL EQUITY AND INCLUSION

Artificial Intelligence (AI) has the potential to significantly enhance educational equity and inclusion by providing personalized learning experiences, bridging gaps in access to resources, and supporting diverse learning needs. This section explores the ways in which AI can promote equity and inclusion in education, examining the benefits, challenges, and future directions for ensuring that AI technologies contribute to a fair and inclusive educational landscape.

Promoting Personalized Learning for Diverse Needs

- **Adaptive Learning Technologies:** AI-powered adaptive learning technologies tailor educational content to the individual needs, strengths, and learning styles of each student. These technologies continuously assess student performance and adjust the difficulty and type of content accordingly. This personalized approach ensures that all students, regardless of their starting point, can progress at their own pace and receive the support they need to succeed.
- **Supporting Students with Disabilities:** AI technologies provide various assistive tools that support students with disabilities. For example, text-to-speech and speech-to-text applications help students with visual and hearing impairments, while predictive text and communication aids support those with speech and language difficulties. AI-driven personalized learning plans can also address the unique needs of students with cognitive or learning disabilities, ensuring they have equal access to education.

Bridging Access Gaps

- **Equitable Access to Educational Resources:** AI can help bridge gaps in access to high-quality educational resources, particularly for students in underserved or remote areas. AI-driven platforms can provide digital textbooks, interactive simulations, and virtual labs that are accessible to all students, regardless of their geographic location. By democratizing access to resources, AI contributes to leveling the playing field.

- **Language Translation and Multilingual Support:** AI-powered language translation tools enable students who speak different languages to access educational content in their preferred language. These tools support multilingual education and help non-native speakers understand and engage with the curriculum. AI can also assist in creating culturally relevant and contextually appropriate learning materials, promoting inclusivity in diverse classrooms.

Enhancing Teacher Support and Professional Development

- **Teacher Empowerment and Professional Development:** AI technologies can support teachers by providing real-time insights into student performance, identifying learning gaps, and suggesting targeted interventions. This data-driven approach enables teachers to tailor their instruction to meet the needs of all students. Additionally, AI-powered professional development platforms offer personalized training opportunities, helping teachers continuously improve their skills and stay updated with the latest educational practices.
- **Reducing Teacher Workload:** AI can automate administrative tasks such as grading, attendance tracking, and lesson planning, reducing the workload on teachers. This allows educators to focus more on teaching, mentoring, and providing individualized support to students. By alleviating administrative burdens, AI enables teachers to dedicate more time and attention to fostering an inclusive learning environment.

Addressing Systemic Inequities

- **Data-Driven Decision Making:** AI-driven data analytics provide valuable insights into systemic inequities within educational institutions. By analyzing data on student performance, demographics, and resource allocation, AI can help identify disparities and inform policy decisions aimed at promoting equity. Educational leaders can use these insights to develop targeted strategies for addressing gaps and improving outcomes for all students.
- **Early Intervention and Support:** Predictive analytics powered by AI can identify students at risk of falling behind or dropping out. By detecting early warning signs, such as declining grades or

attendance issues, AI enables educators to intervene promptly and provide the necessary support. Early intervention programs can be tailored to address the specific needs of at-risk students, helping to prevent long-term academic struggles and ensuring that all students have the opportunity to succeed.

Future Directions for AI in Educational Equity and Inclusion

- **Expanding Access to Technology:** To maximize the impact of AI on educational equity, it is crucial to expand access to technology. This includes providing affordable devices, internet connectivity, and digital literacy training to students and teachers in underserved communities. Collaborative efforts among governments, educational institutions, and technology providers are essential for closing the digital divide.
- **Developing Culturally Responsive AI Tools:** AI tools should be developed with cultural responsiveness in mind, ensuring that they reflect the diverse backgrounds and experiences of students. This involves using inclusive datasets, involving diverse stakeholders in the design process, and continuously evaluating AI systems for bias. Culturally responsive AI tools promote inclusivity and respect for diversity in the classroom.
- **Fostering Global Collaboration:** Global collaboration in AI-driven education can promote knowledge exchange, resource sharing, and the development of best practices for equity and inclusion. International partnerships can address shared challenges and leverage AI technologies to create more inclusive educational systems worldwide. Collaborative initiatives can also promote cultural understanding and global citizenship among students.
- **Continuous Monitoring and Evaluation:** Ongoing monitoring and evaluation of AI-driven educational initiatives are essential for ensuring their effectiveness and equity. Institutions should implement robust evaluation frameworks that assess the impact of AI on student outcomes, inclusivity, and fairness. Regular feedback from students, educators, and stakeholders can inform continuous improvement and guide the ethical use of AI in education.

Conclusion

AI has the potential to transform education by promoting equity and inclusion through personalized learning, assistive technologies, and data-driven insights. By addressing gaps in access to resources, supporting diverse learning needs, and empowering teachers, AI can create a more inclusive and equitable educational landscape. Future directions for AI in education include expanding access to technology, developing culturally responsive tools, fostering global collaboration, and continuously monitoring and evaluating AI initiatives. Through thoughtful and proactive efforts, AI can help ensure that all students, regardless of their background or circumstances, have the opportunity to succeed in education and beyond.

QUESTIONNAIRE

Question 1: How does AI enhance STEAM education?

Answer: AI enhances STEAM (Science, Technology, Engineering, Arts, and Mathematics) education by providing personalized learning experiences, interactive simulations, and real-time feedback. AI-driven tools can adapt to individual learning styles, offering customized challenges and support. For example, AI can power virtual labs where students conduct experiments, engage in coding exercises with immediate debugging assistance, and explore complex scientific concepts through interactive models. This makes STEAM subjects more accessible, engaging, and effective.

Question 2: How does AI facilitate collaborative learning?

Answer: AI facilitates collaborative learning by providing platforms that enable real-time communication, resource sharing, and collaborative problem-solving. AI-driven tools can create virtual study groups, track group interactions, and suggest collaborative activities based on individual strengths and weaknesses. These platforms can analyze group dynamics, offer insights to improve collaboration, and ensure that each member contributes effectively, enhancing the overall learning experience.

Question 3: What is the role of AI in learning analytics?

Answer: AI plays a crucial role in learning analytics by analyzing large datasets to identify trends, predict outcomes, and provide actionable insights. AI algorithms can process data on student performance, engagement, and behavior to identify learning gaps, suggest personalized interventions, and optimize instructional strategies. This data-driven approach helps educators make informed decisions, improve teaching effectiveness, and enhance student learning experiences.

Question 4: How can learning analytics improve educational outcomes?

Answer: Learning analytics can improve educational outcomes by providing real-time feedback, identifying at-risk students, and informing targeted interventions. AI-driven analytics tools can track student progress, highlight areas of difficulty, and recommend personalized learning paths. Educators can use these insights to adjust their teaching methods, offer additional support where needed, and ensure that each student receives a tailored educational experience that maximizes their potential.

Question 5: How is AI transforming creative arts education?

Answer: AI is transforming creative arts education by offering tools that enhance creativity, provide personalized feedback, and enable new forms of artistic expression. AI-driven platforms can generate music, assist with visual arts projects, and offer interactive storytelling experiences. These tools allow students to experiment with different artistic mediums, receive instant feedback on their work, and collaborate on creative projects, expanding the possibilities for innovation and expression in the arts.

Question 6: What are some AI tools used in creative arts education?

Answer: Some AI tools used in creative arts education include DeepArt for visual arts, which uses AI to transform photos into artworks, and Amper Music for music composition, which generates personalized music tracks. Platforms like Runway ML offer AI tools for creative video and design projects, and Google's AI Experiments provide interactive tools for exploring creative coding and digital art. These tools empower students to explore and expand their creative capabilities.

Question 7: How can AI support education for sustainable development?

Answer: AI can support education for sustainable development by providing resources and tools that promote environmental awareness, sustainable practices, and global citizenship. AI-driven platforms can offer personalized learning modules on sustainability topics, simulate environmental scenarios, and analyze data to highlight the impact of various actions. These tools help students understand the importance of sustainability and equip them with the knowledge and skills needed to address environmental challenges.

Question 8: What are some examples of AI applications in sustainable education?

Answer: Examples of AI applications in sustainable education include platforms like Earth Rangers, which use AI to engage students in conservation activities, and AI-driven simulators that model the effects of climate change and resource management. Additionally, AI can power educational games and interactive tools that teach sustainable practices, such as energy conservation and recycling. These applications make learning about sustainability engaging and impactful, encouraging students to adopt environmentally friendly behaviors.

Question 9: How does AI promote educational equity and inclusion?

Answer: AI promotes educational equity and inclusion by providing personalized learning experiences, accessible resources, and support for diverse learning needs. AI-driven tools can adapt to different learning styles, offer real-time feedback, and provide additional support for students with disabilities or those from underserved communities. This ensures that all students have access to quality education and opportunities to succeed, regardless of their background or abilities.

Question 10: What are some AI initiatives that support educational equity and inclusion?

Answer: AI initiatives that support educational equity and inclusion include tools like Kurzweil 3000, which offers text-to-speech and other accessibility features for students with learning disabilities, and platforms like Khan Academy, which provide free, personalized learning resources to students worldwide. AI-driven apps like Be My Eyes assist visually impaired students, and adaptive learning platforms like DreamBox tailor content to individual learning needs, ensuring that all students receive the support they need to thrive.

7

Overcoming Challenges in AI-Driven Education

CHALLENGES IN AI-DRIVEN EDUCATION

The integration of Artificial Intelligence (AI) into the educational sector promises to revolutionize how students learn and how educators teach. However, alongside the numerous benefits, several significant challenges need to be addressed to ensure the effective and equitable implementation of AI-driven educational technologies. This section delves into the key challenges of AI-driven education and suggests strategies to overcome them.

Key Challenges in AI-Driven Education

- **Access and Equity:** AI-driven education has the potential to widen the digital divide. Students from underserved communities may lack access to necessary technologies, such as computers and reliable internet connections, which are critical for utilizing AI-powered educational tools. This disparity can exacerbate existing educational inequalities and hinder the effectiveness of AI-driven initiatives.

- **Bias and Fairness:** AI systems can inherit and perpetuate biases present in the data they are trained on. This can lead to unfair outcomes, such as biased grading, admissions, and disciplinary actions. Ensuring that AI systems are fair and inclusive is crucial to avoid reinforcing existing biases and inequalities in education.
- **Data Privacy and Security:** The deployment of AI in education involves extensive data collection and analysis, raising significant concerns about data privacy and security. Protecting student data from unauthorized access and breaches is paramount. Additionally, institutions must comply with data protection regulations to maintain trust and safeguard student information.
- **Teacher Acceptance and Buy-In:** Teachers play a critical role in the successful implementation of AI in education. However, there may be resistance due to concerns about the potential displacement of teachers, changes in their roles, and the quality of AI-generated insights. Securing teacher buy-in is essential for the smooth integration of AI technologies.
- **Ethical Considerations:** The use of AI in education raises various ethical issues, including the need for transparency in AI decision-making processes, the importance of maintaining human oversight, and the risk of over-reliance on technology. Addressing these ethical concerns is essential to ensure that AI is used responsibly and benefits all stakeholders.

Strategies for Overcoming Challenges

Bridging the Digital Divide

- **Infrastructure Investment:** Governments and private organizations should invest in infrastructure to ensure all students have access to reliable internet and necessary devices.
- **Subsidies and Support:** Providing financial assistance or subsidies for technology and internet access can help underserved communities.
- **Community Programs:** Implement community programs that offer access to technology and training for students and families in underserved areas.

Ensuring Algorithmic Fairness

- **Diverse Data Sets:** Develop AI systems using diverse and representative data sets to minimize biases.
- **Regular Audits:** Conduct regular audits of AI systems to detect and mitigate biases.
- **Inclusive Design Processes:** Involve educators, students, and other stakeholders in the AI development process to ensure the systems meet diverse needs.

Protecting Data Privacy and Security

- **Robust Security Measures:** Implement strong encryption, access controls, and regular security audits to protect student data.
- **Compliance with Regulations:** Ensure compliance with data protection regulations such as GDPR and FERPA.
- **Transparency:** Maintain transparency about data collection, storage, and usage practices, and obtain informed consent from students and parents.

Securing Teacher Acceptance and Buy-In

- **Professional Development:** Offer training programs to help teachers understand and effectively use AI tools in their teaching.
- **Collaborative Implementation:** Involve teachers in the planning and implementation of AI initiatives to address their concerns and incorporate their feedback.
- **Highlighting Benefits:** Demonstrate how AI can assist teachers by reducing administrative tasks, providing personalized student insights, and enhancing teaching effectiveness.

Addressing Ethical Considerations

- **Develop Ethical Guidelines:** Establish clear ethical guidelines for the use of AI in education, emphasizing transparency, accountability, and the importance of human oversight.
- **Maintain Human Oversight:** Ensure that AI complements rather than replaces human decision-making in education.
- **Ethics Training:** Provide ethics training for educators and AI developers to foster a culture of ethical AI use.

AI-driven education holds immense potential to transform the learning landscape, but it also presents several challenges that must be addressed. By focusing on equitable access, algorithmic fairness, data privacy, teacher buy-in, and ethical considerations, we can ensure that AI enhances educational outcomes for all students. Through careful planning, collaboration, and continuous improvement, the educational community can harness the full potential of AI to create a more inclusive, effective, and innovative educational environment.

THE ROLE OF EDUCATORS IN AI-DRIVEN EDUCATION

Educators play a pivotal role in the successful implementation of AI-driven educational technologies. While AI can provide personalized learning experiences, real-time feedback, and administrative efficiencies, it cannot replace the unique human qualities that educators bring to the classroom. This section explores the evolving role of educators in an AI-driven educational landscape and provides strategies for empowering teachers to effectively integrate AI into their teaching practices.

Key Roles of Educators in AI-Driven Education

- **Facilitators of Learning:** In an AI-enhanced educational environment, educators act as facilitators of learning, guiding students through personalized learning paths created by AI systems. Teachers help students navigate AI-driven platforms, interpret AI-generated insights, and apply them to their learning. They provide the human touch that AI cannot, offering encouragement, motivation, and emotional support.
- **Interpreters of Data:** AI systems generate vast amounts of data on student performance, engagement, and progress. Educators play a crucial role in interpreting this data and making informed decisions about instructional strategies and interventions. Teachers use their professional judgment to analyze AI-generated reports, identify trends, and address individual student needs.
- **Designers of Learning Experiences:** Educators are responsible for designing learning experiences that incorporate AI tools effectively. They select appropriate AI-driven resources, integrate them into the curriculum, and create engaging and meaningful activities that leverage AI's capabilities. Teachers ensure that AI tools align with educational goals and enhance rather than replace traditional teaching methods.
- **Ethical Guardians:** As AI becomes more prevalent in education, educators must act as ethical guardians, ensuring that AI is used responsibly and equitably. Teachers advocate for student privacy, monitor AI systems for biases, and ensure that AI-driven decisions are transparent and fair. They uphold ethical standards and promote a culture of responsible AI use in the classroom.
- **Professional Learners:** The integration of AI in education requires educators to continuously update their skills and knowledge.

Teachers must stay informed about the latest AI technologies, understand their applications in education, and engage in ongoing professional development. By embracing a mindset of lifelong learning, educators can effectively adapt to the evolving educational landscape.

Strategies for Empowering Educators in AI-Driven Education

- **Professional Development Programs:** Providing comprehensive professional development programs is essential to empower educators to use AI effectively. Training should focus on building teachers' technical skills, understanding AI-generated data, and integrating AI tools into their teaching practices. Professional development should be ongoing, with opportunities for teachers to learn from experts, collaborate with peers, and stay updated with the latest advancements.
- **Collaborative Implementation:** Involving educators in the planning and implementation of AI initiatives is crucial for securing their buy-in and addressing their concerns. Schools should create collaborative teams that include teachers, administrators, and technology experts to design and implement AI-driven projects. This collaborative approach ensures that AI tools meet the needs of educators and students.
- **Access to Resources and Support:** Providing educators with access to resources and support is vital for the successful integration of AI. Schools should offer technical support, instructional materials, and access to AI-driven tools that align with curricular goals. Creating a supportive environment where teachers can experiment with AI technologies and seek assistance when needed encourages innovation and effective use.
- **Empowering Teacher Leadership:** Empowering teachers to take on leadership roles in AI-driven education initiatives fosters a sense of ownership and accountability. Schools can identify and support teacher leaders who can champion AI projects, mentor colleagues, and share best practices. Recognizing and valuing the contributions of teacher leaders promotes a culture of continuous improvement and collaboration.
- **Encouraging Ethical Practices:** Educators should be encouraged to advocate for ethical AI practices in their classrooms. Schools can provide training on ethical considerations related to AI, including data privacy, algorithmic fairness, and transparency. Teachers should be empowered to voice concerns about AI use and work collaboratively to develop ethical guidelines and policies.

Challenges and Considerations

- **Teacher Resistance to Change:** Some educators may resist adopting AI technologies due to concerns about their impact on teaching roles, workload, and the quality of education. Addressing these concerns through transparent communication, professional development, and demonstrating the benefits of AI can help overcome resistance.
- **Balancing AI and Human Interaction:** Ensuring a balance between AI-driven instruction and human interaction is essential. Educators must find ways to integrate AI tools that complement rather than replace traditional teaching methods. Maintaining meaningful teacher-student interactions is crucial for fostering relationships and supporting student well-being.
- **Equitable Access to AI Tools:** Ensuring that all educators have equitable access to AI tools and resources is a significant challenge. Schools must address disparities in technology access and provide support to teachers in underserved communities. Promoting inclusive access to AI-driven educational resources ensures that all educators can benefit from AI advancements.
- **Continuous Professional Learning:** The rapid pace of technological advancements requires educators to engage in continuous professional learning. Schools must provide ongoing opportunities for teachers to update their skills and knowledge. Encouraging a culture of lifelong learning and professional growth is essential for the effective integration of AI in education.

Educators play a central role in the successful implementation of AI-driven educational technologies. By acting as facilitators of learning, interpreters of data, designers of learning experiences, ethical guardians, and professional learners, teachers can harness the potential of AI to enhance educational outcomes. Empowering educators through professional development, collaborative implementation, access to resources, leadership opportunities, and ethical practices is crucial for overcoming the challenges of AI-driven education. Through these strategies, we can ensure that AI enhances the teaching and learning experience while maintaining the unique human qualities that educators bring to the classroom.

BUILDING AI-READY EDUCATIONAL INSTITUTIONS

To harness the full potential of Artificial Intelligence (AI) in education, it is essential to develop AI-ready educational institutions. This involves creating an infrastructure, culture, and skill set that support the effective implementation of AI technologies. This section outlines the key components and strategies for building AI-ready educational institutions.

Key Components of AI-Ready Educational Institutions

- **Robust Technological Infrastructure:** An AI-ready institution requires a robust technological infrastructure that supports the deployment and integration of AI tools. This includes high-speed internet access, sufficient bandwidth, and up-to-date hardware and software. Ensuring reliable and secure IT systems is crucial for the effective use of AI in education.
- **Data Management and Analytics:** Effective data management and analytics capabilities are essential for AI-driven education. Institutions must have systems in place for collecting, storing, and analyzing large volumes of data. This includes student performance data, engagement metrics, and other relevant information. Data privacy and security measures must also be in place to protect sensitive information.
- **Professional Development and Training:** Continuous professional development and training are critical for educators and administrators to effectively use AI technologies. Institutions should offer training programs that build technical skills, data literacy, and an understanding of AI applications in education. This training should be ongoing to keep pace with technological advancements.
- **Collaborative Culture:** Fostering a collaborative culture is essential for the successful integration of AI. This includes promoting teamwork among educators, administrators, technology staff, and students. Collaboration enables the sharing of best practices, innovative ideas, and collective problem-solving, enhancing the overall effectiveness of AI initiatives.
- **Ethical and Inclusive Practices:** AI-ready institutions must prioritize ethical and inclusive practices in their AI implementations. This involves developing policies and guidelines that ensure transparency, fairness, and accountability in AI use. Institutions should also focus on promoting equity, ensuring that all students have access to AI-driven resources and opportunities.

Strategies for Building AI-Ready Educational Institutions

Investing in Technological Infrastructure

- **Upgrading IT Systems:** Regularly update and maintain IT systems to support AI tools and applications.

- **Expanding Internet Access:** Ensure high-speed internet access throughout the institution, including classrooms, libraries, and administrative offices.
- **Providing Necessary Hardware:** Equip classrooms and labs with the necessary hardware, such as computers, tablets, and smart devices, to support AI-driven learning.

Developing Data Management Systems

- **Implementing Data Analytics Platforms:** Adopt data analytics platforms that can process and analyze large volumes of educational data.
- **Ensuring Data Privacy and Security:** Implement robust data protection measures, such as encryption, secure storage, and compliance with privacy regulations.
- **Training Staff in Data Literacy:** Provide training for educators and administrators on data management, analysis, and interpretation to enhance data-driven decision-making.

Offering Professional Development

- **Creating Training Programs:** Develop comprehensive training programs focused on AI tools, data literacy, and innovative teaching practices.
- **Encouraging Lifelong Learning:** Promote a culture of continuous professional learning and development among educators and staff.
- **Providing Support and Resources:** Offer technical support, instructional materials, and access to AI-driven tools to help educators integrate AI into their teaching practices.

Fostering Collaboration

- **Establishing Collaborative Teams:** Create interdisciplinary teams that include educators, administrators, technology staff, and students to work on AI initiatives.
- **Sharing Best Practices:** Encourage the sharing of best practices and success stories related to AI integration through workshops, seminars, and online forums.
- **Promoting a Collaborative Culture:** Cultivate a culture of collaboration and teamwork by recognizing and rewarding collective efforts and achievements.

Ensuring Ethical and Inclusive AI Practices

- **Developing Ethical Guidelines:** Establish clear ethical guidelines for the use of AI in education, emphasizing transparency, accountability, and fairness.

- **Promoting Equity and Inclusion:** Ensure that AI tools and resources are accessible to all students, including those from underserved communities.
- **Monitoring AI Systems for Bias:** Regularly audit AI systems for biases and take corrective actions to ensure fair and inclusive outcomes.

Case Studies and Examples

- **Arizona State University (ASU):** Arizona State University has embraced AI to enhance its educational offerings and administrative processes. ASU's robust technological infrastructure supports AI-driven initiatives, such as personalized learning platforms and predictive analytics. The university also offers professional development programs to help educators integrate AI into their teaching practices.
- **Stanford University:** Stanford University has established the Stanford Artificial Intelligence Laboratory (SAIL) to explore AI applications in education. The university's commitment to fostering collaboration among researchers, educators, and students has resulted in innovative AI-driven projects. Stanford also prioritizes ethical AI practices, ensuring that its AI initiatives are transparent and inclusive.
- **Georgia State University:** Georgia State University uses AI-driven predictive analytics to improve student retention and success rates. The university's data management systems collect and analyze student performance data, providing insights that inform interventions and support services. Georgia State's commitment to data-driven decision-making and continuous professional development has made it a leader in AI-driven education.

Challenges and Considerations

- **Resource Constraints:** Building AI-ready institutions requires significant investments in technology, training, and infrastructure. Institutions with limited resources may face challenges in securing the necessary funding and support for AI initiatives.
- **Resistance to Change:** Resistance to change can hinder the adoption of AI technologies. Educators and administrators may be reluctant to embrace new tools and practices, fearing the impact on their roles and the quality of education.
- **Ensuring Sustainability:** Ensuring the long-term sustainability of AI initiatives is crucial. Institutions must develop strategies to

maintain and update AI systems, provide ongoing training, and secure funding for continuous improvement.

- **Addressing Ethical Concerns:** Ethical concerns related to AI use, such as data privacy, algorithmic bias, and transparency, must be addressed to build trust and ensure responsible AI implementation. Institutions must develop and enforce ethical guidelines and practices.

Building AI-ready educational institutions involves creating a robust technological infrastructure, developing data management and analytics capabilities, providing continuous professional development, fostering a collaborative culture, and ensuring ethical and inclusive practices. By addressing challenges related to resources, resistance to change, sustainability, and ethical concerns, educational institutions can effectively integrate AI technologies and enhance educational outcomes. Through careful planning, collaboration, and continuous improvement, we can create AI-ready institutions that prepare students for the future and support lifelong learning.

THE FUTURE OF AI IN EDUCATION POLICY

The integration of Artificial Intelligence (AI) in education requires the development of comprehensive policies that ensure its ethical, effective, and equitable use. These policies must address various aspects of AI implementation, including data privacy, algorithmic fairness, and teacher support. This section explores the future of AI in education policy and provides recommendations for developing robust and forward-thinking frameworks.

Key Areas of AI in Education Policy

- **Data Privacy and Security:** Protecting student data is a critical concern in AI-driven education. Policies must ensure that educational institutions and technology providers implement robust data protection measures. This includes encryption, secure storage solutions, and compliance with privacy regulations such as the General Data Protection Regulation (GDPR) and the Family Educational Rights and Privacy Act (FERPA). Regulations should also mandate transparent data usage practices and obtain informed consent from students and parents.
- **Algorithmic Transparency and Accountability:** Policies should promote transparency in AI algorithms used in education. This includes clear documentation of how algorithms are developed, the data they use, and the decision-making processes

they follow. Regulatory frameworks should require regular audits and evaluations of AI systems to ensure fairness and accuracy. Mechanisms for accountability should be established, allowing stakeholders to challenge and appeal AI-driven decisions.

- **Bias and Fairness:** Addressing algorithmic bias is crucial to ensure that AI systems in education are fair and equitable. Policies should mandate the use of diverse and representative datasets in AI development and require regular audits to identify and mitigate biases. Inclusive development practices should involve stakeholders from various backgrounds to ensure that AI systems cater to the needs of all students.
- **Teacher Support and Professional Development:** Policies should provide for the continuous professional development and support of educators. This includes training programs focused on building technical skills, data literacy, and understanding AI applications in education. Policies should also encourage collaboration among educators, technology providers, and policymakers to ensure that AI tools are effectively integrated into teaching practices.
- **Equitable Access to AI Technologies:** Ensuring equitable access to AI technologies is essential to prevent exacerbating existing inequalities. Policies should address the digital divide by providing funding and resources to underserved communities, ensuring that all students have access to the necessary technology and internet connectivity. Initiatives to promote digital literacy and provide training and support for educators and students are also crucial.

Developing Robust Regulatory Frameworks

- **Collaboration and Stakeholder Engagement:** Developing effective policies and regulations for AI in education requires collaboration among governments, educational institutions, technology providers, and other stakeholders. Inclusive policymaking processes should involve input from educators, students, parents, and experts in AI, ethics, and education. This collaborative approach ensures that policies address diverse perspectives and needs.
- **International Standards and Guidelines:** Establishing international standards and guidelines for AI in education can promote consistency and accountability across different regions and institutions. International organizations, such as UNESCO and the International Telecommunication Union (ITU), can play a key role in developing and promoting these standards. Collaboration

among countries can facilitate the exchange of best practices and the development of global regulatory frameworks.

- **Ongoing Monitoring and Evaluation:** Policies and regulations for AI in education should include provisions for ongoing monitoring and evaluation. This ensures that regulatory frameworks remain relevant and effective in addressing emerging challenges and technological advancements. Regular assessments can identify areas for improvement and ensure that policies continue to promote ethical and equitable AI use.
- **Public Awareness and Education:** Raising public awareness about the ethical and social implications of AI in education is essential for informed policymaking and regulation. Educational campaigns and public consultations can engage stakeholders and promote understanding of AI technologies and their impact. This awareness can drive demand for responsible AI practices and support the development of effective policies.

Case Studies and Examples

- **European Union AI Policy:** The European Union (EU) has been proactive in developing policies and regulations for AI. The EU's General Data Protection Regulation (GDPR) sets stringent standards for data privacy and security, applicable to AI systems in education. The EU's proposed AI Act aims to establish a comprehensive regulatory framework for AI, emphasizing transparency, accountability, and fairness. These initiatives provide valuable lessons for developing robust AI policies in education.
- **Singapore's AI Governance Framework:** Singapore has developed a national AI strategy that includes a robust governance framework for AI. The framework emphasizes ethical AI development, transparency, and accountability. Singapore's AI Governance Framework provides guidelines for responsible AI use, including in the education sector. The country's approach highlights the importance of balancing innovation with ethical considerations.
- **UNESCO's AI in Education Initiatives:** UNESCO has been actively involved in promoting ethical AI use in education. The organization has developed guidelines and policy recommendations for integrating AI into educational systems. UNESCO's initiatives emphasize the importance of equitable access, data privacy, and algorithmic fairness. These efforts aim to ensure that AI technologies contribute to inclusive and quality education for all.

Recommendations for Policy and Regulation

- **Establish Comprehensive Data Protection Standards:** Develop and enforce comprehensive data protection standards that safeguard student data and ensure privacy and security. Policies should require educational institutions and technology providers to implement robust data protection measures and comply with relevant regulations.
- **Promote Transparency and Accountability in AI Systems:** Mandate transparency in AI algorithms and decision-making processes. Require regular audits and evaluations of AI systems to ensure fairness and accuracy. Establish mechanisms for accountability, allowing stakeholders to challenge and appeal AI-driven decisions.
- **Address Algorithmic Bias and Promote Fairness:** Develop policies that address algorithmic bias and promote fairness in AI systems. Require the use of diverse and representative datasets in AI development and involve stakeholders from various backgrounds in the development process. Conduct regular audits to identify and mitigate biases.
- **Ensure Ethical AI Development and Use:** Create ethical frameworks for AI development, deployment, and monitoring. Emphasize the importance of human oversight, the avoidance of over-reliance on technology, and the preservation of the essential role of educators. Address broader societal implications of AI in education.
- **Bridge the Digital Divide and Promote Equitable Access:** Implement initiatives to bridge the digital divide and ensure equitable access to AI technologies. Provide funding and resources to underserved communities, promote digital literacy, and offer training and support for educators and students.

The integration of AI into education presents significant opportunities and challenges. Developing comprehensive policies and regulations is essential to ensure the ethical and effective use of AI in education. By addressing data privacy, algorithmic fairness, transparency, accountability, and equitable access, policymakers can create frameworks that promote the responsible use of AI. Collaboration among stakeholders, ongoing monitoring and evaluation, and public awareness are crucial to the success of these efforts. By adopting robust regulatory frameworks, we can harness the potential of AI to enhance education while safeguarding the interests of all stakeholders.

PREPARING STUDENTS FOR AN AI-DRIVEN WORLD

As Artificial Intelligence (AI) continues to reshape industries and job markets, preparing students for an AI-driven world is imperative. This involves equipping students with the skills, knowledge, and mindset necessary to thrive in a future where AI plays a central role. This section explores the strategies for preparing students for an AI-driven world, the skills they need, and the educational approaches that can support their development.

Essential Skills for an AI-Driven World

Technical Skills

- **Coding and Programming:** Understanding the basics of coding and programming languages such as Python, Java, and C++ is crucial for engaging with AI technologies.
- **Data Literacy:** Proficiency in data analysis, interpretation, and visualization helps students make sense of the vast amounts of data generated by AI systems.
- **Machine Learning:** Familiarity with machine learning concepts, algorithms, and tools enables students to understand and develop AI applications.

Cognitive Skills

- **Critical Thinking:** The ability to analyze information, evaluate arguments, and solve complex problems is essential in an AI-driven world.
- **Creative Thinking:** Innovation and creativity are key to developing new AI solutions and applications. Encouraging students to think outside the box fosters these skills.
- **Adaptability:** The rapid pace of technological change requires students to be flexible and adaptable, able to learn new skills and pivot as needed.

Social and Emotional Skills

- **Collaboration:** Working effectively in teams and leveraging diverse perspectives is crucial for success in AI-driven projects.
- **Communication:** Clear and effective communication skills are necessary for explaining complex AI concepts and collaborating with others.
- **Ethical Reasoning:** Understanding the ethical implications of AI and making responsible decisions is vital for the responsible use of AI technologies.

Educational Approaches for an AI-Driven World

Integrating AI into the Curriculum

- **Interdisciplinary Learning:** Incorporate AI concepts into various subjects such as math, science, and humanities to provide a well-rounded understanding of AI's applications.
- **Project-Based Learning:** Use project-based learning to give students hands-on experience with AI technologies, encouraging them to apply their knowledge to real-world problems.
- **AI Literacy Courses:** Develop specific courses focused on AI literacy, covering topics such as machine learning, data science, and ethical AI.

Fostering a Growth Mindset

- **Encouraging Lifelong Learning:** Promote a culture of continuous learning and curiosity, encouraging students to seek out new knowledge and skills throughout their lives.
- **Embracing Failure:** Teach students to view failures as learning opportunities, helping them develop resilience and perseverance.

Providing Access to AI Tools and Resources

- **Hands-On Experience:** Provide students with access to AI tools, software, and platforms that allow them to experiment and build their own AI applications.
- **Mentorship and Guidance:** Connect students with mentors and experts in the AI field who can provide guidance, support, and inspiration.

Creating an Inclusive Learning Environment

- **Equity in Access:** Ensure that all students, regardless of background, have access to AI education and resources.
- **Diverse Perspectives:** Encourage diverse perspectives and representation in AI education to foster innovation and inclusivity.

Case Studies and Examples

- **AI4ALL:** AI4ALL is an organization dedicated to increasing diversity and inclusion in AI education. The program provides summer camps, online courses, and mentorship opportunities to high school students from underrepresented groups. AI4ALL's approach emphasizes hands-on learning, ethical AI, and community building.
- **Code.org:** Code.org offers comprehensive resources for teaching coding and computer science, including AI concepts. The platform

provides curricula, professional development for teachers, and engaging learning activities for students. Code.org's initiatives aim to make computer science education accessible to all students.

- **MIT Media Lab:** The MIT Media Lab's "Learning AI" initiative focuses on integrating AI education into K-12 curricula. The program provides tools, resources, and project-based learning opportunities that help students understand and apply AI technologies. MIT Media Lab's approach emphasizes creativity, collaboration, and real-world problem-solving.

Strategies for Implementation

Collaborating with Industry and Academia

- **Partnerships:** Develop partnerships with industry leaders and academic institutions to provide students with exposure to the latest AI advancements and real-world applications.
- **Internships and Apprenticeships:** Offer internship and apprenticeship programs that give students hands-on experience working with AI technologies in professional settings.

Investing in Teacher Training

- **Professional Development:** Provide teachers with professional development opportunities to build their AI literacy and teaching skills.
- **Resources and Support:** Equip teachers with the resources and support they need to effectively integrate AI into their classrooms.

Promoting Ethical AI Education

- **Ethics Curriculum:** Incorporate discussions on the ethical implications of AI into the curriculum, helping students understand the broader impact of AI technologies.
- **Ethical Guidelines:** Develop and implement ethical guidelines for AI education to ensure responsible and fair use of AI technologies.

Preparing students for an AI-driven world requires a multifaceted approach that combines technical, cognitive, and social skills development. By integrating AI into the curriculum, fostering a growth mindset, providing access to AI tools and resources, and creating an inclusive learning environment, educators can equip students with the skills and knowledge they need to thrive in the future. Through collaboration with industry and academia, investment in teacher training, and a focus on ethical AI education, we can ensure that students are well-prepared to navigate and shape the AI-driven world.

COLLABORATION AND PARTNERSHIPS IN AI EDUCATION

Collaboration and partnerships are critical components for overcoming challenges and ensuring the successful implementation of Artificial Intelligence (AI) in education. By working together, educational institutions, technology companies, policymakers, researchers, and communities can address the complexities of AI integration and maximize its benefits. This section explores the importance of collaboration in AI-driven education, strategies for fostering effective partnerships, and examples of successful collaborative initiatives.

The Importance of Collaboration in AI-Driven Education

- **Leveraging Diverse Expertise:** Collaboration brings together diverse expertise from various fields, including education, technology, psychology, sociology, and data science. This multidisciplinary approach ensures that AI-driven educational initiatives are comprehensive, innovative, and grounded in a deep understanding of both technology and pedagogy.
- **Resource Sharing:** Partnerships facilitate the sharing of resources, such as funding, technology, data, and human capital. Resource sharing can reduce costs, enhance access to cutting-edge tools, and provide broader opportunities for research and development. Collaborative efforts can also attract additional funding from government agencies, private foundations, and industry sponsors.
- **Enhancing Innovation:** Collaborative environments foster innovation by encouraging the exchange of ideas, perspectives, and best practices. Working together, partners can co-create new AI-driven solutions, pilot innovative projects, and scale successful initiatives more effectively. Collaboration accelerates the pace of innovation and ensures that educational practices remain relevant and forward-thinking.
- **Addressing Ethical and Social Considerations:** Ethical and social considerations are integral to the responsible use of AI in education. Partnerships involving diverse stakeholders help identify and address potential ethical issues, such as data privacy, algorithmic bias, and equity. Collaborative decision-making promotes transparency, accountability, and trust in AI technologies.

Strategies for Fostering Effective Partnerships

- **Establishing Clear Objectives and Goals:** Effective partnerships start with clearly defined objectives and goals. Partners should agree on the purpose of the collaboration, the expected outcomes, and the specific roles and responsibilities of each participant. Clear objectives provide a roadmap for the partnership and ensure that all stakeholders are aligned in their efforts.

- **Creating Collaborative Frameworks:** Collaborative frameworks outline the structure, processes, and governance of the partnership. These frameworks include agreements on communication channels, decision-making protocols, resource allocation, and conflict resolution. Well-defined frameworks facilitate smooth and efficient collaboration, minimizing misunderstandings and ensuring accountability.
- **Engaging Diverse Stakeholders:** Inclusive partnerships involve a wide range of stakeholders, including educators, students, parents, technology developers, policymakers, and community members. Engaging diverse stakeholders ensures that multiple perspectives are considered, and that the needs and interests of all groups are addressed. Stakeholder engagement promotes buy-in and support for AI-driven initiatives.
- **Building Trust and Transparency:** Trust and transparency are foundational to successful collaboration. Partners should prioritize open communication, share information openly, and maintain honesty and integrity in their interactions. Regular updates, progress reports, and opportunities for feedback help build trust and keep all stakeholders informed and engaged.
- **Providing Professional Development and Training:** Professional development and training are essential for building the capacity of partners to effectively use AI technologies. Institutions should offer training programs that enhance the AI literacy and technical skills of educators, administrators, and other stakeholders. Continuous learning opportunities ensure that all participants are equipped to contribute meaningfully to the partnership.

Examples of Successful Collaborative Initiatives

- **The EdTech Collaborative:** The EdTech Collaborative is a partnership between educational institutions, technology companies, and non-profit organizations focused on advancing AI-driven education. The collaborative develops and pilots innovative AI tools, conducts research on their impact, and provides professional development for educators. By leveraging the strengths of each partner, the EdTech Collaborative drives innovation and improves educational outcomes.

- **Google AI for Social Good:** Google's AI for Social Good initiative partners with educational institutions, non-profits, and researchers to develop AI solutions that address societal challenges, including education. The initiative provides funding, technology, and expertise to support projects that use AI to enhance learning, improve access to education, and promote equity. Collaborative efforts have resulted in impactful AI-driven educational programs and resources.
- **Microsoft's AI for Accessibility:** Microsoft's AI for Accessibility program partners with schools, non-profits, and developers to create AI solutions that support students with disabilities. The program provides grants, technology, and technical support to projects that use AI to improve accessibility and inclusivity in education. Collaborative projects have developed innovative assistive technologies that empower students with diverse needs.

Challenges and Considerations in Collaboration

- **Aligning Priorities and Expectations:** Partners may have different priorities, expectations, and timelines, which can create challenges in collaboration. Establishing clear objectives and open communication from the outset helps align priorities and manage expectations, ensuring that all partners are working towards common goals.
- **Managing Intellectual Property and Data Sharing:** Intellectual property and data sharing can be complex issues in collaborative projects. Partners should establish agreements that outline the ownership, use, and protection of intellectual property and data. Clear agreements ensure that all parties understand their rights and responsibilities, promoting trust and cooperation.
- **Sustaining Long-Term Collaboration:** Sustaining long-term collaboration requires ongoing commitment, resources, and effort. Partners should establish mechanisms for regular review and evaluation, celebrate successes, and address challenges proactively. Long-term partnerships benefit from a shared vision, continuous engagement, and adaptability to changing circumstances.

Future Directions for Collaboration in AI Education

- **Global Partnerships for Education Equity:** Global partnerships can address educational inequities by leveraging AI to provide access to quality education in underserved regions. Collaborative efforts that involve international organizations, governments, and technology companies can develop scalable AI solutions that promote inclusivity and bridge the digital divide.

- **Research and Development Consortia:** Research and development consortia bring together universities, research institutions, technology providers, and policymakers to advance AI-driven education. These consortia can conduct large-scale studies, share data and findings, and develop best practices for AI integration in education. Collaborative research accelerates the discovery and dissemination of effective AI-driven educational practices.
- **Community-Based AI Initiatives:** Community-based AI initiatives engage local stakeholders in developing and implementing AI solutions that address specific educational challenges. These initiatives empower communities to take an active role in shaping AI-driven education, ensuring that solutions are culturally relevant and responsive to local needs. Community-based collaboration fosters a sense of ownership and sustainability.

Conclusion

Collaboration and partnerships are essential for overcoming challenges and maximizing the benefits of AI in education. By leveraging diverse expertise, sharing resources, enhancing innovation, and addressing ethical considerations, collaborative efforts can drive the successful integration of AI technologies. Effective strategies for fostering partnerships include establishing clear objectives, creating collaborative frameworks, engaging diverse stakeholders, building trust and transparency, and providing professional development. Examples of successful initiatives demonstrate the impact of collaboration on advancing AI-driven education. Future directions include global partnerships, research consortia, and community-based initiatives that promote equity, innovation, and sustainability. Through thoughtful and proactive collaboration, we can harness the transformative potential of AI to create a more inclusive, equitable, and effective educational landscape.

QUESTIONNAIRE

Question 1: How can educational institutions address the challenges of AI implementation?

Answer: Educational institutions can address AI implementation challenges by prioritizing data privacy, investing in technology infrastructure, and providing professional development for educators. Establishing clear data protection policies ensures student information is secure. Investing in necessary hardware and software upgrades enables schools to support AI technologies. Comprehensive training programs help educators understand and effectively integrate AI tools into their teaching practices, fostering a more accepting and innovative educational environment.

Question 2: How can educators prepare for teaching in an AI-driven environment?

Answer: Educators can prepare for teaching in an AI-driven environment by participating in professional development programs, staying informed about AI advancements, and collaborating with peers. Training programs help educators understand AI tools and their applications in the classroom. Keeping up with AI trends ensures teachers can leverage the latest technologies to enhance learning. Collaboration with colleagues allows for the exchange of ideas and best practices, fostering a supportive community for integrating AI in education.

Question 3: What does it mean to build an AI-ready educational institution?

Answer: Building an AI-ready educational institution involves creating an environment that supports the integration and effective use of AI technologies. This includes investing in digital infrastructure, ensuring robust data security measures, and fostering a culture of innovation and continuous learning. An AI-ready institution prioritizes professional development for educators, encourages collaboration, and adopts policies that promote ethical AI use. This holistic approach ensures that both teachers and students are prepared to leverage AI for enhanced educational outcomes.

Question 4: How can schools ensure they are prepared for AI integration?

Answer: Schools can ensure they are prepared for AI integration by conducting needs assessments, developing strategic plans, and investing in necessary resources. Needs assessments help identify gaps in infrastructure and training. Strategic plans outline clear goals and steps for AI implementation, including timelines and responsible parties. Investing in hardware, software, and professional development ensures that educators and students have the tools and skills needed to effectively use AI in the classroom.

Question 5: What is the future of AI in education policy?

Answer: The future of AI in education policy involves developing frameworks that ensure ethical use, data privacy, and equitable access to AI technologies. Policymakers will need to address concerns about algorithmic bias, transparency, and accountability. Policies should promote the integration of AI in ways that enhance learning outcomes while protecting student rights. Additionally, policies will likely focus on funding for digital infrastructure, professional development, and research to continuously improve AI applications in education.

Question 6: How can policymakers support the integration of AI in education?

Answer: Policymakers can support the integration of AI in education by creating clear guidelines for ethical AI use, investing in digital infrastructure, and funding professional development programs. Guidelines should address data privacy, algorithmic fairness, and transparency. Investments in infrastructure ensure schools have the necessary technology to support AI tools. Funding for training programs helps educators develop the skills needed to effectively integrate AI into their teaching practices, promoting widespread and effective use of AI in education.

Question 7: How can educators prepare students for an AI-driven world?

Answer: Educators can prepare students for an AI-driven world by incorporating AI literacy into the curriculum, fostering critical thinking and problem-solving skills, and promoting ethical awareness. Teaching students about AI technologies, their applications, and implications ensures they are informed and capable of navigating an AI-driven future. Encouraging critical thinking helps students evaluate AI outputs and make informed decisions. Emphasizing ethical considerations ensures students understand the responsible use of AI.

Question 8: What skills are essential for students to thrive in an AI-driven world?

Answer: Essential skills for students to thrive in an AI-driven world include AI literacy, digital literacy, critical thinking, problem-solving, and ethical awareness. AI literacy involves understanding AI technologies and their applications. Digital literacy encompasses the ability to use digital tools effectively and responsibly. Critical thinking and problem-solving skills enable students to analyze AI-generated information and address complex challenges. Ethical awareness ensures students consider the broader implications of AI and use it responsibly.

Question 9: Why are collaboration and partnerships important in AI education?

Answer: Collaboration and partnerships are important in AI education because they bring together diverse expertise, resources, and perspectives to enhance AI implementation and innovation. Partnerships between schools, technology companies, universities, and policymakers can facilitate the development and dissemination of AI tools and best practices. Collaborative efforts ensure that AI technologies are tailored to educational needs, promote equity, and are used ethically. These partnerships also provide opportunities for continuous learning and improvement.

Question 10: How can educational institutions form effective partnerships for AI integration?

Answer: Educational institutions can form effective partnerships for AI integration by identifying potential collaborators, establishing clear goals, and fostering open communication. Institutions should seek partnerships with technology providers, research organizations, and other schools to share knowledge and resources. Clear goals ensure that all partners are aligned and working towards common objectives. Open communication facilitates the exchange of ideas, feedback, and best practices, ensuring successful and sustainable AI integration in education.

8

AI and Global Education

COLLABORATION AND PARTNERSHIPS IN AI EDUCATION

Collaborative efforts and strategic partnerships are essential for the successful implementation of AI in education. By fostering cooperation between educational institutions, technology providers, governments, and other stakeholders, we can create a more cohesive and supportive environment for AI-driven education. This section explores the importance of collaboration and partnerships in AI education and provides strategies for building effective alliances.

The Importance of Collaboration and Partnerships

- **Resource Sharing:** Collaboration enables the sharing of resources, such as AI tools, data, and expertise, which can enhance the quality and effectiveness of AI-driven education. Partnerships can help educational institutions access cutting-edge technologies and best practices that may be beyond their individual reach.
- **Innovative Solutions:** Joint efforts between different stakeholders can lead to innovative solutions for educational challenges. By combining diverse perspectives and expertise, partnerships can drive the development of new AI applications and teaching methods that improve learning outcomes.
- **Scalability and Sustainability:** Partnerships can support the scalability and sustainability of AI initiatives. Collaborative projects can pool resources and funding, enabling broader implementation and long-term success. Working together also helps institutions build capacity and resilience to adapt to future challenges.
- **Policy and Advocacy:** Collaboration between educational institutions, governments, and industry leaders can influence policy and advocacy efforts. Partnerships can help shape regulatory frameworks, promote ethical AI use, and advocate for equitable access to AI technologies in education.

Strategies for Building Effective Collaborations and Partnerships

- **Identifying Common Goals:** Successful partnerships are built on shared goals and objectives. Educational institutions and their partners should identify common interests and priorities, such as improving student outcomes, advancing AI literacy, or promoting ethical AI use. Clear and aligned goals provide a strong foundation for collaboration.
- **Leveraging Strengths and Expertise:** Each partner brings unique strengths and expertise to the table. Educational institutions can leverage the technical knowledge of technology providers, the regulatory insights of government agencies, and the practical experience of educators. By recognizing and utilizing these strengths, partnerships can create more effective and innovative solutions.
- **Establishing Clear Roles and Responsibilities:** Defining clear roles and responsibilities for each partner is crucial for successful

collaboration. Establishing a governance structure, communication channels, and decision-making processes helps ensure that all parties are aligned and accountable. Regular meetings and progress updates can maintain momentum and address any challenges that arise.

- **Fostering Open Communication and Trust:** Open communication and trust are key to effective collaboration. Partners should establish transparent communication channels, encourage honest feedback, and build trust through consistent and reliable actions. Trust fosters a collaborative spirit and enables partners to work together effectively towards common goals.
- **Creating Inclusive Partnerships:** Inclusive partnerships that involve diverse stakeholders can drive innovation and equity in AI education. Engaging educators, students, parents, community organizations, and industry leaders ensures that multiple perspectives are considered. Inclusive partnerships help create solutions that address the needs of all learners.

Case Studies and Examples

- **Partnership for AI in Education (PAIE):** The Partnership for AI in Education (PAIE) is a collaborative initiative involving educational institutions, technology companies, and government agencies. PAIE focuses on advancing AI literacy, developing ethical AI guidelines, and promoting equitable access to AI technologies. The partnership leverages the expertise of each member to create comprehensive AI education programs and advocate for supportive policies.
- **IBM's P-TECH Program:** IBM's P-TECH (Pathways in Technology Early College High Schools) program is a partnership between educational institutions, government agencies, and industry leaders. The program provides students with a clear pathway from high school to college and career, focusing on STEM and AI skills. P-TECH offers hands-on learning experiences, mentorship, and internships, preparing students for future job opportunities in technology.
- **AI4K12 Initiative:** The AI4K12 Initiative is a collaboration between the Association for the Advancement of Artificial Intelligence (AAAI), the Computer Science Teachers Association (CSTA), and other stakeholders. The initiative aims to integrate AI education into K-12 curricula by developing guidelines, resources, and professional development programs for teachers. AI4K12

leverages the expertise of educators and AI researchers to create age-appropriate AI learning materials.

Recommendations for Successful Collaborations

- **Developing Memoranda of Understanding (MOUs):** Establishing MOUs can formalize partnerships and outline the terms of collaboration. MOUs should specify the goals, roles, responsibilities, and resource commitments of each partner. Formal agreements help ensure clarity and accountability.
- **Creating Collaborative Learning Communities:** Establishing collaborative learning communities can facilitate knowledge sharing and professional development. These communities can include educators, researchers, and industry experts who collaborate on AI projects, share best practices, and provide mutual support.
- **Pursuing Joint Funding Opportunities:** Collaborative projects can pursue joint funding opportunities to support AI initiatives. Applying for grants, sponsorships, and other funding sources as a partnership can increase the likelihood of securing financial support. Joint funding can enable the implementation of larger-scale and more impactful AI projects.
- **Promoting Public-Private Partnerships:** Public-private partnerships can leverage the strengths of both sectors to advance AI education. Government agencies can provide regulatory support and funding, while private companies can offer technical expertise and innovative solutions. Collaborative efforts can address common challenges and create sustainable AI education programs.

Collaboration and partnerships are essential for the successful implementation of AI in education. By sharing resources, leveraging strengths, and working towards common goals, educational institutions and their partners can create innovative solutions that enhance learning outcomes. Effective collaborations require clear roles, open communication, and trust among partners. Inclusive partnerships that engage diverse stakeholders ensure that AI-driven education addresses the needs of all learners. Through strategic alliances and collaborative efforts, we can build a supportive environment for AI in education and prepare students for an AI-driven world.

AI AND GLOBAL EDUCATION EQUITY

The integration of Artificial Intelligence (AI) in education has the potential to bridge educational gaps and promote global education equity. However, ensuring that AI technologies benefit all students, regardless of their geographic location, socioeconomic status, or access to resources, requires intentional strategies and policies. This section explores the role of AI in promoting global education equity, provides examples of successful initiatives, and discusses strategies for achieving equitable access to AI-driven education.

The Role of AI in Promoting Global Education Equity

- **Expanding Access to Quality Education:** AI can provide access to high-quality educational resources and personalized learning experiences to students in underserved and remote areas. AI-driven platforms can offer adaptive learning materials, virtual tutoring, and online courses that cater to diverse learning needs and levels.
- **Supporting Multilingual Education:** AI-powered language translation and localization tools can break down language barriers, enabling students to access educational content in their native languages. These tools support multilingual education and promote inclusivity by making learning materials accessible to non-native speakers.
- **Enhancing Teacher Support:** AI can assist teachers in underserved areas by providing professional development resources, instructional materials, and real-time feedback on teaching practices. AI-driven tools can help educators improve their skills and deliver more effective instruction, even in resource-constrained environments.
- **Personalized Learning for Diverse Learners:** AI-driven personalized learning platforms can adapt to the unique needs of each student, providing customized learning paths and resources. This personalized approach ensures that students receive the appropriate level of challenge and support, regardless of their background or prior knowledge.
- **Addressing Learning Gaps:** AI can identify learning gaps and provide targeted interventions to help students catch up and stay on track. By analyzing student performance data, AI systems can recommend specific activities, exercises, and resources to address individual learning needs and prevent students from falling behind.

Case Studies and Examples

- **Khan Academy:** Khan Academy is an AI-powered educational platform that provides free, high-quality educational resources to students worldwide. The platform offers personalized learning experiences, adaptive practice exercises, and instructional videos in multiple languages. Khan Academy's mission to provide a free, world-class education to anyone, anywhere exemplifies the potential of AI to promote global education equity.

- **Microsoft Translator:** Microsoft Translator is an AI-driven language translation tool that supports real-time translation and transcription in multiple languages. The tool enables students and educators to access and communicate educational content in their native languages. Microsoft Translator's integration with educational platforms and tools helps bridge language barriers and promote multilingual education.
- **Taleemabad:** Taleemabad is a Pakistan-based edtech platform that uses AI to provide personalized learning experiences to students in underserved areas. The platform offers adaptive lessons, interactive quizzes, and video tutorials in local languages. Taleemabad's AI-driven approach helps address educational disparities and improve learning outcomes for students in remote and low-income communities.

Strategies for Achieving Equitable Access to AI-Driven Education

Investing in Infrastructure

- **Expanding Internet Access:** Governments and organizations should invest in expanding internet connectivity in remote and underserved areas to ensure that all students can access AI-driven educational resources.
- **Providing Devices:** Initiatives to provide affordable devices, such as tablets and laptops, to students in need can help bridge the technology gap and enable access to AI-powered learning tools.

Developing Inclusive AI Systems

- **Diverse and Representative Data:** AI systems should be trained on diverse and representative datasets to ensure that they cater to the needs of all learners and avoid biases.
- **Cultural and Contextual Relevance:** AI-driven educational content should be culturally and contextually relevant to the students it serves, incorporating local languages, examples, and contexts.

Building Capacity and Skills

- **Teacher Training and Support:** Providing professional development and support for teachers in using AI tools can enhance their instructional practices and improve student outcomes.

- **Digital Literacy Programs:** Implementing digital literacy programs for students, teachers, and communities can help build the skills needed to effectively use AI-driven educational technologies.

Forming Public-Private Partnerships

- **Collaborative Efforts:** Governments, educational institutions, technology providers, and non-profit organizations should collaborate to develop and implement AI-driven education initiatives that promote equity.
- **Funding and Resources:** Public-private partnerships can pool resources and funding to support the deployment of AI technologies in underserved areas and ensure their sustainability.

Promoting Policy and Advocacy

- **Supportive Policies:** Governments should develop policies that support the equitable use of AI in education, including regulations that address data privacy, algorithmic fairness, and access to technology.
- **Advocacy for Equity:** Stakeholders should advocate for global education equity and the responsible use of AI through public awareness campaigns, research, and policy engagement.

Challenges and Considerations

- **Digital Divide:** The digital divide remains a significant barrier to equitable access to AI-driven education. Ensuring that all students have access to the necessary technology and internet connectivity is crucial for the success of AI initiatives.
- **Bias and Fairness:** AI systems can perpetuate biases present in the data they are trained on. Ensuring that AI-driven educational tools are fair, unbiased, and inclusive requires ongoing monitoring, evaluation, and adjustment.
- **Sustainability:** Ensuring the sustainability of AI-driven education initiatives is essential. This includes securing long-term funding, maintaining and updating technology, and providing continuous support for educators and students.
- **Ethical Considerations:** The ethical use of AI in education requires transparency, accountability, and human oversight. Developing and enforcing ethical guidelines for AI use is crucial to maintaining trust and ensuring that AI technologies benefit all learners.

AI has the potential to promote global education equity by providing access to quality education, supporting multilingual learning, enhancing teacher support, and personalizing learning experiences. Achieving equitable access to AI-driven education requires investing in infrastructure, developing inclusive AI systems, building capacity and skills, forming public-private partnerships, and promoting supportive policies and advocacy. By addressing challenges related to the digital divide, bias, sustainability, and ethics, we can harness the power of AI to create a more equitable and inclusive educational landscape for all students.

AI AND LIFELONG LEARNING GLOBALLY

In an increasingly interconnected and rapidly evolving world, lifelong learning has become essential for individuals to adapt, grow, and thrive. Artificial Intelligence (AI) plays a pivotal role in promoting lifelong learning globally by providing personalized, accessible, and flexible learning opportunities. This section explores how AI supports lifelong learning, highlights successful global initiatives, and discusses strategies for fostering continuous learning.

The Role of AI in Lifelong Learning

- **Personalized Learning Experiences:** AI-driven platforms can create personalized learning experiences tailored to individual needs, preferences, and goals. By analyzing learner data, AI systems can recommend relevant courses, resources, and activities, ensuring that learners receive the appropriate level of challenge and support. This personalized approach enhances engagement and helps learners achieve their educational and career objectives.
- **Accessible and Flexible Learning:** AI makes learning more accessible and flexible by providing online courses, virtual tutors, and interactive learning materials that can be accessed anytime and anywhere. This flexibility allows learners to fit education into their busy schedules and overcome barriers such as geographic location, physical disabilities, or financial constraints.
- **Real-Time Feedback and Assessment:** AI-powered tools offer real-time feedback and assessment, enabling learners to track their progress and identify areas for improvement. Immediate feedback helps learners adjust their strategies and focus on areas that need attention, promoting continuous improvement and mastery of new skills.
- **Adaptive Learning Paths:** AI can create adaptive learning paths that adjust based on learner performance and progress. These adaptive systems ensure that learners are always working on tasks that are appropriately challenging, preventing frustration and boredom while promoting steady growth and development.

- **Support for Diverse Learning Styles:** AI-driven educational tools can cater to diverse learning styles by offering various formats, such as videos, interactive simulations, reading materials, and hands-on activities. This variety ensures that learners can engage with content in ways that suit their preferences and strengths.

Global Initiatives Supporting Lifelong Learning

- **Coursera:** Coursera is a global online learning platform that partners with universities and organizations to offer courses, specializations, and degrees. The platform uses AI to provide personalized course recommendations, adaptive learning paths, and real-time feedback. Coursera's mission to provide universal access to world-class education exemplifies the potential of AI to promote lifelong learning globally.
- **edX:** edX is an online learning platform founded by Harvard University and MIT that offers courses from leading institutions worldwide. AI powers personalized learning experiences on edX, helping learners discover relevant courses and track their progress. edX's commitment to open access and inclusive education supports lifelong learning for individuals around the globe.
- **Duolingo:** Duolingo is a language-learning platform that uses AI to provide personalized and adaptive language lessons. The platform's gamified approach and real-time feedback make language learning engaging and effective. Duolingo's accessibility and wide range of languages support lifelong learning for diverse learners worldwide.
- **FutureLearn:** FutureLearn is a global online learning platform that offers courses, programs, and degrees from leading universities and organizations. AI-driven features on FutureLearn provide personalized learning experiences, course recommendations, and progress tracking. The platform's focus on social learning and community engagement enhances the lifelong learning experience.

Strategies for Fostering Lifelong Learning Globally

Investing in Digital Infrastructure

- **Expanding Internet Access:** Governments and organizations should invest in expanding internet connectivity to ensure that all individuals have access to online learning resources.
- **Providing Affordable Devices:** Initiatives to provide affordable devices, such as tablets and laptops, can help bridge the technology gap and enable access to AI-powered learning tools.

Promoting Inclusive Learning Environments

- **Cultural and Linguistic Relevance:** Develop educational content that is culturally and linguistically relevant to diverse populations. This ensures that learners can relate to and engage with the material.
- **Supporting Diverse Learners:** Create learning environments that accommodate diverse learning needs and styles, ensuring that all individuals can benefit from AI-driven education.

Building Capacity and Skills

- **Professional Development for Educators:** Provide professional development and training for educators to help them effectively use AI tools and support lifelong learning.
- **Digital Literacy Programs:** Implement digital literacy programs to equip individuals with the skills needed to navigate and utilize AI-powered learning platforms.

Forming Global Partnerships

- **Collaborative Efforts:** Develop partnerships between governments, educational institutions, technology providers, and non-profit organizations to promote lifelong learning initiatives.
- **Resource Sharing:** Share resources, best practices, and innovative solutions to address common challenges and support continuous learning.

Creating Supportive Policies

- **Educational Policies:** Develop policies that support lifelong learning and the integration of AI in education. These policies should address issues such as data privacy, access to technology, and equitable learning opportunities.
- **Funding and Incentives:** Provide funding and incentives for initiatives that promote lifelong learning and the use of AI in education.

Challenges and Considerations

- **Digital Divide:** The digital divide remains a significant barrier to lifelong learning. Ensuring equitable access to technology and internet connectivity is crucial for enabling all individuals to benefit from AI-driven education.
- **Privacy and Security:** Protecting learner data and ensuring privacy and security are essential for building trust in AI-driven educational platforms. Robust data protection measures and compliance with privacy regulations are critical.

- **Bias and Fairness:** AI systems can perpetuate biases present in the data they are trained on. Ensuring that AI-driven educational tools are fair, unbiased, and inclusive requires ongoing monitoring and evaluation.
- **Sustainability:** Ensuring the sustainability of lifelong learning initiatives involves securing long-term funding, maintaining and updating technology, and providing continuous support for learners and educators.

AI has the potential to transform lifelong learning globally by providing personalized, accessible, and flexible learning opportunities. By investing in digital infrastructure, promoting inclusive learning environments, building capacity and skills, forming global partnerships, and creating supportive policies, we can foster a culture of continuous learning that benefits individuals worldwide. Addressing challenges related to the digital divide, privacy, bias, and sustainability is essential to ensure that AI-driven lifelong learning initiatives are effective and equitable. Through collaborative efforts and strategic investments, we can harness the power of AI to support lifelong learning and empower individuals to thrive in a rapidly changing world.

CASE STUDIES FROM DIFFERENT COUNTRIES

Exploring how different countries integrate Artificial Intelligence (AI) into their education systems can provide valuable insights and best practices. These case studies highlight various approaches, successes, and challenges in leveraging AI for educational improvement. This section presents case studies from different countries, showcasing innovative applications of AI in education and their impact.

Case Study: China

Overview: China has made significant strides in incorporating AI into its education system. With substantial investments in AI research and development, the country aims to become a global leader in AI education. AI technologies are widely used to enhance personalized learning, improve administrative efficiency, and support educational equity.

Applications of AI in Education

- **Personalized Learning Platforms:** AI-driven platforms like Squirrel AI and TAL Education Group offer personalized learning experiences tailored to individual student needs. These platforms use adaptive algorithms to analyze student performance and provide customized learning paths and resources.

- **Smart Classrooms:** China has implemented smart classrooms equipped with AI technologies such as facial recognition, emotion analysis, and interactive learning tools. These technologies monitor student engagement, provide real-time feedback, and support differentiated instruction.
- **AI in Teacher Training:** AI-powered tools are used to support teacher training and professional development. Platforms like iFlytek provide resources, feedback, and coaching to help teachers improve their instructional practices and integrate AI technologies into their teaching.
- **Impact and Challenges:** China's AI-driven education initiatives have led to improved student performance, increased engagement, and enhanced teaching effectiveness. However, challenges such as data privacy, algorithmic bias, and the digital divide must be addressed to ensure equitable access and ethical use of AI.

Case Study: United States

Overview: The United States has embraced AI in education through various initiatives led by both public and private sectors. AI technologies are used to support personalized learning, administrative tasks, and data-driven decision-making.

Applications of AI in Education

- **Personalized Learning Platforms:** Platforms like Khan Academy and DreamBox Learning use AI to provide personalized learning experiences. These platforms analyze student data to create adaptive learning paths, offer targeted feedback, and recommend relevant resources.
- **AI in Higher Education:** Universities such as Georgia State University use AI-driven predictive analytics to identify at-risk students and provide timely interventions. AI tools help monitor student progress, predict outcomes, and support academic advising.
- **Virtual Assistants:** AI-powered virtual assistants like IBM Watson are used to provide administrative support, answer student queries, and streamline enrollment processes. These tools enhance efficiency and improve the student experience.
- **Impact and Challenges:** AI-driven education initiatives in the United States have led to increased student engagement, improved academic outcomes, and enhanced administrative efficiency. Challenges include addressing data privacy concerns,

ensuring algorithmic fairness, and promoting equitable access to AI technologies.

Case Study: Finland

Overview: Finland is known for its innovative education system and has integrated AI technologies to enhance teaching and learning. The country's focus on equity and inclusivity ensures that AI-driven education benefits all students.

Applications of AI in Education

- **Personalized Learning and Assessment:** AI tools are used to provide personalized learning experiences and formative assessments. Platforms like Claned analyze student data to offer tailored learning paths and resources, supporting individualized instruction.
- **Teacher Support and Professional Development:** AI-driven platforms like Headai provide resources and coaching for teachers, helping them improve their instructional practices and integrate AI into their teaching. These tools offer feedback and support professional growth.
- **AI in Curriculum Development:** Finland uses AI to support curriculum development and innovation. AI tools analyze educational data to identify trends, inform policy decisions, and ensure that curricula meet the needs of diverse learners.
- **Impact and Challenges:** AI-driven education initiatives in Finland have enhanced personalized learning, supported teacher professional development, and informed curriculum development. Challenges include ensuring data privacy, addressing algorithmic bias, and promoting digital literacy among educators and students.

Case Study: India

Overview: India is leveraging AI to address educational challenges and promote equity and access. AI-driven initiatives aim to improve student learning outcomes, support teacher training, and enhance administrative efficiency.

Applications of AI in Education

- **Adaptive Learning Platforms:** Platforms like BYJU'S and Embibe use AI to provide adaptive learning experiences tailored to individual student needs. These platforms analyze student performance data to offer personalized feedback, resources, and learning paths.

- **AI in Teacher Training:** AI-powered tools support teacher training and professional development. Platforms like CENTA offer resources, feedback, and coaching to help teachers improve their instructional practices and integrate AI technologies into their teaching.
- **AI for Administrative Efficiency:** AI-driven tools are used to streamline administrative tasks such as attendance tracking, grading, and scheduling. These tools enhance efficiency and allow educators to focus more on teaching and learning.
- **Impact and Challenges:** AI-driven education initiatives in India have improved student learning outcomes, supported teacher professional development, and enhanced administrative efficiency. Challenges include addressing the digital divide, ensuring data privacy, and promoting equitable access to AI technologies.

Strategies for Implementing AI in Education Globally

Investing in Digital Infrastructure

- **Expanding Internet Access:** Governments and organizations should invest in expanding internet connectivity to ensure that all individuals have access to online learning resources.
- **Providing Affordable Devices:** Initiatives to provide affordable devices, such as tablets and laptops, can help bridge the technology gap and enable access to AI-powered learning tools.

Promoting Inclusive Learning Environments

- **Cultural and Linguistic Relevance:** Develop educational content that is culturally and linguistically relevant to diverse populations. This ensures that learners can relate to and engage with the material.
- **Supporting Diverse Learners:** Create learning environments that accommodate diverse learning needs and styles, ensuring that all individuals can benefit from AI-driven education.

Building Capacity and Skills

- **Professional Development for Educators:** Provide professional development and training for educators to help them effectively use AI tools and support lifelong learning.
- **Digital Literacy Programs:** Implement digital literacy programs to equip individuals with the skills needed to navigate and utilize AI-powered learning platforms.

Forming Global Partnerships

- **Collaborative Efforts:** Develop partnerships between governments, educational institutions, technology providers, and non-profit organizations to promote lifelong learning initiatives.
- **Resource Sharing:** Share resources, best practices, and innovative solutions to address common challenges and support continuous learning.

Creating Supportive Policies

- **Educational Policies:** Develop policies that support lifelong learning and the integration of AI in education. These policies should address issues such as data privacy, access to technology, and equitable learning opportunities.
- **Funding and Incentives:** Provide funding and incentives for initiatives that promote lifelong learning and the use of AI in education.

Case studies from different countries demonstrate the diverse ways in which AI is being integrated into education systems to enhance teaching and learning. By investing in digital infrastructure, promoting inclusive learning environments, building capacity and skills, forming global partnerships, and creating supportive policies, we can harness the power of AI to support lifelong learning and promote global education equity. Addressing challenges related to the digital divide, privacy, bias, and sustainability is essential to ensure that AI-driven education initiatives are effective and equitable. Through collaborative efforts and strategic investments, we can create a more inclusive and innovative educational landscape for all learners.

STRATEGIES FOR IMPLEMENTING AI IN DIVERSE EDUCATIONAL CONTEXTS

Implementing Artificial Intelligence (AI) in diverse educational contexts requires a nuanced approach that takes into account the unique needs, resources, and cultural dynamics of different learning environments. This section outlines strategies for effectively integrating AI into various educational settings, ensuring that all learners benefit from the advancements in AI technology.

Key Strategies for Implementing AI in Diverse Educational Contexts

- **Understanding Local Needs and Contexts:** Tailoring AI implementations to the specific needs and contexts of different educational settings is essential. This involves understanding the local educational landscape, cultural nuances, language preferences, and specific challenges faced by educators and learners.

- **Building Local Capacity:** Developing the skills and knowledge of local educators, administrators, and students is crucial for the successful integration of AI. Providing training, resources, and ongoing support helps build local capacity and ensures sustainable use of AI technologies.
- **Ensuring Cultural Relevance and Inclusivity:** AI-driven educational tools and content should be culturally relevant and inclusive, reflecting the diversity of learners. This involves incorporating local languages, examples, and contexts into AI applications to enhance engagement and relatability.
- **Leveraging Public-Private Partnerships:** Collaborations between governments, educational institutions, technology providers, and non-profit organizations can facilitate the implementation of AI in education. Public-private partnerships help pool resources, expertise, and funding to support AI initiatives.
- **Promoting Policy Support and Advocacy:** Developing supportive policies and advocating for AI in education are critical for creating an enabling environment. Policies should address issues such as data privacy, equity, access to technology, and the ethical use of AI.

Strategies for Implementation

Conducting Needs Assessments

- **Local Assessments:** Conduct thorough needs assessments to understand the specific educational needs, challenges, and opportunities within a community or region.
- **Stakeholder Engagement:** Engage with local stakeholders, including educators, students, parents, and community leaders, to gather insights and ensure that AI initiatives align with local priorities.

Providing Professional Development and Training

- **Teacher Training Programs:** Offer professional development programs that focus on building educators' skills in using AI tools, data literacy, and integrating AI into teaching practices.
- **Continuous Learning:** Promote a culture of continuous learning and professional growth among educators, ensuring they stay updated with the latest AI advancements and best practices.

Ensuring Equitable Access to Technology

- **Infrastructure Investments:** Invest in infrastructure to expand internet connectivity and provide necessary devices, such as laptops and tablets, to underserved communities.

- **Digital Literacy Initiatives:** Implement digital literacy programs to equip students, educators, and communities with the skills needed to effectively use AI technologies.

Developing Culturally Relevant Content

- **Local Language Support:** Ensure that AI-driven educational tools and content are available in local languages, making them accessible to a wider audience.
- **Contextualized Learning Materials:** Develop learning materials that reflect local cultures, traditions, and real-world contexts, enhancing engagement and relatability.

Fostering Collaboration and Partnerships

- **Public-Private Collaboration:** Establish partnerships between governments, educational institutions, technology companies, and non-profit organizations to support AI initiatives.
- **Knowledge Sharing:** Facilitate knowledge sharing and collaboration among different regions and countries to exchange best practices and innovative solutions.

Developing Supportive Policies and Frameworks

- **Ethical Guidelines:** Develop ethical guidelines for the use of AI in education, emphasizing transparency, accountability, and fairness.
- **Data Privacy and Security:** Implement robust data protection measures to ensure the privacy and security of student data.
- **Equity and Inclusion:** Create policies that promote equitable access to AI technologies and address disparities in educational opportunities.

Case Studies and Examples

- **Brazil's AI in Education Initiative:** Brazil has implemented AI-driven personalized learning platforms to address educational disparities. Platforms like Geekie Lab provide adaptive learning experiences in Portuguese, tailored to individual student needs. The initiative focuses on expanding access to quality education in underserved regions and supporting teacher professional development.
- **Kenya's Digital Learning Program:** Kenya's Digital Learning Program aims to integrate AI and digital technologies into primary education. The program provides tablets with preloaded educational content in local languages, enhancing accessibility and engagement. Teacher training and community involvement are key components of the program's success.

- **Finland's EdTech Ecosystem:** Finland's robust EdTech ecosystem supports the development and implementation of AI-driven educational tools. Collaborations between startups, educational institutions, and the government have led to innovative solutions like AI-powered personalized learning platforms and teacher support tools. Finland's emphasis on inclusivity and cultural relevance ensures that AI benefits all learners.
- **India's National AI Strategy:** India's national AI strategy focuses on leveraging AI to improve educational outcomes and promote equity. Initiatives like the AI for All program aim to integrate AI into the curriculum, provide teacher training, and ensure access to AI technologies in rural and underserved areas. Partnerships with technology companies and non-profit organizations support these efforts.

Challenges and Considerations

- **Digital Divide:** Addressing the digital divide is crucial for ensuring equitable access to AI-driven education. Efforts must focus on expanding infrastructure, providing affordable devices, and promoting digital literacy.
- **Cultural Sensitivity:** Ensuring that AI-driven educational tools and content are culturally sensitive and relevant is essential for engagement and effectiveness. Involving local stakeholders in content development can enhance cultural relevance.
- **Sustainability:** Ensuring the sustainability of AI initiatives involves securing long-term funding, maintaining technology, and providing continuous support for educators and students.
- **Ethical Use of AI:** Developing and enforcing ethical guidelines for AI use in education is critical to addressing concerns related to data privacy, algorithmic bias, and accountability.

Implementing AI in diverse educational contexts requires a tailored approach that considers local needs, cultural relevance, and equity. By conducting needs assessments, providing professional development, ensuring equitable access to technology, developing culturally relevant content, fostering collaboration, and creating supportive policies, we can effectively integrate AI into education systems worldwide. Addressing challenges such as the digital divide, cultural sensitivity, sustainability, and ethical use is essential to ensure that AI-driven education initiatives are successful and benefit all learners. Through strategic planning and collaboration, we can harness the potential of AI to enhance education and promote global education equity.

THE FUTURE OF AI IN GLOBAL EDUCATION

As Artificial Intelligence (AI) continues to advance, its impact on global education will grow, offering new opportunities and presenting unique challenges. The future of AI in education is poised to be transformative, promoting global collaboration, equity, and innovation. This section explores potential future developments in AI-driven education, emphasizing the need for strategic planning, ethical considerations, and continuous adaptation to maximize the benefits of AI for learners worldwide.

Advancements in AI Technologies

- **Next-Generation Learning Platforms:** Future AI-driven learning platforms will offer even more sophisticated adaptive learning experiences. These platforms will leverage advanced algorithms to provide hyper-personalized learning paths, real-time feedback, and dynamic content tailored to individual student needs. Enhanced natural language processing (NLP) and emotional recognition technologies will enable these platforms to understand and respond to students' emotional states, fostering a more engaging and supportive learning environment.
- **Immersive Learning Environments:** AI will drive the development of immersive learning environments that combine virtual reality (VR), augmented reality (AR), and mixed reality (MR) technologies. These environments will allow students to explore complex concepts interactively and experience simulations of real-world scenarios. AI will personalize these experiences to match learners' abilities and preferences, enhancing their understanding and retention of knowledge.
- **AI-Powered Global Classrooms:** AI will facilitate the creation of global classrooms, where students from different countries and cultures can learn together in real-time. AI-driven translation and communication tools will enable seamless interaction across languages and cultural barriers. These global classrooms will promote cross-cultural understanding, collaboration, and the sharing of diverse perspectives.

Promoting Global Education Equity

- **Universal Access to Quality Education:** AI technologies have the potential to democratize access to quality education for learners worldwide. By providing affordable, scalable, and high-quality educational resources, AI can bridge gaps in access to education, particularly in underserved and remote areas. AI-driven platforms can offer courses, textbooks, and interactive learning materials to students regardless of their geographic location.

- **Inclusive Curriculum Design:** The future of AI in education will prioritize inclusive curriculum design that reflects the diverse needs and backgrounds of learners. AI can help develop culturally relevant and contextually appropriate educational content, ensuring that all students see themselves represented in the curriculum. This inclusivity fosters a sense of belonging and engagement among learners.
- **Targeted Interventions and Support:** AI's predictive analytics capabilities will enable educators to identify and support students at risk of falling behind. By analyzing data on student performance, behavior, and engagement, AI can recommend targeted interventions, such as tutoring, counseling, and personalized learning plans. These interventions will help close achievement gaps and ensure that all students receive the support they need to succeed.

Ethical Considerations and Challenges

- **Ensuring Data Privacy and Security:** As AI collects and analyzes vast amounts of educational data, ensuring data privacy and security will be paramount. Robust data protection measures and compliance with international privacy regulations are essential to safeguard student information. Transparent data practices and clear communication about how data is used and protected will build trust among students, parents, and educators.
- **Addressing Algorithmic Bias:** AI algorithms must be designed and tested to prevent and mitigate bias. Ensuring that AI systems are trained on diverse and representative datasets is critical for promoting fairness and equity. Continuous monitoring and auditing of AI algorithms can help identify and address any biases that may arise, ensuring that AI-driven educational tools are inclusive and just.
- **Ethical AI Development and Use:** The development and use of AI in education must adhere to ethical principles, such as fairness, accountability, transparency, and respect for human rights. Institutions should establish ethical guidelines for AI implementation and engage stakeholders in ethical decision-making processes. Educators, policymakers, and technology developers must collaborate to ensure that AI technologies are used responsibly and ethically.

Strategies for Maximizing AI's Impact on Global Education

- **Fostering International Collaboration:** International collaboration is essential for harnessing the full potential of AI in education. Governments, educational institutions, technology companies, and non-profit organizations should work together to share knowledge, resources, and best practices. Collaborative initiatives can address global educational challenges and promote the development of innovative AI-driven solutions.
- **Investing in Research and Development:** Continued investment in research and development is crucial for advancing AI technologies and understanding their impact on education. Funding for AI research should prioritize projects that focus on equity, inclusivity, and ethical considerations. Collaboration between academia and industry can drive innovation and ensure that research findings are translated into practical applications.
- **Building Capacity and Infrastructure:** To maximize the benefits of AI in education, countries must invest in building the necessary capacity and infrastructure. This includes providing access to technology, training educators, and developing robust digital infrastructure. Governments and international organizations can support capacity-building efforts through funding, technical assistance, and policy development.
- **Implementing Inclusive Policies:** Policymakers should develop and implement inclusive policies that promote equitable access to AI-driven educational tools. Policies should address issues such as affordability, accessibility, and digital literacy. Inclusive policies ensure that all students, regardless of their background or circumstances, can benefit from AI technologies.
- **Engaging Communities and Stakeholders:** Engaging communities and stakeholders in the development and implementation of AI-driven educational initiatives is essential for their success. Institutions should involve students, parents, educators, and community leaders in decision-making processes, ensuring that their voices are heard and their needs are addressed. Collaborative engagement fosters trust, buy-in, and support for AI-driven education.

Future Directions and Innovations

- **AI-Enhanced Lifelong Learning:** AI will play a significant role in promoting lifelong learning by providing personalized learning pathways and resources for individuals of all ages. AI-driven platforms can support continuous skill development, career advancement, and personal growth, ensuring that learners remain adaptable and competitive in a rapidly changing world.

- **Sustainable Development Goals (SDGs):** AI can contribute to achieving the United Nations Sustainable Development Goals (SDGs) by promoting quality education, reducing inequalities, and fostering global partnerships. AI-driven educational initiatives should align with the SDGs, ensuring that they contribute to sustainable and inclusive development.
- **AI and the Future of Work:** AI-driven education must prepare students for the future of work by equipping them with the skills needed for an AI-driven economy. This includes technical skills, such as coding and data analysis, as well as critical thinking, creativity, and problem-solving abilities. AI can help identify emerging job market trends and inform curriculum development, ensuring that education remains relevant and future-oriented.

Conclusion

The future of AI in global education is promising, offering opportunities to enhance learning, promote equity, and drive innovation. By advancing AI technologies, fostering international collaboration, addressing ethical considerations, and implementing inclusive policies, we can harness the transformative potential of AI to create a more equitable and effective educational landscape. Through thoughtful and proactive efforts, AI-driven education can empower learners worldwide, preparing them for the challenges and opportunities of the future.

QUESTIONNAIRE

Question 1: How do collaboration and partnerships enhance AI education on a global scale?

Answer: Collaboration and partnerships enhance AI education on a global scale by pooling resources, sharing best practices, and fostering innovation. Global partnerships between educational institutions, technology companies, and governments facilitate the exchange of knowledge and technologies. This collective approach helps address diverse educational challenges, promotes equity, and ensures that AI tools are culturally and contextually relevant. Collaborative initiatives can also drive research and development, leading to more effective and inclusive AI solutions for education worldwide.

Question 2: How can AI promote global education equity?

Answer: AI can promote global education equity by providing personalized learning experiences, improving access to educational resources, and addressing individual learning needs. AI-driven platforms can deliver tailored content to students in remote or underserved areas, ensuring they receive the same quality of education as their urban counterparts. Additionally, AI can help identify and support at-risk students, offering interventions that bridge educational gaps. This promotes inclusivity and ensures that all students have the opportunity to succeed, regardless of their socio-economic background.

Question 3: What are the challenges in using AI to achieve education equity globally?

Answer: Challenges in using AI to achieve education equity globally include the digital divide, data privacy concerns, and potential biases in AI algorithms. The digital divide refers to the disparity in access to technology and internet connectivity, which can hinder the implementation of AI in some regions. Data privacy concerns arise from the need to protect student information. Biases in AI algorithms can perpetuate existing inequalities if not addressed. Overcoming these challenges requires investment in infrastructure, robust data protection policies, and efforts to ensure AI systems are fair and unbiased.

Question 4: How does AI support lifelong learning on a global scale?

Answer: AI supports lifelong learning on a global scale by providing flexible, personalized learning opportunities that adapt to the needs and goals of individual learners. AI-driven platforms offer continuous access to educational content, enabling learners to update their skills and knowledge throughout their lives. These platforms can recommend courses, provide instant feedback, and track progress, making learning more efficient and effective. AI also facilitates access to global educational resources, allowing learners from diverse backgrounds to benefit from high-quality education and training.

Question 5: How has AI impacted education in developing countries?

Answer: AI has impacted education in developing countries by improving access to quality education, providing personalized learning experiences, and supporting teachers with AI-driven tools. For example, in countries like India and Kenya, AI-powered mobile apps and online platforms offer educational content to students in remote areas. These technologies help bridge the educational gap between urban and rural regions, ensuring that all students have access to learning opportunities. Additionally, AI assists teachers in managing classrooms, grading, and providing feedback, enhancing the overall efficiency and effectiveness of education.

Question 6: What are some notable case studies of AI implementation in education from different countries?

Answer: Notable case studies of AI implementation in education include China's use of AI for personalized learning and adaptive assessments, Finland's AI-powered educational initiatives focusing on teacher training and curriculum development, and Kenya's deployment of AI-driven mobile learning apps to reach students in remote areas. In the United States, AI is used to support special education and provide personalized learning experiences through platforms like DreamBox. These case studies demonstrate the diverse applications of AI in education and the potential to enhance learning outcomes globally.

Question 7: What strategies can be used to implement AI in diverse educational contexts?

Answer: Strategies for implementing AI in diverse educational contexts include conducting needs assessments, investing in infrastructure, providing professional development for educators, and involving stakeholders in the planning process. Needs assessments help identify specific requirements and challenges in different educational settings. Investing in infrastructure ensures that schools have the necessary technology and connectivity. Professional development equips educators with the skills to effectively use AI tools. Engaging stakeholders, including students, parents, and community members, ensures that AI implementations are culturally relevant and widely supported.

Question 8: How can schools ensure the successful integration of AI in diverse contexts?

Answer: Schools can ensure the successful integration of AI in diverse contexts by adopting a flexible approach that considers local needs and conditions. This involves customizing AI tools to align with the cultural and educational values of the community. Providing ongoing support and training for educators ensures they are confident in using AI technologies. Additionally, schools should establish partnerships with technology providers and other educational institutions to share resources and best practices. Regular monitoring and evaluation help identify areas for improvement and ensure that AI integration meets its intended goals.

Question 9: What trends are shaping the future of AI in global education?

Answer: Trends shaping the future of AI in global education include the increasing use of AI for personalized learning, the integration of AI with other emerging technologies like VR and AR, and the focus on data-driven decision-making. Personalized learning powered by AI ensures that educational content is tailored to individual needs, enhancing engagement and outcomes. Combining AI with VR and AR creates immersive learning experiences. Data-driven decision-making allows educators to use insights from AI analytics to improve teaching strategies and student support.

Question 10: How can AI contribute to the future of education globally?

Answer: AI can contribute to the future of education globally by making learning more accessible, personalized, and efficient. AI-driven tools can bridge educational gaps by providing resources to underserved communities and adapting content to diverse learning styles. AI enhances administrative efficiency, allowing educators to focus more on teaching. By continuously analyzing data, AI can offer insights into student performance and suggest improvements, fostering a more responsive and effective educational system. The global adoption of AI in education promises to democratize access to quality education and prepare students for a rapidly evolving world.

9

AI and Ethical Leadership In Education

DEFINING ETHICAL LEADERSHIP IN THE AGE OF AI

The integration of Artificial Intelligence (AI) into education brings with it a host of ethical considerations that must be navigated carefully. Ethical leadership in the age of AI involves guiding the implementation and use of AI technologies in ways that are responsible, fair, and aligned with the values of the educational community. This section defines ethical leadership in the context of AI-driven education, outlining its key principles and importance.

Key Principles of Ethical Leadership in AI-Driven Education

- **Transparency:** Ethical leaders ensure that AI systems and processes are transparent. This means openly sharing how AI algorithms work, what data they use, and how decisions are made. Transparency builds trust and allows stakeholders to understand and evaluate the impact of AI technologies on education.
- **Accountability:** Ethical leadership requires taking responsibility for the outcomes of AI systems. Leaders must establish mechanisms for monitoring and evaluating AI-driven decisions, addressing any issues that arise, and being accountable for the effects of AI on students, educators, and the broader educational community.
- **Fairness and Equity:** Ensuring fairness and equity is fundamental to ethical leadership in AI education. Leaders must actively work to eliminate biases in AI systems, promote inclusive practices, and ensure that AI technologies benefit all students, regardless of their background or circumstances.
- **Privacy and Security:** Protecting the privacy and security of student data is a critical component of ethical leadership. Leaders must implement robust data protection measures, comply with relevant privacy regulations, and ensure that data is used responsibly and ethically.
- **Human-Centered Approach:** AI should augment, not replace, the human elements of education. Ethical leaders prioritize the well-being and development of students and educators, ensuring that AI supports rather than undermines human interaction and professional judgment.

The Importance of Ethical Leadership in AI-Driven Education

- **Building Trust:** Trust is crucial for the successful implementation of AI in education. Ethical leadership fosters trust by ensuring transparency, accountability, and fairness in the use of AI technologies. When stakeholders trust that AI is being used responsibly, they are more likely to embrace and support its integration into educational practices.
- **Ensuring Responsible Use of AI:** AI has the potential to greatly enhance education, but it must be used responsibly to avoid unintended consequences. Ethical leadership ensures that AI is implemented in ways that respect the rights and interests of all

stakeholders, prevent harm, and promote positive educational outcomes.

- **Promoting Equity and Inclusion:** AI can either mitigate or exacerbate educational inequalities, depending on how it is used. Ethical leadership is essential for ensuring that AI technologies are designed and deployed in ways that promote equity and inclusion, providing all students with the opportunities and support they need to succeed.
- **Navigating Ethical Dilemmas:** The use of AI in education raises complex ethical dilemmas, such as balancing privacy with the need for data-driven insights or addressing biases in AI algorithms. Ethical leaders are equipped to navigate these dilemmas, making informed decisions that align with ethical principles and the values of the educational community.

Strategies for Fostering Ethical Leadership

Developing Ethical Guidelines and Policies

- **Creating Ethical Frameworks:** Develop comprehensive ethical guidelines and policies for AI use in education, covering transparency, accountability, fairness, privacy, and the human-centered approach.
- **Regular Reviews and Updates:** Ensure that ethical guidelines and policies are regularly reviewed and updated to keep pace with technological advancements and emerging challenges.

Providing Ethics Training and Professional Development

- **Ethics Training Programs:** Implement training programs for educators, administrators, and technology developers focused on ethical considerations in AI use. These programs should cover topics such as data privacy, algorithmic fairness, and responsible AI deployment.
- **Continuous Learning:** Promote continuous learning and professional development in ethics, encouraging stakeholders to stay informed about best practices and emerging issues.

Establishing Mechanisms for Accountability

- **Monitoring and Evaluation:** Establish systems for monitoring and evaluating the impact of AI technologies on education. Regular audits and assessments can help identify and address any ethical concerns.
- **Feedback and Reporting Channels:** Create channels for stakeholders to provide feedback and report ethical issues related

to AI use. Ensuring that concerns are heard and addressed builds trust and accountability.

Engaging Stakeholders in Ethical Decision-Making

- **Inclusive Decision-Making Processes:** Involve a diverse range of stakeholders, including educators, students, parents, and community members, in decision-making processes related to AI use. This inclusive approach ensures that multiple perspectives are considered and that AI systems meet the needs of all users.
- **Ethics Committees and Advisory Boards:** Establish ethics committees or advisory boards to oversee AI initiatives and provide guidance on ethical issues. These bodies can help ensure that AI use aligns with ethical principles and best practices.

Promoting a Culture of Ethical Leadership

- **Leading by Example:** Leaders should model ethical behavior and decision-making, demonstrating a commitment to transparency, accountability, fairness, and the human-centered approach.
- **Fostering Ethical Awareness:** Create an organizational culture that values and prioritizes ethics. Encourage open discussions about ethical challenges and solutions, and celebrate ethical practices and achievements.

Ethical leadership is crucial for the responsible and equitable use of AI in education. By adhering to principles of transparency, accountability, fairness, privacy, and a human-centered approach, educational leaders can ensure that AI technologies benefit all stakeholders. Developing clear ethical guidelines, providing continuous ethics training, establishing accountability mechanisms, engaging stakeholders, and promoting a culture of ethical leadership are essential strategies for fostering ethical practices in AI-driven education. Through ethical leadership, we can harness the potential of AI to enhance education while safeguarding the interests of students, educators, and the broader educational community.

DEVELOPING ETHICAL GUIDELINES FOR AI IN EDUCATION

The integration of Artificial Intelligence (AI) in education necessitates the creation of ethical guidelines to ensure its responsible use. These guidelines serve as a framework for educators, administrators, technology developers, and policymakers to navigate the complexities and ethical dilemmas posed by AI technologies. This section explores the process of developing ethical guidelines for AI in education, highlighting key principles and providing actionable steps.

Key Principles for Ethical Guidelines in AI Education

- **Transparency:** Transparency involves openly sharing information about how AI systems work, the data they use, and the decision-making processes they follow. This principle ensures that stakeholders understand and can trust the AI technologies being implemented.
- **Accountability:** Accountability requires that those who develop, deploy, and use AI systems are responsible for their outcomes. This includes establishing mechanisms for monitoring, evaluating, and addressing the impacts of AI on education.
- **Fairness and Equity:** Fairness and equity focus on eliminating biases in AI systems and ensuring that all students benefit equally from AI technologies. This principle involves designing inclusive AI tools that accommodate diverse needs and backgrounds.
- **Privacy and Security:** Protecting the privacy and security of student data is crucial. Ethical guidelines must ensure that robust data protection measures are in place and that data is used responsibly and ethically.
- **Human-Centered Approach:** A human-centered approach prioritizes the well-being and development of students and educators. AI should augment human capabilities and support human interaction, rather than replace or undermine it.

Steps for Developing Ethical Guidelines for AI in Education

Establishing a Multidisciplinary Team

- **Inclusive Team Composition:** Form a team that includes educators, administrators, technology developers, ethicists, legal experts, and representatives from the student and parent communities. This diverse team ensures that multiple perspectives are considered in the guideline development process.
- **Collaborative Efforts:** Encourage collaboration and open dialogue among team members to identify potential ethical issues and develop comprehensive guidelines.

Conducting a Comprehensive Needs Assessment

- **Identifying Ethical Concerns:** Assess the current use of AI in education to identify potential ethical concerns, such as data privacy risks, algorithmic biases, and impacts on student well-being.
- **Engaging Stakeholders:** Gather input from various stakeholders, including educators, students, parents, and community members, to understand their concerns and priorities related to AI use in education.

Drafting Ethical Guidelines

- **Defining Core Principles:** Based on the needs assessment, define the core principles that will guide the ethical use of AI in education. These principles should reflect the key values and priorities identified by stakeholders.
- **Detailing Specific Practices:** Develop specific practices and protocols for implementing these principles, such as guidelines for data collection and usage, procedures for algorithmic audits, and standards for transparency and accountability.

Reviewing and Refining the Guidelines

- **Seeking Expert Feedback:** Consult with experts in AI ethics, education, and data privacy to review and refine the drafted guidelines. Their feedback can help identify potential gaps and strengthen the guidelines.
- **Conducting Public Consultations:** Hold public consultations to gather feedback from a broader audience, including educators, students, parents, and the community. Incorporate their input to ensure the guidelines are comprehensive and widely accepted.

Implementing the Guidelines

- **Developing Implementation Plans:** Create detailed implementation plans that outline how the guidelines will be applied in practice. These plans should include timelines, responsibilities, and resources needed.
- **Providing Training and Support:** Offer training and support for educators, administrators, and technology developers to ensure they understand and can effectively implement the guidelines.

Monitoring and Evaluating Compliance

- **Establishing Monitoring Mechanisms:** Develop mechanisms for monitoring compliance with the ethical guidelines, such as regular audits, evaluations, and feedback systems.
- **Addressing Non-Compliance:** Create procedures for addressing instances of non-compliance, including corrective actions and accountability measures.

Continuously Reviewing and Updating the Guidelines

- **Regular Reviews:** Schedule regular reviews of the ethical guidelines to ensure they remain relevant and effective in light of evolving AI technologies and educational practices.
- **Incorporating Feedback:** Continuously gather and incorporate feedback from stakeholders to improve and update the guidelines.

Case Studies and Examples

- **The IEEE Global Initiative on Ethics of Autonomous and Intelligent Systems:** The IEEE Global Initiative has developed comprehensive ethical guidelines for the design and implementation of AI systems. These guidelines emphasize transparency, accountability, and inclusivity, providing a valuable framework for educational institutions to adapt and adopt.
- **The UK's Centre for Data Ethics and Innovation (CDEI):** The CDEI provides guidance on the ethical use of AI and data-driven technologies. Their principles of transparency, fairness, and accountability offer a robust foundation for developing ethical guidelines in education.
- **Montgomery County Public Schools (MCPS):** MCPS has established ethical guidelines for AI use in education that prioritize data privacy, algorithmic fairness, and student well-being. Their guidelines include specific practices for data protection, bias audits, and transparent decision-making processes.

Challenges and Considerations

- **Balancing Innovation and Ethics:** Ensuring that ethical guidelines do not stifle innovation while still protecting stakeholders' interests is a significant challenge. Guidelines should promote responsible AI use without hindering technological advancements.
- **Addressing Bias and Fairness:** Eliminating biases in AI systems requires ongoing monitoring and refinement. Ethical guidelines must include robust mechanisms for identifying and addressing biases to ensure fairness and equity.
- **Ensuring Compliance:** Ensuring that all stakeholders adhere to ethical guidelines can be challenging. Clear communication, training, and accountability measures are essential for effective compliance.
- **Adapting to Technological Advancements:** As AI technologies evolve, ethical guidelines must be regularly updated to address new challenges and opportunities. Continuous review and stakeholder engagement are crucial for keeping guidelines relevant.

Developing ethical guidelines for AI in education is essential for ensuring that AI technologies are used responsibly, transparently, and equitably. By establishing a multidisciplinary team, conducting comprehensive needs assessments, drafting and refining guidelines, implementing and monitoring compliance, and continuously updating the guidelines, educational institutions can navigate the ethical complexities of AI integration. Through these efforts, we can harness the potential of AI to enhance education while safeguarding the interests and well-being of all stakeholders.

TRAINING EDUCATORS AND LEADERS FOR ETHICAL AI USE

The integration of Artificial Intelligence (AI) in education requires that educators and leaders are well-equipped to use these technologies ethically and effectively. Comprehensive training programs are essential to build their capacity to navigate the complexities of AI, understand its implications, and make informed decisions that align with ethical principles. This section explores the importance of training for ethical AI use, key components of effective training programs, and strategies for implementation.

The Importance of Training for Ethical AI Use

- **Enhancing Understanding and Competency:** Training programs enhance educators' and leaders' understanding of AI technologies, their applications, and potential impacts. By building competency in AI, they can effectively integrate these tools into their educational practices and decision-making processes.
- **Promoting Ethical Awareness:** Training fosters awareness of ethical considerations related to AI use, such as data privacy, algorithmic bias, and fairness. Educators and leaders can better identify and address ethical dilemmas, ensuring responsible and equitable AI implementation.
- **Supporting Informed Decision-Making:** With proper training, educators and leaders can make informed decisions about AI adoption and use. They can evaluate AI tools critically, considering their benefits, limitations, and ethical implications, and choose solutions that align with their educational goals and values.
- **Building a Culture of Ethical Practice:** Training helps build a culture of ethical practice within educational institutions. By emphasizing the importance of ethics in AI use, training programs encourage a collective commitment to responsible AI practices among all stakeholders.

Key Components of Effective Training Programs

Fundamentals of AI and Machine Learning

- **Introduction to AI:** Provide an overview of AI technologies, including machine learning, neural networks, and natural language processing.

- **Applications in Education:** Explore how AI can be used in educational settings, such as personalized learning, predictive analytics, and administrative support.

Ethical Principles and Guidelines

- **Ethical Frameworks:** Introduce key ethical principles, such as transparency, accountability, fairness, privacy, and a human-centered approach.
- **Case Studies:** Present case studies that illustrate ethical dilemmas and best practices in AI use, helping participants understand real-world implications and solutions.

Data Privacy and Security

- **Data Protection Regulations:** Cover relevant data privacy regulations, such as GDPR and FERPA, and their implications for AI use in education.
- **Best Practices:** Teach best practices for data collection, storage, and usage to ensure the privacy and security of student information.

Addressing Algorithmic Bias and Fairness

- **Understanding Bias:** Explain how biases can arise in AI systems and their impact on educational outcomes.
- **Mitigating Bias:** Provide strategies for identifying, evaluating, and mitigating biases in AI algorithms to ensure fairness and equity.

Human-Centered AI Design

- **Human-AI Interaction:** Explore how AI can augment human capabilities and support educators and students without replacing human interaction.
- **Design Thinking:** Introduce design thinking principles for creating AI tools that prioritize user needs and ethical considerations.

Implementation and Evaluation

- **Practical Implementation:** Offer guidance on how to implement AI tools in educational settings, including integration with existing systems and infrastructure.
- **Evaluation and Monitoring:** Teach methods for evaluating the effectiveness and ethical impact of AI tools, including regular audits and stakeholder feedback.

Strategies for Implementing Training Programs

Creating Accessible and Flexible Learning Opportunities

- **Online Courses and Webinars:** Offer online courses and webinars that provide flexible learning opportunities for educators and leaders to engage with the material at their own pace.

- **Workshops and Seminars:** Conduct in-person workshops and seminars that allow for interactive learning and hands-on practice with AI tools.

Collaborating with Experts and Institutions

- **Partnerships with Universities:** Partner with universities and research institutions to develop and deliver high-quality training programs that leverage expert knowledge and resources.
- **Engagement with Industry Leaders:** Involve industry leaders and AI developers in training programs to provide insights into the latest advancements and best practices.

Providing Ongoing Support and Resources

- **Continuous Professional Development:** Offer continuous professional development opportunities, such as refresher courses, advanced training, and certifications, to keep educators and leaders updated on AI advancements.
- **Resource Libraries:** Create resource libraries that include articles, research papers, case studies, and toolkits to support ongoing learning and reference.

Encouraging Collaborative Learning and Peer Support

- **Learning Communities:** Establish learning communities where educators and leaders can share experiences, discuss challenges, and collaborate on solutions related to AI use.
- **Mentorship Programs:** Develop mentorship programs that pair experienced educators and leaders with those new to AI, providing guidance and support.

Assessing Training Effectiveness

- **Feedback Mechanisms:** Implement feedback mechanisms to gather participants' insights and experiences, ensuring that training programs meet their needs and expectations.
- **Impact Evaluation:** Regularly evaluate the impact of training programs on participants' knowledge, skills, and practices, and make necessary adjustments to improve effectiveness.

Case Studies and Examples

- **The AI4K12 Initiative:** The AI4K12 Initiative offers resources and professional development programs for K-12 educators to integrate AI into their curricula. The initiative provides a framework for teaching AI concepts, ethical considerations, and practical applications, supporting educators in preparing students for an AI-driven future.

- **ISTE AI Explorations Program:** The International Society for Technology in Education (ISTE) offers the AI Explorations Program, which provides training for educators on AI concepts, tools, and ethical considerations. The program includes online courses, webinars, and hands-on workshops, helping educators effectively integrate AI into their teaching practices.
- **The University of Helsinki's Elements of AI Course:** The University of Helsinki offers a free online course called Elements of AI, designed to teach the basics of AI and its ethical implications. The course is accessible to educators and leaders worldwide, promoting a broad understanding of AI and its responsible use.

Challenges and Considerations

- **Resource Constraints:** Limited resources can pose challenges to implementing comprehensive training programs. Securing funding and support from stakeholders is essential to ensure the availability of high-quality training opportunities.
- **Diverse Learning Needs:** Educators and leaders have diverse learning needs and varying levels of familiarity with AI. Training programs must be adaptable and inclusive to accommodate different skill levels and learning styles.
- **Keeping Pace with Technological Advancements:** AI technologies are rapidly evolving, making it challenging to keep training programs up-to-date. Continuous review and updating of training content are necessary to address emerging trends and developments.
- **Ensuring Widespread Participation:** Encouraging widespread participation in training programs can be challenging, especially in large and decentralized educational systems. Effective communication and incentivization strategies can help increase engagement and participation.

Training educators and leaders for ethical AI use is crucial for the responsible and effective integration of AI in education. By enhancing understanding and competency, promoting ethical awareness, supporting informed decision-making, and building a culture of ethical practice, training programs can empower stakeholders to navigate the complexities of AI. Key components of effective training include fundamentals of AI, ethical principles, data privacy, bias mitigation, human-centered design, and practical implementation. Strategies for implementation involve creating accessible learning opportunities, collaborating with experts, providing ongoing support, encouraging collaborative learning, and assessing training effectiveness. Addressing challenges related to resources, diverse learning needs, technological advancements, and participation is essential to ensure the success of training programs. Through comprehensive and continuous training, we can ensure that AI technologies are used ethically and equitably in education, benefiting all learners.

CASE STUDIES OF ETHICAL AI IMPLEMENTATION

Ethical implementation of Artificial Intelligence (AI) in education requires careful planning, adherence to ethical guidelines, and a commitment to transparency, accountability, and fairness. Examining case studies of successful ethical AI implementation can provide valuable insights and best practices for educators, administrators, and policymakers. This section presents several case studies that highlight how different educational institutions have navigated the ethical challenges of AI and achieved positive outcomes.

Case Study: Montgomery County Public Schools (MCPS), USA

Overview: Montgomery County Public Schools (MCPS) in Maryland, USA, has implemented AI-driven tools to support personalized learning, enhance administrative efficiency, and improve student outcomes. The district's commitment to ethical AI use involves rigorous adherence to data privacy standards, transparent communication with stakeholders, and ongoing evaluation of AI systems.

Ethical Practices

- **Data Privacy and Security:** MCPS prioritizes the privacy and security of student data. The district complies with federal and state regulations, such as the Family Educational Rights and Privacy Act (FERPA), and implements robust data protection measures, including encryption, secure storage, and restricted access.
- **Transparency and Stakeholder Engagement:** MCPS maintains transparency by clearly communicating the purposes, benefits, and potential risks of AI systems to stakeholders. The district engages parents, students, and educators through regular updates, public forums, and feedback channels, ensuring that their concerns and suggestions are addressed.
- **Bias Mitigation:** To ensure fairness, MCPS conducts regular audits of AI algorithms to identify and mitigate biases. The district collaborates with AI developers to refine algorithms, ensuring they are equitable and inclusive.

- **Professional Development:** MCPS provides professional development and training for educators on the ethical use of AI tools. Training programs focus on data literacy, ethical considerations, and practical implementation strategies, empowering educators to use AI responsibly and effectively.
- **Impact:** The ethical implementation of AI in MCPS has led to improved student engagement, personalized learning experiences, and enhanced administrative efficiency. The district's commitment to transparency, accountability, and fairness has built trust among stakeholders and ensured the responsible use of AI technologies.

Case Study: University of Edinburgh, UK

Overview: The University of Edinburgh has integrated AI technologies into its teaching and learning practices, focusing on personalized learning, predictive analytics, and administrative support. The university's ethical approach emphasizes transparency, fairness, and the human-centered design of AI systems.

Ethical Practices

- **Transparency and Accountability:** The University of Edinburgh promotes transparency by providing detailed information about AI systems, including their design, data usage, and decision-making processes. The university has established clear accountability mechanisms, ensuring that AI developers and users are responsible for the outcomes of AI-driven decisions.
- **Inclusive Design and Fairness:** The university adopts an inclusive design approach, involving diverse stakeholders in the development and evaluation of AI tools. This collaborative process helps ensure that AI systems are fair, equitable, and meet the needs of all students.
- **Data Privacy and Ethical Guidelines:** The University of Edinburgh has developed comprehensive ethical guidelines for AI use, emphasizing data privacy, security, and responsible data management. The university complies with the General Data Protection Regulation (GDPR) and implements strict data protection measures.
- **Human-Centered AI:** The university's AI initiatives prioritize the augmentation of human capabilities rather than the replacement of human interaction. AI tools are designed to support educators and students, enhancing the learning experience while maintaining the centrality of human relationships.

- **Impact:** The ethical integration of AI at the University of Edinburgh has enhanced personalized learning, improved student retention, and streamlined administrative processes. The university's commitment to ethical practices has fostered a positive and supportive learning environment, benefiting students and educators alike.

Case Study: Singapore's Ministry of Education (MOE)

Overview: Singapore's Ministry of Education (MOE) has implemented AI-driven initiatives to enhance educational outcomes, support teacher professional development, and improve administrative efficiency. The MOE's ethical approach focuses on transparency, data privacy, and equitable access to AI technologies.

Ethical Practices

- **Transparency and Stakeholder Communication:** The MOE ensures transparency by regularly communicating AI initiatives, goals, and progress to stakeholders. Public consultations and feedback mechanisms are established to involve educators, parents, and students in the decision-making process.
- **Data Privacy and Security:** The MOE adheres to stringent data privacy regulations and implements robust security measures to protect student data. Policies and practices are in place to ensure that data is used responsibly and ethically, with consent from students and parents.
- **Equitable Access and Inclusivity:** The MOE's AI initiatives aim to provide equitable access to AI technologies for all students, regardless of their socioeconomic background. Programs and resources are tailored to address the diverse needs of learners, ensuring that AI benefits are distributed fairly.
- **Teacher Training and Support:** The MOE provides extensive training and support for teachers on the ethical use of AI. Professional development programs focus on building AI literacy, understanding ethical considerations, and integrating AI tools into teaching practices.
- **Impact:** The ethical implementation of AI by Singapore's MOE has led to improved educational outcomes, enhanced teacher capabilities, and increased administrative efficiency. The ministry's focus on transparency, data privacy, and equitable access has ensured that AI technologies are used responsibly and inclusively.

Case Study: Finnish National Agency for Education (EDUFI), Finland

Overview: The Finnish National Agency for Education (EDUFI) has integrated AI technologies into the national education system, focusing on personalized learning, curriculum development, and teacher support. EDUFI's ethical approach emphasizes fairness, inclusivity, and data protection.

Ethical Practices

- **Fairness and Inclusivity:** EDUFI ensures that AI systems are designed to be fair and inclusive, addressing the diverse needs of all students. The agency involves various stakeholders in the development and evaluation of AI tools, ensuring that they are equitable and culturally relevant.
- **Data Privacy and Security:** EDUFI implements strict data privacy and security measures, complying with national and international regulations. The agency ensures that student data is collected, stored, and used responsibly, with a focus on protecting privacy and security.
- **Transparency and Public Engagement:** EDUFI promotes transparency by openly sharing information about AI initiatives, including goals, methodologies, and outcomes. Public engagement activities, such as forums and consultations, involve educators, parents, and students in the ethical use of AI.
- **Professional Development for Educators:** EDUFI provides professional development programs that focus on AI literacy, ethical considerations, and practical implementation strategies. These programs equip educators with the knowledge and skills needed to use AI responsibly and effectively.
- **Impact:** The ethical integration of AI by EDUFI has enhanced personalized learning, supported curriculum development, and improved teacher support. EDUFI's commitment to fairness, inclusivity, and data protection has built trust among stakeholders and ensured the responsible use of AI technologies.

These case studies demonstrate the importance of ethical practices in the implementation of AI in education. By prioritizing transparency, accountability, fairness, data privacy, and a human-centered approach, educational institutions can navigate the ethical challenges of AI and achieve positive outcomes. Key strategies include developing comprehensive ethical guidelines, engaging stakeholders, providing professional development, and ensuring equitable access to AI technologies. Through ethical leadership and responsible practices, we can harness the potential of AI to enhance education while safeguarding the interests and well-being of all stakeholders.

BUILDING TRUST IN AI-DRIVEN EDUCATION

Building trust is essential for the successful implementation of Artificial Intelligence (AI) in education. Trust ensures that stakeholders, including educators, students, parents, and the broader community, feel confident in the ethical use and potential benefits of AI technologies. This section explores strategies for building and maintaining trust in AI-driven education, emphasizing transparency, accountability, stakeholder engagement, and continuous improvement.

Strategies for Building Trust in AI-Driven Education

Ensuring Transparency

- **Open Communication:** Clearly communicate the goals, processes, and outcomes of AI initiatives. Explain how AI systems work, what data they use, and how decisions are made. Transparency helps demystify AI and build confidence in its use.
- **Public Reporting:** Regularly publish reports on the performance, impact, and ethical considerations of AI systems. Sharing success stories, challenges, and lessons learned fosters a culture of openness and accountability.

Demonstrating Accountability

- **Clear Responsibility:** Define and communicate the roles and responsibilities of all parties involved in AI implementation, including developers, educators, administrators, and policymakers. Ensure that everyone understands their duties and obligations.
- **Ethical Guidelines:** Develop and adhere to comprehensive ethical guidelines for AI use in education. These guidelines should cover data privacy, algorithmic fairness, transparency, and accountability.
- **Feedback Mechanisms:** Establish channels for stakeholders to provide feedback, report concerns, and ask questions about AI initiatives. Actively respond to feedback and address any issues raised.

Engaging Stakeholders

- **Inclusive Decision-Making:** Involve a diverse range of stakeholders in the development, implementation, and evaluation of AI systems. This includes educators, students, parents, community members, and AI experts. Inclusive decision-making ensures that multiple perspectives are considered and that AI tools meet the needs of all users.

- **Educational Workshops:** Conduct workshops and seminars to educate stakeholders about AI technologies, their applications, and ethical considerations. Providing knowledge and understanding helps build trust and support for AI initiatives.

Ensuring Data Privacy and Security

- **Robust Data Protection:** Implement strong data protection measures, such as encryption, secure storage, and access controls, to safeguard student information. Compliance with data privacy regulations, such as GDPR and FERPA, is essential.
- **Informed Consent:** Obtain informed consent from students and parents before collecting and using data. Clearly explain what data will be collected, how it will be used, and the measures in place to protect privacy.

Addressing Bias and Ensuring Fairness

- **Bias Audits:** Regularly audit AI algorithms to identify and mitigate biases. Ensure that AI systems are designed and tested using diverse and representative data sets to promote fairness and equity.
- **Equitable Access:** Ensure that all students, regardless of their background or circumstances, have access to AI-driven educational tools and resources. Address any barriers to access, such as the digital divide, and provide necessary support.

Continuous Improvement and Adaptation

- **Ongoing Evaluation:** Continuously monitor and evaluate the performance and impact of AI systems. Use data-driven insights to make informed adjustments and improvements.
- **Stakeholder Feedback:** Regularly solicit feedback from stakeholders to understand their experiences and perspectives. Incorporate their input into the ongoing development and refinement of AI tools.
- **Adaptation to Changes:** Stay informed about advancements in AI technology and evolving ethical standards. Adapt AI initiatives to reflect new developments and emerging best practices.

CASE STUDIES AND EXAMPLES

EdTech Sandbox Initiative, USA

Overview: The EdTech Sandbox Initiative in the USA focuses on piloting AI-driven educational tools in a controlled, transparent, and ethical manner. The initiative involves educators, students, parents, and AI experts in the decision-making process.

Trust-Building Practices

- **Transparency:** The initiative maintains transparency by openly sharing project goals, methodologies, and outcomes with stakeholders.
- **Stakeholder Engagement:** Regular meetings, workshops, and public forums are held to gather feedback and address concerns.
- **Accountability:** Clear roles and responsibilities are defined for all participants, ensuring accountability throughout the project.
- **Impact:** The EdTech Sandbox Initiative has successfully built trust among stakeholders, leading to increased support for AI-driven educational tools and improved student outcomes.

TeachFX, USA

Overview: TeachFX is an AI-powered tool that provides teachers with feedback on their classroom interactions to improve instructional practices. The company emphasizes ethical use and data privacy.

Trust-Building Practices

- **Data Privacy:** TeachFX ensures data privacy by implementing strong protection measures and complying with relevant regulations.
- **Transparency:** The company openly communicates how data is collected, used, and protected, and provides clear explanations of the AI algorithms used.
- **Stakeholder Feedback:** TeachFX actively solicits feedback from teachers and administrators to refine and improve the tool.
- **Impact:** TeachFX has gained the trust of educators by prioritizing data privacy and transparency, leading to widespread adoption and positive impacts on teaching practices.

NSW Department of Education, Australia

Overview: The New South Wales (NSW) Department of Education in Australia has implemented AI-driven tools to enhance personalized learning and administrative efficiency. The department's ethical approach focuses on transparency, stakeholder engagement, and continuous improvement.

Trust-Building Practices

- **Transparency:** The NSW Department of Education provides detailed information about AI initiatives, including goals, processes, and outcomes, to stakeholders.

- **Stakeholder Engagement:** The department engages educators, students, parents, and community members through consultations, surveys, and public forums.
- **Continuous Improvement:** Regular evaluations and stakeholder feedback are used to continuously improve AI tools and address any concerns.
- **Impact:** The NSW Department of Education has successfully built trust in its AI initiatives, resulting in enhanced learning experiences and greater administrative efficiency.

Challenges and Considerations

- **Overcoming Skepticism:** Building trust in AI-driven education requires overcoming skepticism and resistance from stakeholders who may have concerns about data privacy, algorithmic bias, and the potential impact on human interaction.
- **Ensuring Consistency:** Consistently applying ethical guidelines and practices across all AI initiatives is crucial for maintaining trust. Any lapses or inconsistencies can undermine stakeholder confidence.
- **Adapting to Rapid Changes:** The rapid pace of AI advancements can make it challenging to keep stakeholders informed and up-to-date. Continuous communication and education are essential to address this challenge.
- **Balancing Innovation and Ethics:** Striking a balance between leveraging AI for innovation and adhering to ethical principles can be challenging. Ensuring that ethical considerations are integral to AI development and implementation is crucial.

Building trust in AI-driven education is essential for the successful and ethical integration of AI technologies. By ensuring transparency, demonstrating accountability, engaging stakeholders, protecting data privacy, addressing bias, and committing to continuous improvement, educational institutions can foster a culture of trust and support. These strategies not only enhance the effectiveness and acceptance of AI in education but also safeguard the interests and well-being of all stakeholders. Through ethical leadership and responsible practices, we can harness the potential of AI to create a more inclusive, equitable, and innovative educational landscape.

ENSURING LONG-TERM ETHICAL COMPLIANCE IN AI-DRIVEN EDUCATION

As Artificial Intelligence (AI) becomes increasingly integrated into educational systems, ensuring long-term ethical compliance is crucial for maintaining trust, equity, and effectiveness. This section explores strategies for sustaining ethical compliance in AI-driven education, focusing on the development of robust frameworks, continuous monitoring, stakeholder engagement, and adaptive practices.

Establishing Robust Ethical Frameworks

- **Comprehensive Ethical Guidelines:** Developing comprehensive ethical guidelines is the first step towards ensuring long-term compliance. These guidelines should address key areas such as data privacy, algorithmic bias, transparency, accountability, and inclusivity. Institutions must collaborate with ethicists, educators, technologists, and policymakers to create guidelines that reflect diverse perspectives and ethical considerations.
- **Ethics Committees and Advisory Boards:** Establishing ethics committees and advisory boards helps oversee the implementation and adherence to ethical guidelines. These bodies should include representatives from various stakeholder groups, including educators, students, parents, and AI experts. Ethics committees can provide ongoing guidance, review AI initiatives, and address ethical concerns as they arise.
- **Regular Ethical Audits:** Conducting regular ethical audits ensures that AI-driven educational tools and practices remain compliant with established guidelines. Audits should assess data privacy practices, algorithmic fairness, and the overall impact of AI technologies on students and educators. Independent auditors can provide objective evaluations and recommendations for improvement.

Continuous Monitoring and Evaluation

- **Real-Time Monitoring Systems:** Implementing real-time monitoring systems allows institutions to track the performance and impact of AI tools continuously. These systems can identify potential ethical issues, such as biases in AI algorithms or breaches of data privacy, and alert relevant authorities for immediate action. Continuous monitoring helps maintain ethical standards and address problems proactively.
- **Feedback Mechanisms:** Establishing robust feedback mechanisms enables stakeholders to report ethical concerns and provide input on AI initiatives. Institutions should create accessible channels for students, educators, parents, and community members to share

their experiences and suggestions. Regularly reviewing and acting on feedback fosters a culture of transparency and accountability.

- **Impact Assessments:** Conducting periodic impact assessments evaluates the long-term effects of AI on education. These assessments should examine academic outcomes, equity, student well-being, and overall effectiveness. By analyzing the impact of AI initiatives, institutions can make data-driven decisions to enhance ethical compliance and educational outcomes.

Engaging Stakeholders in Ethical Practices

- **Stakeholder Involvement in Decision-Making:** Involving stakeholders in decision-making processes ensures that diverse perspectives are considered in ethical discussions. Institutions should engage educators, students, parents, and community leaders in developing and implementing AI initiatives. Collaborative decision-making promotes transparency and trust, fostering a shared commitment to ethical practices.
- **Ethics Education and Awareness:** Raising awareness and educating stakeholders about ethical AI use is essential for sustaining long-term compliance. Institutions should offer ethics training programs for educators, administrators, and students, covering topics such as data privacy, algorithmic bias, and responsible AI use. Promoting ethical literacy helps stakeholders make informed decisions and advocate for ethical practices.
- **Community Outreach and Engagement:** Engaging the broader community in discussions about AI and ethics fosters a culture of accountability and inclusivity. Institutions can organize workshops, seminars, and public forums to discuss the ethical implications of AI in education and gather community input. Community outreach initiatives strengthen relationships and ensure that AI-driven education aligns with societal values.

Adaptive and Resilient Practices

- **Flexible Ethical Guidelines:** Ethical guidelines should be flexible and adaptable to evolving technological advancements and societal changes. Institutions must regularly review and update guidelines to address new ethical challenges and incorporate emerging best practices. Adaptive guidelines ensure that ethical standards remain relevant and effective in a rapidly changing landscape.
- **Scalable Ethical Frameworks:** Developing scalable ethical frameworks allows institutions to expand ethical practices across

different contexts and levels of education. Scalable frameworks can be tailored to the unique needs of various educational settings, from K-12 schools to higher education institutions. Ensuring scalability promotes consistent ethical standards across the educational ecosystem.

- **Innovative Ethical Solutions:** Embracing innovation in ethical practices helps address complex ethical dilemmas associated with AI use. Institutions should explore new methodologies, such as participatory design and co-creation, to develop ethical AI solutions. Innovative approaches to ethics encourage creative problem-solving and enhance the effectiveness of ethical frameworks.

Case Studies and Examples

- **EdTech Ethics Consortium:** The EdTech Ethics Consortium is a collaborative initiative involving educational institutions, technology companies, and non-profit organizations. The consortium develops and promotes ethical guidelines for AI use in education, conducts regular audits, and provides training programs. Through collective efforts, the consortium ensures long-term ethical compliance and fosters trust in AI technologies.
- **AI Ethics Lab at Stanford University:** Stanford University's AI Ethics Lab conducts research on the ethical implications of AI and develops practical guidelines for responsible AI use. The lab collaborates with educators, policymakers, and industry leaders to create scalable ethical frameworks and innovative solutions. The lab's work informs ethical practices in AI-driven education and promotes ongoing dialogue about ethical challenges.
- **UK Data Ethics Framework:** The UK Data Ethics Framework provides a comprehensive guide for ethical data use in public sector projects, including education. The framework outlines principles for transparency, accountability, and fairness, and includes practical tools for ethical decision-making. Educational institutions in the UK use the framework to ensure ethical compliance in AI initiatives and protect student data.

Challenges and Considerations

- **Balancing Innovation and Ethics:** Balancing the drive for innovation with the need for ethical compliance can be challenging. Institutions must prioritize ethical considerations while exploring new AI applications, ensuring that ethical standards are not compromised in pursuit of technological advancements.

- **Addressing Global Ethical Variations:** Ethical standards and cultural values vary across different regions and societies. Developing global ethical guidelines that respect diverse perspectives requires careful consideration and collaboration. Institutions must engage in cross-cultural dialogue to create inclusive and contextually appropriate ethical frameworks.
- **Sustaining Ethical Commitment:** Sustaining long-term ethical commitment requires continuous effort and vigilance. Institutions must foster a culture of ethics, provide ongoing support and resources, and remain adaptable to new ethical challenges. Ensuring sustained commitment to ethics is essential for building trust and maintaining the integrity of AI-driven education.

Conclusion

Ensuring long-term ethical compliance in AI-driven education involves establishing robust ethical frameworks, continuous monitoring and evaluation, stakeholder engagement, and adaptive practices. By developing comprehensive guidelines, conducting regular audits, and fostering a culture of ethics, educational institutions can maintain trust and promote equity in AI use. Engaging stakeholders in ethical discussions, raising awareness, and embracing innovation in ethical practices are essential for sustaining ethical compliance. Through thoughtful and proactive efforts, we can navigate the ethical challenges of AI in education and create a fair, inclusive, and effective educational landscape.

QUESTIONNAIRE

Question 1: What is ethical leadership in the context of AI in education?

Answer: Ethical leadership in the context of AI in education involves guiding the implementation and use of AI technologies in a way that prioritizes fairness, transparency, accountability, and respect for all stakeholders. Ethical leaders ensure that AI tools enhance learning without compromising privacy or perpetuating biases. They promote policies that protect student data, foster inclusive practices, and maintain a balance between technological advancements and human-centric education. Ethical leadership requires ongoing reflection and adaptation to uphold these principles in the dynamic landscape of AI.

Question 2: Why is ethical leadership crucial in AI-driven education?

Answer: Ethical leadership is crucial in AI-driven education to ensure that the deployment of AI technologies aligns with moral and ethical standards. It helps prevent misuse of AI, protects student privacy, and promotes equitable access to educational resources. Ethical leaders advocate for transparency in AI algorithms and decisions, ensuring that AI systems are used responsibly. By prioritizing ethical considerations, leaders can build trust among students, parents, and educators, fostering an environment where AI enhances learning while safeguarding individual rights.

Question 3: What should ethical guidelines for AI in education include?

Answer: Ethical guidelines for AI in education should include principles of transparency, fairness, accountability, privacy, and inclusivity. They should outline how AI data is collected, stored, and used, ensuring student data privacy and security. Guidelines should address algorithmic fairness, preventing biases that could disadvantage any student group. They should also establish clear accountability mechanisms for AI decisions and promote inclusivity by ensuring that AI tools are accessible to all students, regardless of their background or abilities. Regular review and updates to these guidelines are essential to keep pace with technological advancements.

Question 4: How can schools develop effective ethical guidelines for AI use?

Answer: Schools can develop effective ethical guidelines for AI use by involving a diverse group of stakeholders, including educators, students, parents, technologists, and ethicists, in the drafting process. This ensures that multiple perspectives are considered. Schools should research existing ethical frameworks and adapt them to their specific context. Regular training and workshops can help educators understand and implement these guidelines. Continuous monitoring and evaluation are necessary to assess the effectiveness of the guidelines and make adjustments as needed.

Question 5: Why is training educators and leaders important for ethical AI use in education?

Answer: Training educators and leaders is important for ethical AI use in education because it equips them with the knowledge and skills to implement AI technologies responsibly. Training helps educators understand the ethical implications of AI, including data privacy, algorithmic bias, and transparency. It ensures they can make informed decisions about AI integration in their teaching practices and leadership roles. By promoting ethical AI use, training helps build trust and confidence among students, parents, and the broader educational community.

Question 6: What should be included in training programs for ethical AI use?

Answer: Training programs for ethical AI use should include an overview of AI technologies and their applications in education, discussions on ethical principles such as privacy, fairness, and transparency, and strategies for identifying and mitigating biases in AI systems. Programs should also cover data protection policies, legal and regulatory frameworks, and case studies of ethical and unethical AI use. Hands-on workshops and scenario-based learning can help educators and leaders apply ethical guidelines in practical situations.

Question 7: How can trust be built in AI-driven education?

Answer: Trust in AI-driven education can be built through transparency, communication, and stakeholder engagement. Schools should openly communicate how AI technologies are used, what data is collected, and how it is protected. Involving students, parents, and educators in the development and implementation of AI policies fosters a sense of ownership and accountability. Providing clear explanations of AI decisions and ensuring that AI tools are fair and unbiased also contribute to building trust. Regular feedback mechanisms and addressing concerns promptly further enhance trust.

Question 8: Why is trust important in AI-driven education?

Answer: Trust is important in AI-driven education because it ensures the successful adoption and use of AI technologies. When students, parents, and educators trust AI tools, they are more likely to engage with and benefit from them. Trust mitigates fears about data privacy and misuse, promoting a positive and collaborative educational environment. Without trust, AI initiatives may face resistance, limiting their effectiveness and potential to enhance learning outcomes. Building trust ensures that AI technologies are used responsibly and ethically, fostering a supportive educational ecosystem.

Question 9: How can long-term ethical compliance in AI-driven education be ensured?

Answer: Long-term ethical compliance in AI-driven education can be ensured through continuous monitoring, regular updates to ethical guidelines, and ongoing training for educators and administrators. Establishing a dedicated ethics committee to oversee AI initiatives and address emerging ethical issues is crucial. Schools should conduct periodic audits of AI systems to identify and rectify biases or other ethical concerns. Encouraging a culture of ethical reflection and dialogue among all stakeholders helps maintain a commitment to ethical standards over time.

Question 10: What role do policies play in ensuring ethical compliance in AI-driven education?

Answer: Policies play a critical role in ensuring ethical compliance in AI-driven education by providing a clear framework for the responsible use of AI technologies. They establish standards for data privacy, algorithmic transparency, and accountability, guiding the development and implementation of AI tools. Policies also outline procedures for addressing ethical issues and ensuring that AI systems are regularly evaluated and updated. By embedding ethical considerations into institutional policies, schools can ensure that AI use aligns with broader educational goals and values, promoting a sustainable and ethical approach to AI integration.

10

The Long-Term Impact of AI on Education

AI-DRIVEN INNOVATION IN EDUCATION

Artificial Intelligence (AI) is rapidly transforming various sectors, and education is no exception. AI-driven innovation in education holds the promise of revolutionizing how we teach, learn, and manage educational systems. This section explores the multifaceted ways in which AI is driving innovation in education, discussing its potential long-term impacts, benefits, challenges, and the future of AI-driven educational ecosystems.

Personalized Learning Experiences

- **Adaptive Learning Technologies:** AI-powered adaptive learning systems tailor educational content to the individual needs and learning pace of each student. These systems analyze data on student performance, preferences, and behaviors to provide customized learning pathways. This personalization ensures that students receive the right level of challenge and support, enhancing their engagement and achievement.
- **Intelligent Tutoring Systems:** Intelligent Tutoring Systems (ITS) leverage AI to provide personalized instruction and feedback. These systems mimic the capabilities of human tutors by offering explanations, hints, and real-time feedback. ITS can identify and address specific learning gaps, helping students master concepts more effectively.
- **Content Recommendation Engines:** AI-driven recommendation engines suggest relevant resources, such as articles, videos, and exercises, based on students' learning profiles and progress. These recommendations help students discover new materials that align with their interests and needs, fostering a more engaging and self-directed learning experience.

Enhanced Educational Tools and Resources

- **Automated Assessment and Feedback:** AI enables automated grading of assignments and exams, providing immediate and objective feedback to students. This automation saves educators time and allows them to focus on more complex tasks. Additionally, AI can analyze patterns in student responses to offer personalized feedback and identify areas for improvement.
- **Natural Language Processing (NLP) Applications:** NLP technologies, such as chatbots and virtual assistants, support students in various ways, including answering questions, providing explanations, and facilitating study sessions. These AI tools are available 24/7, offering students immediate assistance and reducing their reliance on human intervention.
- **Virtual and Augmented Reality (VR/AR):** AI-enhanced VR and AR applications create immersive learning environments that enable students to explore complex concepts interactively. For

example, virtual labs allow students to conduct experiments in a safe and controlled digital environment, while augmented reality overlays provide real-time information and visualizations.

Administrative Efficiency and Decision-Making

- **Predictive Analytics for Student Success:** AI-powered predictive analytics models analyze historical and real-time data to identify students at risk of falling behind or dropping out. These models can predict academic performance and suggest timely interventions, such as tutoring or counseling, to support student success.
- **Streamlined Administrative Processes:** AI-driven automation streamlines administrative tasks, such as scheduling, enrollment, and record-keeping. This efficiency reduces the administrative burden on educators and administrators, allowing them to focus more on teaching and student support.
- **Data-Driven Decision-Making:** AI tools analyze vast amounts of educational data to generate actionable insights for decision-makers. These insights inform curriculum development, resource allocation, and policy-making, leading to more effective and data-driven educational practices.

Fostering Collaboration and Communication

- **AI-Supported Collaborative Learning:** AI facilitates collaborative learning by connecting students with peers, mentors, and experts worldwide. AI-powered platforms can match students with complementary skills and interests, fostering collaborative projects and discussions. These interactions enhance social learning and expose students to diverse perspectives.
- **Enhanced Teacher-Student Communication:** AI tools, such as messaging apps and virtual meeting platforms, improve communication between teachers and students. AI can facilitate personalized communication, track interactions, and provide insights into student engagement and well-being.
- **Global Learning Communities:** AI enables the creation of global learning communities where students and educators can share knowledge, resources, and experiences. These communities promote cultural exchange and collaboration, enriching the educational experience.

Addressing Challenges and Ethical Considerations

- **Data Privacy and Security:** The use of AI in education raises concerns about data privacy and security. It is essential to implement robust data protection measures and ensure compliance with privacy regulations to safeguard student information.
- **Algorithmic Bias and Fairness:** AI algorithms can perpetuate biases present in the training data, leading to unfair outcomes. Addressing algorithmic bias involves using diverse and representative data sets, conducting regular audits, and developing inclusive AI systems.
- **Equitable Access to AI Technologies:** Ensuring equitable access to AI-driven educational tools is crucial to avoid exacerbating existing educational inequalities. Efforts must focus on providing access to technology and resources for all students, regardless of their socioeconomic background.

The Future of AI-Driven Education

- **Lifelong Learning and Skills Development:** AI supports lifelong learning by providing personalized learning opportunities beyond traditional education. AI-driven platforms can help individuals continuously develop new skills and adapt to changing job market demands.
- **AI-Driven Research and Innovation:** AI accelerates educational research by analyzing large data sets, identifying trends, and generating new insights. This research informs the development of innovative educational practices and technologies, driving continuous improvement in education.
- **Sustainable Education Practices:** AI can contribute to sustainable education practices by optimizing resource use, reducing waste, and promoting environmentally friendly initiatives. For example, AI can optimize energy use in educational facilities and support digital learning, reducing the need for physical materials.
- **Integration with Emerging Technologies:** The integration of AI with other emerging technologies, such as the Internet of Things (IoT) and blockchain, can create more efficient and secure educational ecosystems. For instance, IoT devices can monitor classroom environments and provide data for optimizing learning conditions, while blockchain can ensure secure and transparent credentialing.

AI-driven innovation in education offers immense potential to transform teaching, learning, and administrative processes. By leveraging AI technologies, educators can create personalized, engaging, and effective learning experiences that meet the diverse needs of students. However, it is essential to address the ethical considerations and challenges associated with AI use, such as data privacy, algorithmic bias, and equitable access. Through responsible and thoughtful implementation, AI can drive significant improvements in education, preparing students for the future and fostering a culture of continuous learning and innovation.

THE LONG-TERM IMPACT OF AI ON LEARNING AND TEACHING

Artificial Intelligence (AI) is poised to revolutionize learning and teaching, bringing profound changes to educational paradigms. Its long-term impact spans various aspects of education, including personalized learning, teaching methodologies, curriculum development, and student assessment. This section explores the transformative potential of AI in education, highlighting its benefits, challenges, and future implications.

Personalized Learning

- **Customized Learning Paths:** AI enables the creation of personalized learning paths tailored to individual student needs, abilities, and interests. By analyzing data on student performance, preferences, and behaviors, AI systems can design customized curricula that adapt to each learner's pace and style. This personalization enhances engagement, motivation, and academic achievement.
- **Real-Time Feedback and Adaptation:** AI-powered tools provide real-time feedback on student performance, allowing for immediate adjustments to the learning process. Intelligent tutoring systems and adaptive learning platforms can modify instruction based on student responses, ensuring that learners receive the appropriate level of challenge and support at all times.
- **Enhanced Learning Experiences:** AI enhances the learning experience by incorporating multimedia, interactive simulations, and gamification. These elements make learning more engaging and immersive, catering to diverse learning styles and preferences. AI can also recommend supplementary resources, such as videos, articles, and exercises, that align with individual interests and needs.

Transforming Teaching Methodologies

- **Data-Driven Instruction:** AI empowers teachers with data-driven insights into student performance, enabling them to tailor their instruction more effectively. By analyzing patterns and trends in student data, educators can identify areas where students struggle and adjust their teaching strategies accordingly. This data-driven approach leads to more targeted and effective instruction.
- **Automated Administrative Tasks:** AI automates routine administrative tasks, such as grading, attendance tracking, and scheduling, freeing up teachers to focus on instructional and interactive activities. Automation reduces the administrative burden on educators, allowing them to devote more time and energy to teaching and student support.
- **Professional Development:** AI supports teacher professional development by providing personalized learning opportunities and resources. AI-driven platforms can recommend professional development courses, articles, and workshops based on individual teacher needs and interests. Additionally, AI can facilitate peer collaboration and knowledge sharing among educators.

Curriculum Development and Innovation

- **Dynamic Curriculum Design:** AI enables dynamic and responsive curriculum design that can adapt to changing educational needs and contexts. By analyzing data on student performance, industry trends, and emerging technologies, AI can inform the development of curricula that are relevant, future-oriented, and aligned with real-world demands.
- **Interdisciplinary Learning:** AI supports interdisciplinary learning by integrating content from various subjects and facilitating cross-curricular connections. AI-driven platforms can identify and highlight links between different disciplines, encouraging students to apply knowledge and skills across diverse contexts.
- **Innovative Learning Models:** The integration of AI fosters innovative learning models, such as flipped classrooms, blended learning, and project-based learning. These models leverage AI to provide flexible, student-centered learning experiences that promote critical thinking, creativity, and collaboration.

Revolutionizing Student Assessment

- **Continuous and Formative Assessment:** AI enables continuous and formative assessment, providing ongoing insights into student progress. AI-driven assessment tools can evaluate student performance in real-time, offering immediate feedback and identifying areas for improvement. This continuous assessment supports a growth mindset and encourages students to take an active role in their learning.

- **Authentic Assessment:** AI facilitates authentic assessment by evaluating complex tasks and real-world problem-solving. AI-driven tools can assess student projects, presentations, and collaborative work, providing a more comprehensive and accurate measure of student learning and skills.
- **Personalized Assessment:** AI allows for personalized assessment that takes into account individual learning styles and preferences. AI-driven assessment tools can adapt to different formats, such as written responses, oral presentations, and interactive tasks, ensuring that each student can demonstrate their knowledge and skills in the most effective way.

Enhancing Student Engagement and Motivation

- **Gamification and Interactive Learning:** AI incorporates gamification and interactive elements into the learning process, making education more engaging and enjoyable. By introducing game-like features, such as points, badges, and leaderboards, AI-driven platforms motivate students to participate actively and strive for continuous improvement.
- **Social and Collaborative Learning:** AI supports social and collaborative learning by connecting students with peers, mentors, and experts worldwide. AI-powered platforms can facilitate group projects, discussions, and knowledge sharing, fostering a sense of community and collaboration among learners.
- **Intrinsic Motivation:** AI-driven personalized learning experiences enhance intrinsic motivation by aligning educational content with students' interests and goals. When students perceive learning as relevant and meaningful, they are more likely to engage deeply and persist in their efforts.

Addressing Equity and Accessibility

- **Supporting Diverse Learners:** AI has the potential to support diverse learners, including those with special educational needs and disabilities. AI-driven tools can provide tailored accommodations, such as speech-to-text, text-to-speech, and customized learning materials, ensuring that all students have equal access to education.

- **Bridging the Digital Divide:** While AI offers numerous benefits, it is essential to address the digital divide to ensure equitable access to AI-driven educational tools. Efforts must focus on providing affordable technology, internet access, and digital literacy training for all students, regardless of their socioeconomic background.
- **Inclusive Education:** AI promotes inclusive education by identifying and addressing barriers to learning. AI-driven analytics can detect patterns that indicate learning difficulties or disparities, enabling timely interventions and support for students who need it most.

Preparing Students for the Future

- **Developing 21st Century Skills:** AI-driven education equips students with essential 21st-century skills, such as critical thinking, problem-solving, collaboration, and digital literacy. These skills are crucial for success in an increasingly complex and technology-driven world.
- **Lifelong Learning and Adaptability:** AI fosters a culture of lifelong learning by providing continuous learning opportunities beyond traditional education. AI-driven platforms support skill development, career advancement, and personal growth, preparing students to adapt to changing job market demands and technological advancements.
- **Ethical and Responsible AI Use:** Educating students about the ethical and responsible use of AI is crucial for their future roles as informed citizens and professionals. AI-driven education should include discussions on data privacy, algorithmic bias, and the societal impact of AI, fostering a generation of ethical and responsible AI users.

Challenges and Considerations

- **Ethical Implications:** The use of AI in education raises ethical considerations, such as data privacy, algorithmic bias, and the potential for increased surveillance. It is essential to develop and enforce ethical guidelines to ensure that AI technologies are used responsibly and equitably.
- **Teacher Training and Support:** Effective integration of AI requires comprehensive teacher training and ongoing support. Educators must be equipped with the knowledge and skills to use AI tools effectively and ethically, and they should have access to continuous professional development opportunities.

- **Sustainability and Scalability:** Ensuring the sustainability and scalability of AI-driven educational initiatives involves securing long-term funding, maintaining infrastructure, and continuously updating technology. Collaborative efforts among governments, educational institutions, and technology providers are essential for sustainable implementation.
- **Balancing Human Interaction and Technology:** While AI offers numerous benefits, it is crucial to balance technology use with human interaction. Educators play a vital role in fostering relationships, providing emotional support, and facilitating social learning. AI should augment, not replace, these human elements.

The long-term impact of AI on learning and teaching is profound, offering opportunities for personalized learning, innovative teaching methodologies, dynamic curriculum development, and comprehensive student assessment. By addressing ethical considerations and challenges, educational institutions can harness the transformative potential of AI to enhance education and prepare students for the future. Through thoughtful and responsible implementation, AI-driven education can create a more inclusive, equitable, and effective learning environment for all.

FUTURE VISIONS: AI IN 2050 EDUCATION

By 2050, Artificial Intelligence (AI) will have profoundly transformed education, creating a future where learning is more personalized, accessible, and integrated with technology than ever before. This section explores future visions of AI in education, imagining the innovations and advancements that could shape how we teach and learn. It considers the potential benefits, challenges, and ethical implications of AI-driven education in the mid-21st century.

Personalized and Adaptive Learning Environments

- **Hyper-Personalized Learning Paths:** In 2050, AI will enable hyper-personalized learning paths tailored to the unique needs, interests, and goals of each student. Advanced AI algorithms will continuously analyze data on student performance, preferences, and behaviors, adjusting curricula in real-time to optimize learning outcomes. This level of personalization will ensure that every student can learn at their own pace and receive the support they need to succeed.
- **Intelligent Learning Companions:** AI-driven intelligent learning companions will act as personal tutors, mentors, and motivators for students. These companions will leverage natural

language processing, emotional recognition, and adaptive learning technologies to provide personalized instruction, encouragement, and feedback. They will be able to anticipate students' needs and offer just-in-time support, making learning more engaging and effective.

- **Immersive and Experiential Learning:** Virtual and augmented reality (VR/AR) technologies, powered by AI, will create immersive and experiential learning environments. Students will be able to explore historical events, conduct scientific experiments, and interact with virtual simulations, enhancing their understanding and retention of complex concepts. AI will personalize these experiences to match individual learning styles and preferences.

Revolutionizing Teaching and Educator Roles

- **AI-Augmented Educators:** By 2050, educators will work alongside AI systems that augment their teaching capabilities. AI will handle routine administrative tasks, such as grading and attendance, allowing teachers to focus on high-value activities like mentoring and personalized instruction. AI will provide real-time insights into student performance, enabling educators to make data-driven decisions and tailor their teaching strategies.
- **Continuous Professional Development:** AI will facilitate continuous professional development for educators by identifying skill gaps, recommending relevant training programs, and providing real-time feedback on teaching practices. AI-driven platforms will enable peer collaboration and knowledge sharing, fostering a culture of lifelong learning among educators.
- **Collaborative Teaching Models:** AI will support collaborative teaching models, where educators from different disciplines and geographic locations can co-teach and share resources. AI-driven platforms will facilitate seamless communication and coordination, enabling teachers to create interdisciplinary learning experiences that enrich students' education.

Transforming Curriculum and Content Delivery

- **Dynamic and Responsive Curricula:** Curricula in 2050 will be dynamic and responsive, continuously evolving based on real-time data and feedback. AI will analyze trends in student performance, industry needs, and societal changes to inform curriculum updates, ensuring that education remains relevant and future-oriented.

- **Universal Access to Quality Education:** AI will democratize access to quality education by providing free or low-cost learning resources to students worldwide. AI-driven platforms will offer multilingual and culturally relevant content, breaking down language barriers and promoting inclusivity. This universal access will help bridge educational gaps and promote global equity.
- **AI-Generated Content:** AI will play a significant role in content creation, generating high-quality educational materials, such as textbooks, videos, and interactive simulations. AI-driven content will be customized to meet the diverse needs of learners, making education more engaging and effective.

Enhancing Student Assessment and Evaluation

- **Holistic and Continuous Assessment:** AI will enable holistic and continuous assessment, providing a comprehensive view of student progress. AI-driven assessment tools will evaluate a wide range of skills, including critical thinking, creativity, collaboration, and emotional intelligence. Continuous assessment will offer real-time feedback, helping students and educators track progress and identify areas for improvement.
- **Competency-Based Education:** AI will support competency-based education, where students advance based on their mastery of skills and knowledge rather than time spent in class. AI-driven platforms will assess student competencies through various methods, including project-based learning, simulations, and real-world applications, ensuring that students are well-prepared for future challenges.
- **Ethical AI in Assessment:** Ensuring the ethical use of AI in assessment will be crucial. AI systems will need to be transparent, fair, and unbiased, providing accurate and equitable evaluations of student performance. Ethical guidelines and regular audits will help maintain the integrity of AI-driven assessments.

Promoting Lifelong Learning and Skill Development

- **AI-Driven Lifelong Learning Platforms:** By 2050, AI-driven lifelong learning platforms will support continuous education and skill development. These platforms will offer personalized learning experiences, career guidance, and access to a vast array of courses and resources. AI will help individuals identify and pursue learning opportunities that align with their career goals and personal interests.

- **Just-in-Time Learning:** AI will facilitate just-in-time learning, providing individuals with the knowledge and skills they need at the moment they need them. AI-driven systems will analyze job market trends, professional requirements, and individual career paths to recommend relevant learning opportunities, ensuring that learners remain competitive and adaptable.
- **Global Learning Ecosystems:** AI will create global learning ecosystems that connect learners, educators, and institutions worldwide. These ecosystems will promote knowledge exchange, cultural understanding, and collaborative problem-solving, enriching the educational experience and fostering global citizenship.

Addressing Challenges and Ethical Considerations

- **Data Privacy and Security:** As AI systems collect and analyze vast amounts of data, ensuring data privacy and security will be paramount. Robust data protection measures, compliance with privacy regulations, and transparent data practices will be essential to safeguard student information and maintain trust.
- **Algorithmic Bias and Fairness:** Preventing algorithmic bias and ensuring fairness in AI systems will be critical. Diverse and representative data sets, regular audits, and inclusive AI design practices will help mitigate biases and promote equitable outcomes for all students.
- **Human-Centric AI Design:** AI-driven education must prioritize human-centric design, ensuring that technology enhances rather than replaces human interaction. Educators will continue to play a vital role in fostering relationships, providing emotional support, and guiding students' personal and social development.
- **Ethical AI Governance:** Establishing ethical AI governance frameworks will be essential to oversee the development and use of AI in education. These frameworks will include guidelines for transparency, accountability, and ethical decision-making, ensuring that AI technologies are used responsibly and for the greater good.

Imagining the Classroom of 2050

- **Smart Classrooms:** Classrooms in 2050 will be equipped with advanced AI technologies, such as interactive displays, IoT devices, and adaptive learning environments. AI will monitor and optimize classroom conditions, such as lighting, temperature, and seating arrangements, to enhance student comfort and focus.

- **Flexible Learning Spaces:** Learning spaces will be flexible and adaptable, designed to support various teaching and learning activities. AI-driven systems will configure spaces to facilitate individual study, group work, and experiential learning, promoting a dynamic and interactive educational environment.
- **Seamless Integration of Technology:** Technology will be seamlessly integrated into the learning experience, with AI-driven devices and applications enhancing collaboration, creativity, and critical thinking. Students will use AI tools to conduct research, create projects, and engage with interactive content, making learning more engaging and relevant.

Preparing for the Future of AI in Education

- **Fostering Digital Literacy:** Developing digital literacy skills will be essential for students, educators, and administrators to navigate and thrive in an AI-driven educational landscape. Digital literacy programs will focus on critical thinking, ethical AI use, and the responsible management of digital information.
- **Collaborative Efforts:** Collaborative efforts among governments, educational institutions, technology providers, and researchers will drive the development and implementation of AI in education. Partnerships will facilitate knowledge exchange, resource sharing, and the co-creation of innovative solutions.
- **Continuous Research and Innovation:** Ongoing research and innovation will be crucial to explore the full potential of AI in education and address emerging challenges. Investment in research will support the development of new AI applications, best practices, and ethical guidelines, ensuring that AI-driven education remains effective and responsible.

The future of AI in education by 2050 promises to be transformative, offering unprecedented opportunities for personalized learning, innovative teaching, and global collaboration. By addressing challenges and ethical considerations, we can harness the power of AI to create a more inclusive, equitable, and effective educational landscape. Through thoughtful and responsible implementation, AI-driven education will prepare students for the complexities of the future, fostering a culture of lifelong learning and adaptability.

AI AND THE EVOLUTION OF EDUCATIONAL SYSTEMS

Artificial Intelligence (AI) is driving a fundamental evolution in educational systems worldwide. This transformation encompasses not only teaching and learning but also how educational institutions operate, make decisions, and engage with their communities. This section explores how AI is reshaping educational systems, examining its impact on governance, policy, curriculum, assessment, and equity.

Transforming Educational Governance and Policy

- **Data-Driven Policy Making:** AI enables data-driven policy making by analyzing vast amounts of educational data to inform decisions. Predictive analytics and machine learning models can identify trends, predict outcomes, and suggest interventions. This approach leads to more effective and evidence-based policies that enhance educational outcomes.
- **Transparent and Accountable Systems:** AI increases transparency and accountability in educational governance. Automated reporting and analytics provide real-time insights into the performance of schools, educators, and students. This transparency ensures that stakeholders can monitor progress, identify areas for improvement, and hold institutions accountable.
- **Efficient Resource Allocation:** AI optimizes resource allocation by analyzing data on student needs, school performance, and funding requirements. AI-driven tools can recommend the most efficient use of resources, ensuring that funds are directed where they are needed most and have the greatest impact.
- **Streamlined Administrative Processes:** AI automates administrative processes, such as enrollment, scheduling, and record-keeping, reducing the workload on educational staff. This automation increases efficiency, reduces errors, and allows administrators to focus on strategic planning and student support.

Innovative Curriculum and Instructional Design

- **Dynamic Curriculum Development:** AI facilitates dynamic curriculum development that evolves based on real-time data and feedback. Curricula can be continuously updated to reflect the latest knowledge, skills, and industry demands. AI-driven platforms can tailor curricula to meet the diverse needs of students and ensure relevance.
- **Interdisciplinary Learning:** AI supports interdisciplinary learning by identifying connections between different subjects and promoting cross-curricular projects. AI-driven tools can help students apply knowledge from various disciplines to solve complex problems, fostering a more holistic understanding of the world.

- **Experiential and Project-Based Learning:** AI enhances experiential and project-based learning by providing tools and resources for hands-on, real-world learning experiences. AI can simulate real-world scenarios, guide students through projects, and offer feedback, making learning more engaging and applicable.

Revolutionizing Assessment and Evaluation

- **Continuous and Formative Assessment:** AI enables continuous and formative assessment, providing ongoing feedback to students and educators. AI-driven assessment tools can evaluate student performance in real-time, identify learning gaps, and suggest personalized interventions to support continuous improvement.
- **Competency-Based Assessment:** AI supports competency-based assessment, where students progress based on their mastery of skills and knowledge rather than time spent in class. AI-driven platforms can assess a wide range of competencies through various methods, such as simulations, projects, and real-world applications.
- **Holistic Student Evaluation:** AI facilitates holistic student evaluation by considering multiple dimensions of student performance, including academic achievement, social-emotional development, and critical thinking skills. This comprehensive approach provides a more accurate and complete picture of student progress.

Promoting Equity and Inclusion

- **Personalized Learning for Diverse Needs:** AI enables personalized learning experiences that cater to the diverse needs of students, including those with special educational needs and disabilities. AI-driven tools can provide customized support, accommodations, and learning materials, ensuring that all students have equal opportunities to succeed.
- **Bridging the Digital Divide:** Efforts to bridge the digital divide are essential to ensure equitable access to AI-driven educational tools. This includes providing affordable technology, internet access, and digital literacy training to underserved communities. By addressing these disparities, AI can promote greater equity in education.
- **Inclusive Curriculum Design:** AI supports the development of inclusive curricula that reflect diverse cultures, perspectives, and experiences. AI-driven content creation tools can generate materials that are culturally relevant and accessible to all students, fostering a more inclusive learning environment.

Enhancing Community Engagement and Collaboration

- **AI-Driven Community Platforms:** AI-powered community platforms facilitate collaboration and communication among students, educators, parents, and community members. These platforms can connect stakeholders, share resources, and support collaborative projects, enhancing the sense of community and engagement.
- **Parent and Guardian Involvement:** AI tools can provide parents and guardians with real-time updates on their child's progress, enabling more informed and proactive involvement in their education. AI-driven communication platforms can facilitate regular and meaningful interactions between educators and families.
- **Global Educational Networks:** AI supports the creation of global educational networks that connect institutions, educators, and students worldwide. These networks promote knowledge exchange, cultural understanding, and collaborative learning, enriching the educational experience for all participants.

Preparing for Future Workforce Demands

- **Alignment with Industry Needs:** AI helps align educational programs with current and future workforce demands. By analyzing job market trends and industry requirements, AI can inform curriculum development and ensure that students acquire the skills and knowledge needed for success in the evolving job market.
- **Skill Development and Lifelong Learning:** AI supports continuous skill development and lifelong learning by providing personalized learning pathways and resources. AI-driven platforms can guide individuals through career transitions, professional development, and upskilling, ensuring that they remain competitive and adaptable.
- **Real-World Learning Experiences:** AI facilitates real-world learning experiences, such as internships, apprenticeships, and project-based learning. AI-driven tools can connect students with industry partners, provide mentorship, and simulate workplace scenarios, preparing students for the challenges of the workforce.

Ethical Considerations and Challenges

- **Data Privacy and Security:** Ensuring data privacy and security is a critical challenge in the implementation of AI in education. Robust data protection measures, compliance with privacy regulations, and transparent data practices are essential to safeguard student information and maintain trust.

- **Algorithmic Bias and Fairness:** Addressing algorithmic bias and ensuring fairness in AI systems is crucial to prevent discriminatory outcomes. This involves using diverse and representative data sets, conducting regular audits, and adopting inclusive AI design practices.
- **Human-Centric AI Design:** AI-driven educational systems must prioritize human-centric design, ensuring that technology enhances rather than replaces human interaction. Educators will continue to play a vital role in fostering relationships, providing emotional support, and guiding students' personal and social development.
- **Ethical AI Governance:** Establishing ethical AI governance frameworks is essential to oversee the development and use of AI in education. These frameworks should include guidelines for transparency, accountability, and ethical decision-making, ensuring that AI technologies are used responsibly and for the greater good.

AI is driving a significant evolution in educational systems, transforming how we teach, learn, and manage education. By leveraging AI, educational institutions can create more personalized, efficient, and equitable learning environments that prepare students for the future. However, addressing ethical considerations and challenges, such as data privacy, algorithmic bias, and equitable access, is crucial to ensure the responsible and effective use of AI. Through thoughtful and inclusive implementation, AI has the potential to revolutionize education and create a more inclusive, innovative, and effective educational landscape for all.

PREPARING FOR A CONTINUALLY EVOLVING AI LANDSCAPE

As Artificial Intelligence (AI) continues to advance and integrate into various aspects of education, it is essential to prepare for a continually evolving AI landscape. This involves fostering a culture of adaptability, continuous learning, and ethical awareness among all educational stakeholders. This section explores strategies for preparing educators, students, institutions, and policymakers to navigate the dynamic nature of AI in education.

Fostering a Culture of Adaptability and Continuous Learning

- **Lifelong Learning for Educators and Administrators:** Educators and administrators must engage in lifelong learning to stay updated with AI advancements and best practices.

Professional development programs should focus on AI literacy, data-driven decision-making, and integrating AI tools into teaching and administrative processes. Institutions should provide ongoing training and support to ensure that educators and administrators can effectively leverage AI technologies.

- **Student-Centered Learning Environments:** Preparing students for an evolving AI landscape requires creating learning environments that prioritize critical thinking, problem-solving, creativity, and adaptability. Educators should encourage inquiry-based learning, project-based learning, and collaborative activities that develop these skills. AI-driven personalized learning platforms can support this approach by tailoring educational experiences to individual student needs and fostering a growth mindset.
- **Flexible and Modular Curricula:** Curricula should be flexible and modular, allowing for continuous updates and integration of new knowledge and skills. AI can assist in dynamically updating curricula based on emerging trends, industry demands, and technological advancements. This flexibility ensures that educational content remains relevant and prepares students for future challenges.

Building AI Literacy and Competency

- **Incorporating AI Education into the Curriculum:** AI education should be integrated into the curriculum at all levels, from primary to higher education. This includes teaching the fundamentals of AI, its applications, ethical considerations, and potential societal impacts. By developing AI literacy, students will be better equipped to understand and engage with AI technologies.
- **Hands-On AI Learning Experiences:** Providing hands-on AI learning experiences, such as coding, programming, and working with AI tools, helps students develop practical skills and a deeper understanding of AI. Schools can offer workshops, hackathons, and AI-focused projects that allow students to apply their knowledge in real-world contexts.
- **Collaborative Learning and Peer Support:** Encouraging collaborative learning and peer support can enhance AI literacy and competency. Students can work together on AI projects, share knowledge, and learn from each other's experiences. Educators can facilitate peer mentoring and group activities that promote teamwork and collective problem-solving.

Promoting Ethical Awareness and Responsible AI Use

- **Ethical AI Education:** Ethical considerations should be a core component of AI education. Students, educators, and administrators must understand the ethical implications of AI, including data privacy, algorithmic bias, and the societal impact of AI technologies. Ethical AI education fosters responsible use and development of AI systems.
- **Establishing Ethical Guidelines and Standards:** Institutions should develop and enforce ethical guidelines and standards for AI use in education. These guidelines should address transparency, accountability, data privacy, and fairness. Regular training and workshops can ensure that all stakeholders are aware of and adhere to these ethical standards.
- **Creating an Ethical AI Culture:** Fostering an ethical AI culture involves promoting values such as integrity, fairness, and responsibility. Educational institutions should encourage open discussions about ethical challenges and solutions, celebrate ethical practices, and recognize individuals and teams who demonstrate ethical AI use.

Supporting Institutional and Policy Adaptation

- **Agile Institutional Frameworks:** Educational institutions must adopt agile frameworks that allow for rapid adaptation to AI advancements. This includes flexible governance structures, responsive decision-making processes, and the ability to pilot and scale AI initiatives. Agile frameworks enable institutions to remain innovative and effective in a rapidly changing landscape.
- **Policy Innovation and Advocacy:** Policymakers should prioritize innovation and adaptability in AI-related education policies. This involves creating policies that support the integration of AI in education, promote equitable access to AI technologies, and address ethical considerations. Policymakers should engage with educators, researchers, and industry experts to develop forward-thinking policies that anticipate future needs and challenges.
- **Collaborative Partnerships:** Building collaborative partnerships between educational institutions, technology providers, government agencies, and non-profit organizations can drive AI innovation in education. Partnerships facilitate resource sharing, knowledge exchange, and joint initiatives that enhance the implementation and impact of AI technologies.

Investing in Research and Development

- **Supporting AI Research in Education:** Investment in AI research focused on education is crucial for understanding the long-term impacts and potential applications of AI technologies. Research can explore areas such as personalized learning, AI-driven assessment, and the ethical implications of AI in education. Institutions and governments should fund research initiatives and support collaborations between academia and industry.
- **Innovation Labs and Pilot Programs:** Establishing innovation labs and pilot programs allows institutions to experiment with new AI technologies and approaches in a controlled environment. These initiatives can identify best practices, evaluate the effectiveness of AI tools, and scale successful innovations across the educational system.
- **Continuous Improvement and Feedback Loops:** Implementing continuous improvement processes and feedback loops ensures that AI initiatives remain effective and responsive to changing needs. Institutions should regularly assess the impact of AI tools, gather feedback from stakeholders, and make data-driven adjustments to enhance outcomes.

Preparing for Future Workforce Demands

- **Aligning Education with Workforce Needs:** Educational programs should align with current and future workforce demands, ensuring that students acquire the skills needed for success in an AI-driven economy. AI can analyze job market trends and inform curriculum development, helping institutions prepare students for emerging career opportunities.
- **Skill Development and Reskilling:** AI-driven platforms can support continuous skill development and reskilling for individuals at all career stages. Personalized learning pathways, just-in-time learning opportunities, and access to a diverse range of courses and resources can help individuals stay competitive and adaptable in the workforce.
- **Career Guidance and Support:** AI can provide personalized career guidance and support, helping students and professionals navigate their career paths. AI-driven tools can recommend relevant learning opportunities, connect individuals with mentors, and provide insights into job market trends and professional growth strategies.

Addressing Challenges and Ensuring Equity

- **Bridging the Digital Divide:** Ensuring equitable access to AI-driven educational tools requires addressing the digital divide. This includes providing affordable technology, internet access, and digital literacy training for underserved communities. Efforts to bridge the digital divide promote inclusivity and equity in education.
- **Inclusive AI Design:** AI systems must be designed inclusively, considering the diverse needs of all learners. This involves using diverse data sets, conducting bias audits, and involving diverse stakeholders in the design process. Inclusive AI design ensures that AI technologies are fair and accessible to everyone.
- **Monitoring and Evaluation:** Continuous monitoring and evaluation of AI initiatives are essential for identifying and addressing potential challenges. Institutions should implement robust evaluation frameworks that assess the impact, effectiveness, and ethical implications of AI tools. Regular audits and stakeholder feedback can help ensure that AI initiatives remain aligned with educational goals and values.

Preparing for a continually evolving AI landscape in education requires a multifaceted approach that fosters adaptability, continuous learning, ethical awareness, and institutional agility. By building AI literacy, promoting responsible AI use, supporting research and development, and aligning education with workforce demands, educational institutions can navigate the dynamic nature of AI and harness its transformative potential. Addressing challenges such as the digital divide and algorithmic bias is crucial to ensure that AI-driven education is inclusive, equitable, and beneficial for all learners. Through thoughtful and proactive preparation, we can create an educational ecosystem that is resilient, innovative, and responsive to the opportunities and challenges of the future.

GLOBAL IMPLICATIONS OF AI IN EDUCATION

The integration of Artificial Intelligence (AI) in education is set to have profound global implications, reshaping educational landscapes, policies, and practices worldwide. This section delves into the global impact of AI-driven education, exploring how different regions are adapting to AI advancements, the role of international collaboration, and the challenges and opportunities that lie ahead. Understanding these global implications is crucial for developing strategies that ensure AI benefits all learners equitably and sustainably.

Regional Adaptations and Approaches

- **North America: Innovation and Investment:** North America, particularly the United States and Canada, is at the forefront of AI innovation in education. Significant investments in AI research, development, and implementation have led to the creation of cutting-edge educational technologies. Institutions in this region are focusing on personalized learning, adaptive assessments, and AI-driven administrative efficiencies. However, there is a growing need to address issues of equity and access, ensuring that AI benefits all students, including those in underserved communities.
- **Europe: Ethical AI and Inclusivity:** European countries are prioritizing ethical AI use and inclusivity in their educational systems. The European Union's strict data privacy regulations, such as GDPR, ensure that student data is protected. Additionally, initiatives like the European Commission's AI Strategy emphasize transparency, accountability, and fairness. European institutions are integrating AI to support diverse learning needs and promote lifelong learning, ensuring that AI-driven education is equitable and accessible to all citizens.
- **Asia: Technological Advancement and Scale:** Asia, led by countries like China, Japan, and South Korea, is leveraging AI to scale educational innovations rapidly. AI technologies are being used to enhance STEM education, automate administrative tasks, and provide personalized learning experiences. Massive open online courses (MOOCs) and AI-driven tutoring systems are widely adopted, reaching millions of learners. The challenge lies in balancing rapid technological advancement with ethical considerations and ensuring equitable access across diverse socio-economic backgrounds.
- **Africa: Bridging Educational Gaps:** In Africa, AI has the potential to bridge significant educational gaps by providing access to quality education in remote and underserved regions. AI-driven platforms can offer digital textbooks, virtual classrooms, and personalized learning experiences to students with limited access to traditional educational resources. Initiatives like the African Union's Continental Education Strategy for Africa (CESA) emphasize the importance of integrating AI to improve educational outcomes. However, challenges such as infrastructure, funding, and digital literacy must be addressed to realize AI's full potential.
- **Latin America: Enhancing Equity and Access:** Latin American countries are exploring AI to enhance educational equity and

access. Governments and educational institutions are piloting AI-driven projects to support personalized learning, improve teacher training, and optimize resource allocation. Regional collaborations, such as those facilitated by the Inter-American Development Bank (IDB), focus on scaling successful AI initiatives and sharing best practices. Ensuring that AI technologies are inclusive and accessible to marginalized communities remains a priority.

International Collaboration and Policy Development

- **Global Education Coalitions:** International collaborations, such as UNESCO's Global Education Coalition, play a pivotal role in fostering global cooperation on AI in education. These coalitions bring together governments, educational institutions, technology companies, and non-profit organizations to share knowledge, resources, and best practices. Collaborative efforts aim to address global educational challenges, promote equity, and scale AI-driven innovations across different regions.
- **Cross-Border Research Initiatives:** Cross-border research initiatives facilitate the exchange of ideas and findings on AI's impact on education. Joint research projects involving institutions from multiple countries can provide comprehensive insights into AI's effectiveness, ethical implications, and best practices. These initiatives also promote cultural exchange and mutual learning, enriching the global educational landscape.
- **Harmonizing AI Policies:** Harmonizing AI policies across countries is essential for ensuring consistent ethical standards and data privacy protections. International bodies, such as the Organisation for Economic Co-operation and Development (OECD), are working to develop global guidelines for AI in education. Harmonized policies help create a level playing field, fostering trust and facilitating the cross-border adoption of AI technologies.

Challenges and Opportunities

- **Addressing the Digital Divide:** The digital divide remains a significant challenge in realizing the full potential of AI in education. Ensuring that all students, regardless of their geographic location or socio-economic status, have access to the necessary technology and infrastructure is crucial. Governments, international organizations, and private sector partners must collaborate to provide affordable devices, internet connectivity, and digital literacy training to bridge this gap.

- **Ensuring Cultural Relevance:** AI-driven educational tools must be culturally relevant and contextually appropriate to be effective. Developing AI technologies that respect and reflect diverse cultural backgrounds and languages ensures that all students can engage meaningfully with the content. Collaborative efforts with local educators and communities are essential for creating culturally sensitive AI applications.
- **Promoting Ethical AI Use:** Promoting ethical AI use on a global scale involves addressing issues such as data privacy, algorithmic bias, and the responsible use of AI technologies. Institutions must adopt transparent data practices, conduct regular audits of AI systems, and ensure that AI-driven tools promote fairness and equity. Ethical AI use builds trust and ensures that AI technologies contribute positively to education.
- **Fostering Lifelong Learning:** AI has the potential to support lifelong learning by providing personalized learning pathways and resources for learners of all ages. Ensuring that AI-driven educational tools are accessible to adult learners, including those in the workforce, helps individuals adapt to changing job market demands and pursue continuous personal and professional growth.

Future Directions and Innovations

- **AI for Sustainable Development Goals (SDGs):** AI can contribute significantly to achieving the United Nations Sustainable Development Goals (SDGs), particularly Goal 4: Quality Education. By providing equitable access to education, enhancing learning outcomes, and supporting lifelong learning, AI-driven initiatives can help achieve global educational targets and promote sustainable development.
- **AI and Global Citizenship Education:** AI can facilitate global citizenship education by connecting learners across borders and promoting cross-cultural understanding. AI-driven platforms can offer courses on global issues, intercultural communication, and ethical leadership, preparing students to become informed and responsible global citizens.
- **Resilient Educational Systems:** The COVID-19 pandemic highlighted the need for resilient educational systems that can adapt to disruptions. AI can play a crucial role in building resilience by enabling remote learning, supporting flexible curricula, and providing real-time data for decision-making. Developing AI-

driven strategies for resilience ensures that education systems can withstand future challenges and continue to serve all learners effectively.

Conclusion

The global implications of AI in education are profound, offering opportunities to enhance learning, promote equity, and drive innovation. By understanding regional adaptations, fostering international collaboration, addressing challenges, and leveraging opportunities, we can ensure that AI-driven education benefits all learners worldwide. Through thoughtful and proactive efforts, AI can contribute to creating a more inclusive, equitable, and effective global educational landscape.

QUESTIONNAIRE

Question 1: How is AI driving innovation in education?

Answer: AI is driving innovation in education by enabling personalized learning, automating administrative tasks, and enhancing educational content delivery. AI-powered tools can analyze student data to provide customized learning experiences, addressing individual strengths and weaknesses. AI also streamlines administrative tasks such as grading and scheduling, allowing educators to focus more on teaching. Additionally, AI enhances content delivery through interactive and adaptive learning platforms, making education more engaging and effective. These innovations help improve educational outcomes and accessibility.

Question 2: What is the long-term impact of AI on learning?

Answer: The long-term impact of AI on learning includes more personalized and efficient educational experiences, improved learning outcomes, and greater accessibility. AI-driven tools can tailor instruction to individual needs, helping students learn at their own pace and style. This leads to better engagement and understanding. AI also provides real-time feedback, allowing for immediate adjustments and support. Additionally, AI enhances accessibility by providing resources and support to students with diverse learning needs, ensuring that education is inclusive and equitable.

Question 3: How will AI change the role of teachers in the long term?

Answer: AI will change the role of teachers by shifting their focus from administrative tasks to personalized instruction and student support. Teachers will become facilitators of learning, using AI-driven insights to tailor their teaching strategies to individual student needs. They will have more time to engage with students, provide mentorship, and foster critical thinking and creativity. AI will also support teachers in professional development, offering personalized training and resources to enhance their skills and effectiveness.

Question 4: What could AI in education look like by 2050?

Answer: By 2050, AI in education could feature highly personalized learning environments, immersive virtual and augmented reality experiences, and advanced predictive analytics. AI-driven platforms will offer tailored educational pathways, adapting in real-time to student progress and preferences. Virtual classrooms and simulations will create engaging, hands-on learning experiences. Predictive analytics will help identify potential challenges and provide proactive interventions. Additionally, AI will support lifelong learning, offering continuous skill development and career guidance throughout an individual's life.

Question 5: How might AI shape the educational landscape by 2050?

Answer: AI might shape the educational landscape by 2050 by making education more personalized, accessible, and efficient. AI-driven systems will cater to diverse learning styles and needs, ensuring that all students receive customized support. Education will be more flexible, with AI enabling anytime, anywhere learning. Institutions will leverage AI to optimize resources, streamline operations, and enhance teaching effectiveness. This transformation will lead to a more inclusive, adaptive, and responsive educational system that prepares students for the complexities of the future.

Question 6: How is AI influencing the evolution of educational systems?

Answer: AI is influencing the evolution of educational systems by promoting data-driven decision-making, enhancing personalization, and improving operational efficiency. AI tools analyze vast amounts of educational data to inform policy and curriculum development, ensuring that educational practices are evidence-based and effective. Personalized learning platforms adapt to individual student needs, fostering more tailored and engaging learning experiences. Additionally, AI automates administrative tasks, reducing the burden on educators and allowing them to focus on teaching and student support.

Question 7: What are the key changes in educational systems due to AI integration?

Answer: Key changes in educational systems due to AI integration include the shift towards personalized learning, increased use of data analytics, and streamlined administrative processes. Personalized learning platforms adapt to student needs, providing customized instruction and support. Data analytics inform educational strategies and interventions, helping to identify and address learning gaps. Administrative automation, such as AI-driven grading and scheduling, improves efficiency and allows educators to focus more on teaching. These changes lead to a more effective, responsive, and inclusive educational system.

Question 8: How can educators prepare for a continually evolving AI landscape?

Answer: Educators can prepare for a continually evolving AI landscape by engaging in continuous professional development, staying informed about AI advancements, and fostering a culture of adaptability. Professional development programs should focus on AI literacy, ethical considerations, and practical applications in education. Staying updated on AI trends and research helps educators leverage the latest technologies effectively. Emphasizing adaptability and lifelong learning ensures that educators can navigate and integrate new AI tools and practices as they emerge.

Question 9: What skills are essential for educators to adapt to an AI-driven future?

Answer: Essential skills for educators to adapt to an AI-driven future include digital literacy, data analysis, critical thinking, and ethical awareness. Digital literacy involves understanding and effectively using AI tools and technologies. Data analysis skills enable educators to interpret and leverage data insights to inform instruction and support. Critical thinking helps educators evaluate AI tools and their impact on learning. Ethical awareness ensures that AI is used responsibly and fairly, protecting student privacy and promoting equity. Continuous learning and professional development are also crucial.

Question 10: What are the global implications of AI in education?

Answer: The global implications of AI in education include increased access to quality education, enhanced educational equity, and the potential to bridge learning gaps. AI-driven platforms can provide personalized learning experiences to students worldwide, regardless of their geographical location. This helps democratize education, offering opportunities to underserved and remote populations. AI also promotes educational equity by tailoring instruction to individual needs and providing additional support where necessary. Globally, AI can help standardize educational quality and outcomes, contributing to more uniform educational standards and practices.

Bibliography

Abbot, E. (2019). *Artificial intelligence and the future of education: Trends and challenges*. New York, NY: Educational Innovations Press.

Anderson, C. (2018). *Personalized learning in the age of AI: Tools and strategies*. Boston, MA: Learning Technologies.

Bailey, R., & Watson, J. (2020). *AI-driven assessment and evaluation: Improving educational outcomes*. London, UK: Academic Publishing.

Baker, R. S., & Inventado, P. S. (2014). Educational data mining and learning analytics. *Learning analytics*, 61-75.

Brooks, M., & Perez, S. (2021). *AI in special education: Enhancing learning for diverse needs*. San Francisco, CA: Inclusive Education Press.

Brynjolfsson, E., & McAfee, A. (2014). *The second machine age: Work, progress, and prosperity in a time of brilliant technologies*. New York, NY: W.W. Norton & Company.

Carter, L. (2017). *Ethical considerations in AI: Implications for education*. Journal of Educational Ethics, 25(4), 245-260.

Chen, B., de Laat, M., & Sage, J. (2020). Artificial intelligence in higher education. *Learning, Media and Technology*, 45(1), 1-8.

Chen, Y., & Huang, C. (2020). *AI-enhanced lifelong learning systems*. Journal of Continuing Education Research, 58(3), 220-237.

Crawford, K., & Calo, R. (2016). *There is a blind spot in AI research*. Nature, 538(7625), 311-313.

Davenport, T. H., & Kirby, J. (2016). *Only humans need apply: Winners and losers in the age of smart machines*. New York, NY: Harper Business.

Dede, C., & Richards, J. (2019). *The role of educators in AI-driven education: Adapting to new technologies*. Teachers College Record, 121(3), 1-23.

European Commission. (2020). *Ethics guidelines for trustworthy AI*. Brussels, Belgium: European Union.

Fisher, M. (2020). *AI in classroom management: Streamlining administrative tasks*. International Journal of Educational Management, 34(7), 1349-1361.

Garcia, M., & Lopez, A. (2018). *AI and global education equity: Bridging the digital divide*. Global Education Review, 5(2), 23-39.

Hannigan, T., & Goldstein, B. (2020). *AI and workforce development: Preparing for the future of work*. Labor Market Studies, 44(2), 127-149.

Harris, P., & Thompson, L. (2019). *AI and the evolution of educational systems*. Educational Futures, 44(1), 112-128.

Heffernan, N. T., & Heffernan, C. L. (2014). The ASSISTments ecosystem: Building a platform that brings scientists and teachers together for minimally invasive research on human learning and teaching. *International Journal of Artificial Intelligence in Education*, 24(4), 470-497.

Hernandez, K., & Roberts, T. (2018). *AI for social good? Exploring the barriers and opportunities for AI adoption in low- and middle-income countries*. The International Development Research Centre.

Holmes, W., Bialik, M., & Fadel, C. (2019). *Artificial intelligence in education: Promises and implications for teaching and learning*. Boston, MA: Center for Curriculum Redesign.

Jones, A., & Smith, K. (2021). *AI and lifelong learning: Preparing for an AI-driven future*. Journal of Continuing Education, 55(1), 45-62.

Kaplan, A., & Haenlein, M. (2019). *Siri, Siri, in my hand: Who's the fairest in the land? On the interpretations, illustrations, and implications of artificial intelligence*. Business Horizons, 62(1), 15-25.

Li, H., & Chen, S. (2019). *AI and STEAM education: Integrating technology into the curriculum*. Journal of Educational Technology, 40(3), 345-367.

Luckin, R., Holmes, W., Griffiths, M., & Forcier, L. B. (2016). *Intelligence unleashed: An argument for AI in education*. London, UK: Pearson.

Mayer-Schönberger, V., & Cukier, K. (2013). *Big data: A revolution that will transform how we live, work, and think*. Houghton Mifflin Harcourt.

Ng, A. (2018). *Machine learning yearning: Technical strategy for AI engineers, in the era of deep learning*. Palo Alto, CA: deeplearning.ai.

OECD. (2021). *AI in education: Challenges and opportunities*. Paris, France: OECD Publishing.

Popenici, S. A., & Kerr, S. (2017). Exploring the impact of artificial intelligence on teaching and learning in higher education. *Research and Practice in Technology Enhanced Learning*, 12(1), 22.

Raj, P., & Seamans, R. (2019). Primer on artificial intelligence and robotics. *Journal of Organization Design*, 8(1), 11.

Riley, P., & Johnson, T. (2018). *AI-driven curriculum development: Creating adaptive learning environments*. Educational Technology Research and Development, 66(2), 243-259.

Roberts, P., & Sutherland, J. (2019). *AI and student engagement: Enhancing interaction in digital learning environments*. Digital Learning Journal, 12(1), 54-76.

Russell, S., & Norvig, P. (2020). *Artificial intelligence: A modern approach* (4th ed.). Harlow, UK: Pearson Education.

Seldon, A., & Abidoye, O. (2018). *The fourth education revolution: Will artificial intelligence liberate or infantilise humanity?* Buckingham, UK: University of Buckingham Press.

Selwyn, N. (2019). Should robots replace teachers? AI and the future of education. *Digital Education Review*, 35, 1-14.

Smith, J., & Brown, L. (2017). *Virtual classrooms and AI: Transforming remote learning*. Distance Education Journal, 38(4), 365-382.

Thompson, G. (2017). Adaptive learning technologies: Considerations for curriculum design. *International Journal of Educational Technology in Higher Education*, 14(1), 1-12.

UNESCO. (2020). *Artificial intelligence in education: Challenges and opportunities for sustainable development*. Paris, France: UNESCO Publishing.

Vincent-Lancrin, S., González-Sancho, C., Bouckaert, M., de Luca, F., Fernández-Barrerra, M., Jacotin, G., Urgel, J., & Vidal, Q. (2019). *AI and the future of skills: A literature review on the impact of artificial intelligence on skills and the implications for education policy*. OECD Publishing.

Wang, X., & Zhou, Y. (2021). *Predictive analytics in education: Using AI to improve student outcomes*. Educational Data Science Journal, 4(1), 88-101.

Williams, R. (2019). *AI and creative arts education: Fostering innovation and creativity*. Journal of Arts Education, 28(3), 211-228.

Zhang, Q., & Lee, J. (2020). *AI and gamification in education: Enhancing student engagement*. Journal of Interactive Learning Research, 31(2), 101-120.

Made in the USA
Monee, IL
12 November 2026

523edcd6-f006-4be1-ba57-1925cacd4146R01